BLACK DIAMONDS
FROM THE TREASURE STATE

RAILROADS PAST AND PRESENT

H. Roger Grant and Thomas Hoback, editors

Recent titles in the Railroads Past and Present series

Pennsylvania Railroad
Albert J. Churella

Electric Indiana
Carlos Arnaldo Schwantes

Sunset Cluster
H. Roger Grant

The Railroad Photography of Phil Hastings
Tony Reevy

The Station Agent and the American Railroad Experience
H. Roger Grant

The Diesel That Did It
Wallace W. Abbey

Crossroads of a Continent
Peter A. Hansen, Don L. Hofsommer, and Carlos Arnaldo Schwantes

Narrow Gauge in the Tropics
Augustus J. Veenendaal, Jr.

Amtrak, America's Railroad
Geoffrey H. Doughty, Jeffrey T. Darbee, and Eugene Harmon

The Panama Railroad
Peter Pyne

Last Train to Texas
Fred W. Frailey

Transportation and the American People
H. Roger Grant

American Steam Locomotives
William L. Withuhn

My Life with Trains
Jim McClellan

The Railroad Photography of Lucius Beebe and Charles Clegg
Tony Reevy

Chicago Union Station
Fred Ash

John W. Barriger III
H. Roger Grant

Riding the Rails
Robert D. Krebs

Wallace W. Abbey
Scott Lothes and Kevin P. Keefe

Branch Line Empires
Michael Bezilla with Luther Gette

Indianapolis Union and Belt Railroads
Jeffrey Darbee

Railroads and the American People
H. Roger Grant

Derailed by Bankruptcy
Howard H. Lewis

Electric Interurbans and the American People
H. Roger Grant

The Iron Road in the Prairie State
Simon Cordery

The Lake Shore Electric Railway Story
Herbert H. Harwood, Jr. and Robert S. Korach

The Railroad That Never Was
Herbert H. Harwood, Jr.

BLACK DIAMONDS FROM THE TREASURE STATE

The Incredible Saga of the Montana, Wyoming & Southern, and Yellowstone Park Railroads

Robert A. Schalla

INDIANA UNIVERSITY PRESS

This book is a publication of

INDIANA UNIVERSITY PRESS
Office of Scholarly Publishing
Herman B Wells Library 350
1320 East 10th Street
Bloomington, Indiana 47405 USA

iupress.org

Manufactured in the United States of America

First Printing 2024

Library of Congress Cataloging-in-Publication Data

Names: Schalla, Robert A., author.
Title: Black diamonds from the treasure state : the incredible saga of the Montana, Wyoming & Southern, and Yellowstone park railroads / Robert A. Schalla.
Description: Bloomington, Indiana : Indiana University Press, [2024] | Series: Railroads past and present | Includes bibliographical references and index.
Identifiers: LCCN 2023029019 (print) | LCCN 2023029020 (ebook) | ISBN 9780253068194 (hardback) | ISBN 9780253068217 (ebook)
Subjects: LCSH: Railroads—United States—History. | Yellowstone National Park. | Northern Pacific Railway Company—History. | Montana, Wyoming & Southern Railroad Company—History. | BISAC: TRANSPORTATION / Railroads / History | BUSINESS & ECONOMICS / Corporate & Business History
Classification: LCC HE2751 .S33 2024 (print) | LCC HE2751 (ebook) | DDC 385.0979—dc23/eng/20230824
LC record available at https://lccn.loc.gov/2023029019
LC ebook record available at https://lccn.loc.gov/2023029020

This book is dedicated to the memory of my good friend

JOHN FREDLUND,

whose grandparents John and Frances Chesarek owned the First and Last Chance Saloon and Boarding House in Bearcreek during the town's heyday.

CONTENTS

PREFACE

HAVING BEEN CAPTIVATED AT AN EARLY AGE BY A. B. GUTHRIE Jr.'s vision of Montana in his classic *The Big Sky*, I had the unmistakable good fortune in early 1989 to be offered a job in Billings, Montana. As the old saying goes, "I wasn't born here, but I came as quick as I could." Perhaps a year after my arrival, some of my associates and newfound friends insisted that I be exposed to some of the area's important cultural activities. As a result, one weekend I found myself in the town of Bearcreek, where the main activity appeared to be drinking beer while watching pigs run around an oval racetrack at the local saloon. Having never attended a pig race, I was impressed. Those little guys can really fly when there is food at the other end of the line. But my most lasting impression from my visit to Bearcreek was the discovery that a railroad had once run through the town. At first there seemed to be little evidence of this, but there on the wall of the saloon was a photograph of a coal mine with lines of railcars parked in front. Having been afflicted with a lifelong fascination with railroads, I asked the bartender if the photo had been taken nearby. "Oh, yeah," he replied, "that's the Smith Mine, it's just up the road." Amazing, I thought, I have to learn more.

Having a full-time job distracted me from further investigation for a number of years, but in the summer of 2003, my interest was renewed when I learned that an old engine house just outside the town of Belfry was about to be torn down due to a state highway project. This discovery prompted a field trip with two friends, and upon my return, I was inspired to begin a search for photographs. Amazingly, I found numerous photos of this little railroad in museums and archives scattered across the country. My search also led me to an excellent article by historian Jon Axline in the Montana Historical Society's quarterly. Now I was really interested. My first thought was to see if I could assemble enough photos to publish a simple album with just enough text to tie the pictures together. But as I began to delve into the subject, a very interesting story began to emerge—something completely different from what I had expected.

My initial research revealed a somewhat shadowy character variously identified as Frank Hall, F. A. Hall, or possibly even S. A. Hall. Little seemed to be known of this individual except that he was the man credited with building the railroad to Bearcreek. Further digging soon brought Frank A. Hall to life, and he quickly became the focus of my story. My efforts to learn more about him led me from Montana to Milwaukee, Wisconsin; St. Paul, Minnesota; and back. Soon I was digging into the history of a little-known railroad far from Bearcreek on Bozeman Pass where Hall had made his initial foray into the railroad business.

The story of Frank Hall, his life and business dealings exceeded my most sanguine expectations. Along the way I was introduced to a fascinating tableau of notable turn-of-the-century businessmen and eccentric characters. Starting with Yankee Jim George, an itinerant prospector, the story led me to visionary civil engineer Philip M. Gallaher, and from there on to Boston financier Elijah Smith. Two presidents of the Northern Pacific Railway loomed large as well. I now realized this wasn't going to be a story limited to an insignificant twenty-five-mile-long short line railroad in southern Montana, for its tentacles reached far beyond the Clarks Fork and Bear Creek valleys. There was intrigue, backstabbing, train wrecks, and heroes and villains who unexpectedly emerged from the woodwork. All of this was more than I had expected or could have hoped for. As some might say, "you can't make this stuff up." Now I knew that I had a story worth telling.

In the late nineteenth century, railroads played a crucial role in the development of Montana's economy. Beginning with the chance discovery of coal in 1866, the saga of Frank Hall's railroad follows early efforts to bring rail transport to both the New World Mining District, near the northeast corner of Yellowstone National Park, and the Red Lodge–Bear Creek Coal Field in south-central Montana. It includes

Northern Pacific's early, unsuccessful efforts to build a railroad through the National Park and then follows the struggles of various privately financed schemes aimed at developing the vast mineral wealth of both these regions.

In 1905, Frank Hall finally succeeded in financing a railroad to the coal fields, but his plan to continue the line up the rugged Clarks Fork Canyon to the National Park ran afoul of Northern Pacific president Howard Elliott. The story of the construction and operation of the Yellowstone Park Railroad and its successor, the Montana, Wyoming & Southern, delves into the motivations and backgrounds of the individuals involved and their ultimate triumphs and failures. The story is historically important because it reveals how a major corporation worked to control and limit competition within what was perceived to be its exclusive sphere of economic interest. Despite enduring years of interference by the Northern Pacific and setbacks attributable to the line's poor construction and lack of equipment, the management of this short line railroad persevered and maintained a critical transportation link that spurred the development of not only the Bear Creek coal field but also the expansion of agriculture in the upper Clarks Fork Valley. The railroad's construction also resulted in the creation of three new towns. One of the few privately owned rail lines in the state, it maintained its independence for nearly fifty years. At a time when Montana's economy depended on black diamonds for its heat and energy, Frank Hall's little railroad ensured that some of the highest-quality coal in state was available to private, commercial, and industrial consumers.

ACKNOWLEDGMENTS

SIMPLY STATED, THIS STORY WOULD HAVE NOT BEEN WRITTEN without the encouragement and support of Montana historian Jon Axline. At the inception of this project, Jon not only shared his knowledge and photographs but also generously donated all of his research files on the subject to me. He graciously reviewed early drafts of the manuscript and offered numerous helpful suggestions and insights. Although I am not a historian by training, my initial meeting with Jon inspired me to dive deep into my research and fearlessly begin to connect the dots.

The few hours I spent discussing railroad history with Bill and Jan Taylor at their home near Lolo, Montana, probably unbeknownst to them, was immensely important to this project as well. Their practical advice on writing, publishing, and research helped convince me that I could do this.

My good friend Geoffrey Stone willingly waded through several early drafts of the manuscript and offered numerous insights into western history and railroads. His comments, corrections, and advice greatly improved the final product. I am also indebted to Gary Hughes for his assistance in creating the regional maps and to Jo Wiggins for sharing his extensive map database and preparing the detailed map of Belfry. Denver attorney Chris Hayes helped guide me through the arcane technicalities of several legal proceedings, Steve Durrett contributed his insights into corporate finance, and Dave Bickerstaff contributed much appreciated last-minute help with computer graphics. Thanks must also go out to all the museum personnel and archivists across the country who graciously endured my repeated inquiries and requests. The assistance and guidance received from the editors and staff at Indiana University Press made the publication process a seamless endeavor. Numerous other individuals contributed their support and encouragement in various ways during the several years spent on this project, and I thank you all.

Finally, I must extend my warmest heartfelt thanks to my patient and supportive wife Jeannine, who not only put up with my reclusive and compulsive behavior during my research and writing but also cheerfully read several drafts of the manuscript. Her insights and encouragement helped to bring this project to fruition.

Needless to say, I have done my best to piece together a story that I believe to be true and accurate, but in some cases, I was forced to rely on scattered and disparate bits of information. In the end, I bear full responsibility for any errors of fact, omission, or interpretation.

BLACK DIAMONDS
FROM THE TREASURE STATE

1

"Treat Him in Every Way as an Irresponsible Fellow"

ON A BLUSTERY DAY IN LATE JANUARY 1891, FRANK AVERY Hall, a small-time businessman from Milwaukee, Wisconsin, stepped off a train at the Northern Pacific depot in Helena, Montana, and made his way uptown to the New Merchants' Hotel. Located on Broadway not far from the state capitol building, the recently refurbished New Merchants' was known for its elegant bar, billiard room, restaurant, and wide hallways carpeted with crimson velvet. One of the swankier establishments in Helena, it was the sort of place where prominent businessmen and politicians gathered to discuss the day's events over a glass of good whiskey and a fine cigar. For Frank Hall, the up-and-coming president of Reliance Wire Works, the hotel's opulence must have been appealing. A parlor-level room with steam heat and electric lights cost him just $1.25 per night on the European plan; an upgrade to the American plan, with all meals included, added as little as $1.25 more.[1]

Tall, thin, and clean-shaven with dark, wavy hair, Frank Hall possessed boyish good looks, a flamboyant personality, and wry wit. At age twenty-three, he was brimming with self-confidence and ready to take on the world. Born in New York in 1868, the timing and circumstances of his move to Milwaukee are unknown, but in 1886, at the age of no more than eighteen, he and W. N. Fitzgerald, the son of a well-known local ship inspector, purchased Charles Goehner's wire works plant in Racine, Wisconsin. Hall and Fitzgerald changed the company name to Reliance Wire Works and immediately announced plans to invest $10,000 in order to expand operations. Where they got the money for this ambitious venture is unknown, but it suggests they may have come from families of at least modest wealth and had connections to the local business community. The *Green Bay Weekly Gazette* described Fitzgerald as a "promising young businessman." Considering his ambitious nature and entrepreneurial flair, this portrayal could, no doubt, have been applied to Frank Hall as well. Said to be well known in the area, both Hall and Fitzgerald were previously associated with the manufacturing concern E. P. Allis & Company, an important employer in Milwaukee that would soon become known worldwide as farm equipment manufacturer Allis-Chalmers.[2]

A purveyor of fences, vine trainers, office railing, and window guards, Reliance Wire Works did not file Articles of Association with the Wisconsin Secretary of State until March 1887, by which time Hall and Fitzgerald had brought in a third, somewhat older partner, named Oscar F. Lindman. Hall's trip to Montana four years later was likely prompted by the reluctance of a certain Fred M. Wilson to make good on a $453.85 bill owed to Hall's company. Hall sued Wilson and eventually won a judgment against him. Whether he ever received payment is unknown; however, the trip west piqued Hall's interest in the Treasure State, and he would soon return.[3]

With one plant operating in Racine, in late 1892 Hall changed the company name to Reliance Wire and Iron Works and in a bold move acquired the Beloit Architectural Works in Beloit, Wisconsin. This expansion added a second plant to his operations but appears to have left Reliance financially overextended. Just a year later, deep in debt, Reliance Wire and Iron was bankrupt, a victim of the Panic of 1893. Reliance Wire's failure may have been the first time Hall faced financial ruin, but it would not be the last. As the country slipped into a serious economic depression, 1894 found Hall both out of work and out of money. His activities and financial struggles during the next several years are obscure, but he returned to Montana several times, visiting Butte in 1895 and Helena a year later. Whether he was seeking employment or business opportunities is unknown.[4]

In November 1897, Hall once again ventured out to the Treasure State. This time as the representative of a Chicago syndicate that hoped to raise $30,000 to underwrite the construction of a rye whiskey distillery. Having developed his skills as both a persuasive and elegant speaker,

Hall diligently pursued his sponsors' goals by making presentations in Billings, Great Falls, and Bozeman. As an enticement, he described how the distillery would provide a much-needed boost to the local economy while it produced forty barrels of "a splendid brand of rye whiskey" per day. He went on to explain that the plant would benefit local farmers by providing a yearly market for 120,000 bushels of rye. Hall's arguments were persuasive, but despite his best efforts, he was unable to raise the capital his backers sought and his mission ended in failure. But his activities did not go unnoticed. The *Billings Weekly Gazette* described him as presenting his proposal in a "very favorable and pleasing light." For Frank Hall the *Gazette*'s praise meant little. When he returned to Milwaukee, he was once again out of work and ready to take on whatever might come next.[5]

Despite his numerous setbacks, the indefatigable Milwaukee salesman and promoter once again headed west to Montana in February 1898, this time to begin work on a highly speculative railroad project. In the late 1890s, promoters were making fortunes in the railroad business, and having become intrigued with the business opportunities in Montana, Hall was anxious to try his hand at this new and potentially lucrative profession. His partners in this new enterprise were Willis A. Ritchie and William Wallace Davenport Turner, two well-respected businessmen from Spokane, Washington. Their plan was to build a one-hundred-mile-long railroad that would cross the Gallatin Valley and then follow the Gallatin River through miles of uninhabited wilderness to a place called Dodge Creek, where Ritchie and Turner believed there was a vast coalfield.[6]

Ritchie, a thin man with prominent ears that accentuated his narrow face, was a renowned architect who had invested in numerous mining ventures in several western states. Although he had begun his career in Winfield, Kansas, in 1889 he moved to Seattle and relocated to Spokane four years later. During this time, he was responsible for the design of numerous public buildings and county courthouses throughout the state of Washington, one of the more notable being the famous Jefferson County courthouse in Port Townsend. Hall's other partner, William W. D. Turner, a sturdy-looking man with dark, wavy hair and a bushy mustache was born and raised in Missouri. An attorney by training,

Turner had served in the Union army during the Civil War and attained the rank of colonel. When the war ended, he moved to Wisconsin and opened a law office in Ripon, about forty miles northwest of Milwaukee. He served in the state legislature for a time before deciding there was more opportunity out west.

Turner's move to Spokane proved his instincts were correct, and he soon made a fortune investing in gold and silver mines, most notably the Le Roi mine near Rossland in British Columbia. How Frank Hall, a whiskey distillery promoter and ex-president of a bankrupt wire company, became acquainted with these two prominent Washington businessmen is a mystery. In Turner's case, there may have been a Wisconsin connection. What that connection might have been is unclear, unless it involved some tie to Hall's extended family. The fact that Turner departed Wisconsin in 1885, when Hall was a teenager, makes it seem unlikely they would have ever crossed paths. Why Turner and Ritchie took Hall on as their partner is an even greater mystery. Having no prior railroad experience, Hall's youth and energy might have been enough to impress them. Or perhaps they were swayed by his witty, gregarious personality and persuasive salesman's charm. Spokane's *Spokesman-Review* added to the mystery by describing Hall as "a moneyed man" from Milwaukee, which seems an unlikely appellation given his apparent lack of success in recent business activities. Perhaps Hall portrayed himself as "a moneyed man" to gain Turner and Ritchie's trust. If this was the case, they should have looked into his background a little more closely.[7]

Articles of Incorporation for the Gallatin Railroad Company of Spokane were filed in late February 1898 with William Turner, Willis Ritchie, and Frank Hall listed as officers and Llewellyn A. Luce of Bozeman serving as the firm's general counsel. The seemingly incongruous name originated from a decision to incorporate the company in Washington State, where the filing fee was a mere $7.75, rather than in Montana, where it would have cost $503. The railroad the partners envisioned was a huge undertaking that would start at Three Forks, Montana, extend

Map of south-central Montana showing the Crow Cession of 1882 and railroad development through 1900. NP (Northern Pacific); YPR (Yellowstone Park Railway); proposed lines: GRR (Gallatin Railroad); RF&CC (Rocky Fork & Cooke City); BCF&CC (Billings, Clark's Fork & Cooke City); BR (Boulder River route).

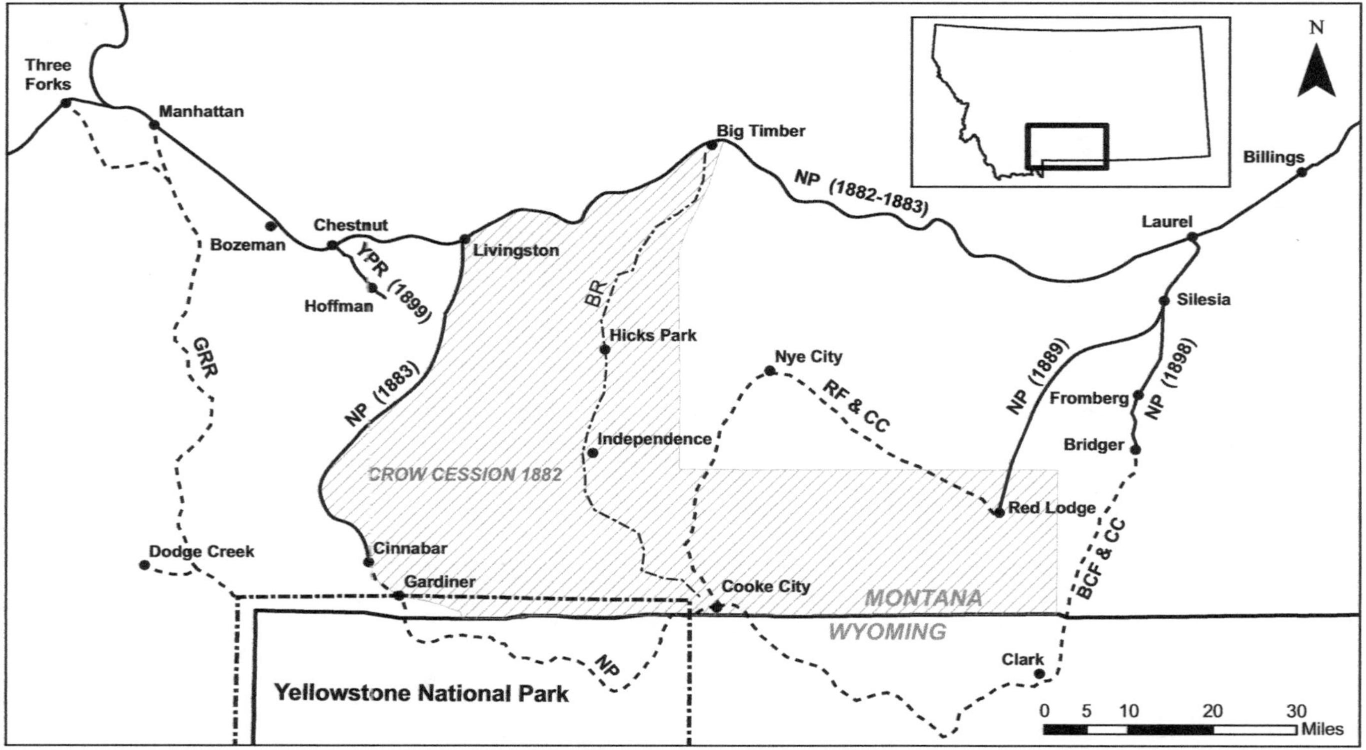
N
Three Forks
Manhattan
Bozeman
Chestnut
YPR (1899)
Hoffman
Livingston
Big Timber
NP (1882-1883)
Billings
Laurel
Silesia
NP (1889)
NP (1898)
Fromberg
Bridger
Red Lodge
BCF & CC
RF & CC
Nye City
Hicks Park
BR
Independence
CROW CESSION 1882
NP (1883)
GRR
Dodge Creek
Cinnabar
Gardiner
Cooke City
MONTANA
WYOMING
Clark
NP
Yellowstone National Park
0 5 10 20 30
Miles

eastward across the agricultural lands of the Gallatin Valley, and then follow the Gallatin River south up its narrow, rugged canyon to Dodge Creek (present-day Taylor Fork of the Gallatin). Here Willis Ritchie confidently claimed, "There are some very rich and extensive coal fields . . . which the company has purchased." He went on to explain, "The coal fields embrace thousands of acres and the road is designed with only one object in view, and that is to provide means of transportation to get our product to the market." According to Ritchie they had already completed a survey of the proposed route and had interested "a number of eastern capitalists" in the project. The problem with Ritchie's plan was that the coalfields did not exist. Although a few coal beds were present in the Dodge Creek area, none of them constituted a commercial deposit. Ritchie, it appears, had been grossly misinformed by whoever sold him the property.[8]

Once the incorporation papers were signed, Frank Hall, the company's vice president and general manager, assumed responsibility for day-to-day operations and moved to Bozeman. But he soon headed east to New York to meet with Ritchie's "eastern capitalists" and to Washington, DC, to discuss their proposed route with government officials. Upon his return in April, he announced that permission had been granted by the federal government to run their line all the way to Yellowstone National Park, an extension that was probably not part of Willis Ritchie's original plan. Curiously, at the same time, he made no mention of Ritchie's supposed East Coast investors. Nevertheless, Hall was enthused about his new venture and was convinced that local farmers would be supportive. His next move was to solicit their help by requesting they donate land for the right-of-way and complete the grading of the roadbed across their property for free. Sadly for Hall, his appeals for voluntary support fell on deaf ears.[9]

While Hall was busy trying to garner local support, the project suffered a severe setback when Willis Ritchie, perhaps having received discouraging news from his investors, or possibly more accurate information regarding the coal lands he had purchased, dropped out of the project. William Turner, seemingly unconcerned, promptly replaced him with his younger brother George, an attorney who had recently been elected to the US Senate. An agreement was soon formalized to give Hall and each of the Turner brothers one-third of the company stock. Hall retained his position as vice president and general manager.[10]

In mid-June 1898, Hall optimistically informed the *Anaconda Standard* that the first fifty miles of the Gallatin Railroad would be completed that summer, enough he said, to bring in most of that year's wheat crop. Then, in an apparent overreach of his geographic knowledge, he also claimed that when complete the railroad would reach to within three miles of Mammoth Hot Springs. Having likely never visited the area, Hall did not elaborate on exactly how he planned to navigate his way through the several mountain ranges between the Gallatin River and Mammoth. In the end, it was just a lot of fanciful talk, a talent that Hall seems to have cultivated to some great extent during his years as a salesman. As spring passed into summer and the anticipated local support failed to materialize, he came to realize that locals had little interest in a railroad up the Gallatin Valley. When William Turner arrived in Bozeman in late June to meet with Hall, he found him despondent. Although the lack of local support was a major setback, Hall and Turner soon learned that a group of coal mine operators in the Trail Creek area south of Bozeman Pass, having been rebuffed by the Northern Pacific Railway (NP), were anxious to have someone build a railroad to their mines.[11]

The Livingston Coal Field, of which Trail Creek was a part, had been an important source of fuel for the NP and smelters across Montana since 1883, but by 1898, much of the production was in decline. Mines near the NP mainline at Timberline had closed in 1895 and operations at Cokedale, near Livingston, were nearing their economic limit. The only remaining mines of any significance were located on the mainline at Chestnut and Mountain Side. But just a few miles to the south, on the hillsides above Meadow and Trail Creeks, thick beds of the same high-quality bituminous coal lay virtually untouched due to the lack of reliable transportation. The group that approached Hall and Turner was led by influential state senator Charles W. Hoffman who saw a great opportunity in the development of these resources. Hoffman's experience in the area went back many years, having previously operated mines at both

Timberline and Chestnut. Being aware of the coal along Trail Creek, as early as 1888 Hoffman had proposed the construction of a railroad to tap those reserves, but ten years later, his vision remained unfulfilled.[12]

According to the *Helena Daily Independent*, after meeting with Hoffman, Hall made several trips to the area and "ascertained the nature and extent of its coal," a considerable achievement for someone with no training in either geology or engineering. With this presumed knowledge, Hall convinced William Turner to return to Bozeman to have a look for himself. Turner, who had a bit more experience evaluating mining properties, liked what he saw, negotiated a tonnage guarantee with Hoffman, and then authorized the start of construction. Although a short branch line to some coal mines was not part of their broader vision for a regional carrier servicing the Gallatin Valley and Yellowstone National Park, the Gallatin Railroad partners seem to have concluded that the Trail Creek branch might be a worthwhile step toward getting their larger venture started. Having made the decision to proceed, Hall excitedly announced on June 28 that they were seeking construction bids and then boldly predicted that trains would be running on what he referred to as the first section of the Gallatin Railroad within ninety days.[13]

How the partners intended to finance a project with a total cost likely to exceed $100,000 is unknown. But Hall's initial step was to seek the help of the NP, and in July, he traveled to St. Paul, Minnesota, to meet with NP president Charles S. Mellen. A tall, balding man with a prominent chin and commanding presence, the forty-five-year-old Mellen lacked a college education but had nevertheless managed to work his way to the top of his profession. Given his background, it can be imagined that Mellen was somewhat amused when Hall, a dapper, smooth-talking thirty-year-old from Bozeman with no railroad experience, sat down in this office and tried to convince him that the NP should take a mortgage on a yet to be built branch line in Montana.[14]

Despite Hall's obvious inexperience in finance, Mellen listened to his proposal with interest and then patiently explained to him not only the legal pitfalls involved in his scheme but also the fact that a mortgage would amount to little more than an unsecured loan, something the NP was not willing to consider. Nonetheless Mellen was intrigued and

Charles S. Mellen, Northern Pacific Railway president (1897–1903). Mellen's dealings with Frank Hall left him both frustrated and unimpressed. (Minnesota Historical Society).

saw enough benefit in the potential traffic from the Trail Creek mines that he decided to support the project. Because of NP's tight finances, rather than a cash loan, Mellen offered to supply Hall with construction materials from company stockpiles, the cost of which would be repaid over time. Then, having taken the measure of Hall, Mellen allowed that he was willing to go through with the deal only if Hall could furnish "a note of your Company, endorsed personally by responsible parties." By this, there is little doubt, he meant the Turner brothers.[15]

The Turners soon agreed to Mellen's terms, but funding for the remainder of the project remained an issue. Where these funds eventually came from is unknown, but it is likely that the Turners invested their own money and convinced some of their associates in Spokane to buy into the venture as well. Additional funding may have come from Charles Hoffman and the other mine owners. However the money was raised, it was soon clear that contracts were let and work begun before the project was fully funded. Whether this was an oversight or a decision driven by the desire to move forward before winter is unclear.

According to one account, the motivation was the tonnage agreement with Hoffman that stipulated a completion date for the line. It could also have been influenced by assurances from Frank Hall that he could easily raise more money once construction was under way. Regardless of the circumstances, in August 1898, Hall opened a "handsome office" in the Bozeman City Hall and the Gallatin Railroad partners let a contract to the firm of Cook and Woldson to build an eleven-mile branch from the NP mainline near Chestnut to the mines on Trail Creek.[16]

Named for Colonel John D. Chesnut, who opened the first coal mine in the area in 1867, the town of Chestnut was located just east of the narrow canyon of rugged limestone and quartzite outcrops that carries Rocky Creek to the broad alluvial plain on the outskirts of Bozeman. Situated four miles west of the summit of Bozeman Pass on the north side of the canyon in a grassy alcove surrounded by steeply tilted gray and tan beds of sandstone with interbedded coal, the Chestnut or Rocky Canyon mine had been operated by the NP since 1891. A mile to the east was an even larger complex called the Mountain Side Mine.[17]

The railroad that Hall and the Turners planned to build would start about a half mile east of Chestnut at a siding near the Mountain Side Mine and swing through a tight 180-degree curve to the southwest past the mine workings before turning southeast to follow Meadow Creek's wooded south bank up a broad U-shaped valley on a grade that gradually increased from 1 to 3 percent. After about six miles, the line flattened as it emerged from the trees and crossed a low, grassy divide into the Trail Creek drainage. From that point, it was less than a mile to a stagecoach stop called Mountain House and the Hoffman mine. The Cox, or Kountz, mine was about a mile beyond the Hoffman and the Cook and Bell mine (later Maxey Bros. or Chimney Rock mine) about three miles farther down the drainage to the southeast. The valley sides and floor being composed of mostly stream gravel and shale would present no major construction problems. The entire route would use light fifty-six-pound rail supplied by the NP spiked to locally cut, rough-hewn ties laid on a narrow, unballasted roadbed. Although the grades were reasonable, curvature at one point was near ten degrees, close to the maximum allowed on an industrial type railroad.[18]

A month after signing the construction contract William Turner gave a detailed account of their plans to a reporter from the Spokane *Spokesman-Review* that was picked up by the *Anaconda Standard*. According to Turner, the line to Trail Creek was just the beginning. He explained that in addition to the coal mine branch, they still intended to build a one-hundred-mile-long regional line starting at a point near Bozeman, or possibly Manhattan near the Altenbrand elevators, that would follow the Gallatin River and terminate near the petrified forest in Yellowstone National Park. According to Turner, their principal goal was to tap the area's rich agricultural lands, specifically its world-renowned barley crop, while at the same time providing tourists with an alternate route to the park. He explained that visitors arriving via the NP's Park Branch, or his new line, could traverse the park and depart via the other railroad. The Gallatin line would thus capture half of the ever-increasing tourist traffic. With this in mind, he also informed the reporter that to more accurately describe their new vision, he and his partners had decided to change the name of their company to the Yellowstone Park Railway. Then, with a promoter's zeal, or perhaps just an overactive imagination and a lot of misinformation, Turner went on to describe the great coal, asbestos, gold, and copper deposits to be found along the railroad's proposed route—all of which would prove to be illusory.[19]

Turner's plans for the Yellowstone Park Railway made no more sense than the earlier Gallatin Railroad. Construction up the Gallatin River canyon would be an expensive and daunting task with little prospect of significant returns. The proposed terminus near the northwest corner of Yellowstone National Park, some twenty miles south of present-day Big Sky, was an area of mostly uninhabited wilderness and investors giving the project the least scrutiny would have realized there was little merit in Turner's proposal. Nonetheless, confident of their ultimate success, and hoping to establish himself as a prominent member of the local business community, in November 1898, Hall vacated his office in city hall and moved into even more spacious accommodations in the Masonic Block of Bozeman's central business district at the corner of West Main and South Tracy Avenue. According to one report, Hall spared no expense in making all of the rooms in his new office comfortable and elegant with new paint, paper, and furniture. The new company was incorporated in Montana in December and capitalized at $1.5 million, each of the three partners contributing $1,000 to the start-up.[20]

A new railroad was the kind of news that generated excitement and attracted attention across the state. With construction about to commence, on August 2, 1898, Frank Hall advertised for twenty tie makers with the promise that the company would pay "top wages." Three weeks after posting his ad in the *Helena Daily Independent,* when only about two miles of brush had been cleared from the right-of-way, that same paper eagerly reported that "those who saw the smoke from the successive brush piles could almost imagine they saw a locomotive rushing around the mountain." Riding a wave of local enthusiasm, two months later Hall let it be known that as soon as the line was complete, he would offer an excursion to anyone in Bozeman who wished to visit the mining camps or just wanted to ride on his new railroad.[21]

Due to numerous delays, the railroad was not completed as planned. It was early 1899 before tracks finally reached the Hoffman Mine, and there, with only seven miles of the eleven-mile branch completed, the project stalled. This hiatus was likely due to the project's inadequate funding, as construction to that point had not been without its share of problems. As early as November, it appears that Hall had failed to make a required payment to the NP. When this issue was brought to light by NP's Second Vice President John W. Kendrick, Hall's glib response was that there must have been a misunderstanding about when the payment was due. Hall then turned the table on Kendrick and complained that NP was not supplying the promised rails in a timely manner. "We have our ties distributed ahead of us and had figured on completing the line to the mine by next Tuesday, weather permitting," Hall told Kendrick in a December 1 letter, "and here we are, tied up completely without a rail after receiving advice that another shipment was being loaded." Hall's response appears to have been little more than a subterfuge, as he was probably out of money and attempting to buy time while seeking additional investors. In January, as work ground to a halt, the general contractor, Cook and Woldson, filed a mechanic's lien against the Yellowstone Park Railway (née Gallatin Railroad) for unpaid construction

John W. Kendrick, general manager and later second vice-president of the Northern Pacific Railway. Kendrick hoped that the Yellowstone Park Railway would be the first and last time the NP had to deal with Frank Hall, but his wishful prognostications went unfulfilled. (Minnesota Historical Society).

bills. Hall and the Turners disputed the contractor's claim and refused to pay, saying that the railroad had been overcharged. The crux of the disagreement was the volume of dirt and rock that had been excavated during construction. But, again, this could have simply been another distraction aimed at buying time for Hall to raise more money.[22]

As the year wore on, troubles for Hall and the Yellowstone Park Railway did not abate, and in March 1899, when payment for rails and fasteners had still not been received, Charles Mellen ceased to be amused by Hall's behavior. Having done what he could to support the project, he wrote to John Kendrick, stating: "I have been disappointed in my dealings with Mr. Hall so many times that I do not feel like taking any more chances. I think his intentions are all right but he has been unable thus far to carry out his agreements and unless we protect ourselves we may find ourselves worse off than at the present time." A month later, when payment was still not forthcoming, his patience exhausted, Mellen again wrote to Kendrick, saying:

> What I want from Mr. Hall is some money and not so much talk about what he is going to do some time with somebody else. . . . I want him to pay up, and then he will have the right to do some talking such as he has been indulging in for some time back.
>
> I have no faith in him or his promises. . . . Treat him in every way as an irresponsible fellow connected with an irresponsible concern, hereafter.[23]

While Hall was increasingly a source of frustration and irritation for the NP, Mellen's assessment, that his intentions were good, was probably accurate, but as with Reliance Wire Works, he lacked the business acumen to properly manage the company and, in his eagerness to complete the project, had allowed it to become seriously overextended. Caught in a bind, Hall was trying to talk his way out, a pattern he would repeat with varying degrees of success in the future.

By the time the tracks reached the Hoffman Mine, it was abundantly clear that the Yellowstone Park Railway was in serious financial trouble; Hall's only remaining hope was that revenue from coal shipments could be used to settle the company's debts and eventually complete the line. But even this proved to be difficult. Using a leased locomotive, the first coal was not shipped until May, a delay likely caused by winter weather and a soggy, unstable roadbed. At that point, securing outside financing for either the Trail Creek line or William Turner's grandiose scheme for a railroad to Yellowstone National Park seemed increasingly unlikely as investors had shown little interest in either project. Despite these setbacks, the partners celebrated the line's completion with an inspection tour. A photo of the event shows Frank Hall attired in a morning coat, white shirt, and straw boater hat seated on a cross tie while the Turner brothers and Charles Hoffman, along with their wives, proudly stand at the rear of a NP caboose chartered for the occasion. Things were not going well, and an air of tension seems to pervade the scene as the Turner brothers' stoic expressions hint at their growing disillusionment with their young partner.[24]

With operations just getting underway, in early summer the situation took a turn for the worse when the dispute with Cook and Woldson ended up in court. When a preliminary hearing was held in Bozeman during August, Philip M. Gallaher, a recognized expert in railroad construction from Billings, was among the witnesses called to testify. Frank Hall, having been named as a defendant, was probably present during Gallaher's testimony, and this event likely led to their first meeting. Within a year, this chance encounter would result in the two of them working together in a most unlikely partnership. But for now, Frank Hall was on his own.[25]

As time and the court battle wore on, having grown disenchanted with Hall's managerial skills, as well as his increasingly problematic relationship with the NP, the Turner brothers found themselves in an awkward position. Not wanting their reputations tarnished by Hall's questionable business antics, the Turners concluded that something had to be done. So, in September 1899, the Turners approached Hall and convinced him to sell out. Hall, who probably reveled in the status and attention his position provided, might have resisted, as he stayed on the job until at least mid-October. But in the end, William Turner presumably made Hall's departure sufficiently rewarding to ensure his agreement. Because Frank Hall was by now well known to NP's upper management, John Kendrick was pleased to hear of this development and wrote to President Mellen stating hopefully that Hall "will presumably leave for 'fields green and pastures new.'" While his behavior may have frustrated the Turners and left NP's upper management wary of him, Hall's overall reputation does not appear to have suffered. Newspapers across Montana continued to herald him as a well-known railroad promoter, the man who had built the state's newest railroad and spurred the development of an important new coalfield. Deserved or not, these were accolades Hall would proudly carry into the future.[26]

With Hall out of the picture, William Turner moved to Bozeman and assumed the role of general manager. Seeing little hope for their planned extension to the National Park, and not wanting to be saddled with the details of daily operations on the branch line, in late October, the Turner brothers met with President Mellen and John Kendrick and worked out a ten-year lease agreement. But several issues had to be resolved before the NP would assume operations. Among them was the need to improve the existing roadbed and complete the four-mile extension to the Cook and Bell mine. NP engineers who inspected the line complained that it was poorly located and shoddily constructed, requiring not only ballast but also widening, improved drainage, and, in places, additional fill to even the grade. It can only be assumed that these deficiencies were the result of Hall's efforts to economize and complete the line despite its inadequate funding. These complaints, along with the four-mile extension, were settled when the Turners agreed to deposit about $45,000 into an NP account. A year after the line was completed, the *Anaconda Standard* enthusiastically sang the praises of the little-known Yellowstone Park Railway. In an effusive article, the *Standard* claimed the line would "add much to the wealth of Montana," ultimately extend its line another fifty or sixty miles to reach the National Park and offer "a new route to Wonderland"—improbable prophesies all.[27]

Having removed Frank Hall from its management and leased the railroad to the NP, one outstanding issue remained: the dispute with Cook and Woldson. When in June 1903, after four years of haggling, the court finally found the case in the contractor's favor, the Turner brothers were no longer concerned with the outcome, William having moved to southern California and George being occupied in Washington, DC, with his duties as US senator from Washington. This left the NP to deal with the problem. Faced with foreclosure on a property it had leased, operated, maintained, and improved during the past several years, the NP reluctantly agreed to pay Cook and Woldson the $14,077 it was owed. Although long gone, the outcome of this dispute probably did little to improve NP management's opinion of Frank Avery Hall. And despite John Kendrick's wishful prediction that he would move on to "pastures new," Hall was not done with the railroad business or the NP. He was still intent on building a railroad to Yellowstone National Park, and it would not be long before their paths crossed again.[28]

2

“The Line Is Remarkable for Cheapness”

TWENTY-FIVE YEARS BEFORE FRANK HALL FIRST SET FOOT IN Montana a chance discovery by an itinerant prospector named James George set into motion a series of events that would inexorably alter the course of Hall’s life. Born in Vermont on September 18, 1841, James George grew up in Pennsylvania, where he received a rudimentary education that ended at age twelve when his family headed west to Iowa. Tall and thin with dark mischievous eyes, in 1857, at age sixteen, George left the family farm “on the toe of his father’s boot” and crossed the plains of Kansas in the company of the US Army’s Utah Expedition under the command of future Confederate general Albert Sidney Johnston. Five years later, he arrived in the Montana Territory, lured, no doubt, by stories of the riches being discovered in the gold fields near Bannack. Little is known of his early exploits except that the gold of Bannack and nearby Virginia City eluded him. Although he would later gain notoriety as the operator of a toll road leading to Yellowstone National Park and assume the moniker “Yankee Jim,” in 1866 James George was just another prospector hoping to strike it rich.[1]

Spurred on by dreams of sudden wealth, in the summer of 1866 Yankee Jim George joined an expedition led by respected explorer Jefferson J. Standifer, who planned to work his way east from Bozeman in search of gold along the foot of the Snow Mountains, as the Beartooth Range was then known. Because Standifer’s planned route passed through wild country claimed by hostile Indian tribes, prospecting would be a dangerous endeavor. For Yankee Jim George, traveling with a group of one hundred well-armed men afforded protection against attack and the possible loss of horses and supplies. But despite these ever-present dangers, individuals occasionally split off from the group to work on their own. This seems to have been the case the day that Yankee Jim stumbled on a thick layer of black rock on a steep, grass-and-sage-covered hillside above a broad valley not far from the mountain front. Being eight or ten feet thick it must have been quite notable. Yankee Jim knew immediately that it was coal and even to his untrained eye it must have looked like good stuff. But just the same, he knew it was worthless. Located deep within Crow tribal lands and miles from any possible market, it was little more than a curiosity. Even so, he may have picked up a sample or two before logging the location away in his mind and moving on. Another sixteen years would pass before anyone gave serious consideration to exploiting his discovery. Even then, few imagined that the broad valley with the swift-running stream lined with willows and aspen, later called Rocky Fork or Rock Creek, would one day be the site of one of southern Montana's most important coal mining towns, a place called Red Lodge.[2]

Coal was the fuel of the industrial revolution and Yankee Jim George's discovery had been 60 million years in the making, the product of a huge swampy forest with bogs and lakes that stretched as far east as North Dakota and covered much of southern Montana and northeast Wyoming. Occurring on both sides of the Rock Creek valley and extending four miles to the east into the Bear Creek valley, the coal he had found was not a single bed but one of nine mineable coal-bearing intervals distributed within an 825-foot-thick section of sandstone, siltstone, and shale. Although these deposits were initially considered high-grade subbituminous, geologists would later elevate much of this coal to bituminous rank based on its high heat content and resistance to weathering. This was especially true of the coal found along Bear Creek, which geologists judged to be superior to that found just a few miles away in Red Lodge. Because nearly everything in the late nineteenth century

Facing, James "Yankee Jim" George as he appeared around 1900. A prospector, hunter, and toll road operator, his serendipitous discovery of coal along Rock Creek in 1866 led to the development of the Red Lodge–Bear Creek Coal Field. (Yellowstone Gateway Museum of Park County 2006.044.1875).

was powered by coal, promoters and mine developers soon recognized Yankee Jim George's discovery as a huge and potentially valuable resource. Fifty years after his fateful discovery the US Geological Survey designated it the Red Lodge–Bear Creek Coal Field and estimated the total coal in place at over 1.23 billion tons.[3]

About four years after Yankee Jim George discovered coal along Rock Creek, thirty-one-year-old Adam "Horn" Miller and three other prospectors followed the Yellowstone River deep into the Absaroka Mountains in search of gold. After days of fruitless work Miller and his partners found themselves in a high mountain valley surrounded by craggy peaks and dense forest. Here they came upon stream gravels with traces of gold and notable showings of galena (lead ore). Encouraged, they expanded their search but, within a few days, were ambushed by a band of native inhabitants who surrounded their camp and ran off their horses. Narrowly escaping death, Miller and his partners abandoned their endeavor and headed home. But they soon returned, and on the south-facing slope of a mountain that would one day bear his name, Horn Miller staked a claim on an outcrop of argentiferous (silver-bearing) galena. There were indications of gold, copper, and zinc ore in the area as well. Miller named his claim "Shoo-fly." Other members of the party staked claims nearby, some rich in silver, others rich in copper. Miller had made the discovery of a lifetime, and it was not long before news of his success reached the outside world. Soon legions of hopeful fortune seekers were packing up shovels and pickaxes in preparation for their trek to the high mountains, an area that one day would be called the New World Mining District.[4]

Located near the headwaters of the Clarks Fork of the Yellowstone, just beyond the northeast corner of what would soon be Yellowstone National Park, the New World Mining District was created by the intrusion of molten rock from deep within the Earth's crust between 43 and 53 million years ago. Encompassing an area of about forty square miles the mining district comprises several geologically complex ore bodies, some rich in silver and lead, others rich in copper or gold. But just like the coalfield Yankee Jim George had found, this new mining district was within the recently established Crow Indian Reservation. This being a mere technicality for anxious fortune seekers, within a year or two more than a hundred miners were working claims in the area. Although miners who staked claims on stream-gravel gold placers found them to be a disappointment, the bedrock lodes were rich. The problem the miners faced was the areas' remoteness. With only rough trails, and later crude wagon roads as a means of transport, it was difficult to bring in needed equipment and only the most valuable ores were worth hauling out. Despite this limitation, claims continued to be developed and the small mining camp that sprang up in the bottom of a broad glacial valley near the southwest corner of the district was soon named Cooke City by area miners who hoped to entice capitalist Jay Cooke into helping them develop the district.[5]

During the late 1870s, increased mining activity and the construction of furnaces for smelting ore resulted in friction with the Crow tribe. Landownership soon became a contentious issue. Fearing an eruption of violence, in 1880, government officials met with tribal leaders to negotiate a treaty. The result was an agreement that ceded 1.5 million acres of Crow tribal land to the federal government. The ceded lands included both the New World Mining District and the Red Lodge–Bear Creek Coal Field. Ratification of the treaty by Congress on July 10, 1882, opened both areas to full-scale development.[6]

Having failed to strike it rich, Yankee Jim George returned from the Standifer expedition and took a job as a hunter for the Crow Indian Agency. A few years later, he acquired the toll road for which he became well known and settled into a cabin in a narrow canyon above the Yellowstone River just north of Yellowstone National Park. Here George soon established a reputation as a purveyor of tall tales and by demanding a kiss from every pretty girl who ventured down his rough-built tollway. When Congress ratified the Treaty of 1882, Yankee Jim and three partners saddled up and headed back to the broad valley where he had made his 1866 discovery. Despite it still being many miles from any potential market, each of them staked an adjoining 160-acre claim; other speculators soon followed.[7]

In the New World Mining District news of the treaty's ratification prompted local investor George Eaton to purchase a number of claims from disgruntled miners and then partner with Cheyenne, Wyoming, bankers Sturgis & Lane to build the Republic, or Cooke City smelter. The Republic smelter was not the first in the district, but when it became operational in 1884, it was the largest and most modern. Although reducing ores from some parts of the district proved to be problematic, mixing them with the near pure lead-silver ore from the Shoo-fly and other mines on Miller Mountain allowed the production of several hundred tons of lead-silver bullion in 1886. Despite this early success, it soon became apparent that hauling the heavy ingots out of the mountains by wagon was a money-losing proposition. Reuben Rickard, the smelter's superintendent, recommended that a plant be built to extract the silver from the mixture. His plan was to ship the silver and retain the lead on site until reliable, cost-effective transportation could be provided. But Eaton and his partners could not afford the investment in a new plant. Seeing little hope of ever making the smelter profitable Rickard resigned, and after the brief spike in activity in 1886, mining in the New World District dropped off dramatically. What both Cooke City and the Red Lodge–Bear Creek Coal Field desperately needed was a reliable, economic transportation link to the outside world. In the latter half of the nineteenth century, that meant a railroad, and by 1886, there were a number of promoters with plans to build one.[8]

Because the financial Panic of 1873 had driven financier Jay Cooke into bankruptcy, the Northern Pacific (NP) Railroad's transcontinental line from Lake Superior to the Pacific Coast had remained stalled in Bismarck, Dakota Territory, for almost seven years. But in the winter of 1879, after reorganizing, the railroad once again began to build west across the boundless prairies and sculpted badlands of the Dakota and Montana Territories. When the line reached a point fifty miles west of the confluence of the Yellowstone and Bighorn Rivers, it bypassed the pioneer riverside settlement of Coulson in favor of a newly platted town named for the company's ex-president Frederick Billings, who happened to own large tracts of land in the area. The tracks reached there in March 1882. After the customary speeches and celebrations, the graders and track crews pushed west up the Yellowstone Valley and reached Livingston at the foot of Bozeman Pass in January 1883. From there, work continued until a final gold spike, which signified the completion of the nation's first northern transcontinental railroad, was driven at Independence Creek, Montana, on September 8, 1883.[9]

With the territory between Bismarck and the Pacific Coast now ripe for development, before the final spike was driven, branch lines off the transcontinental route were being proposed and built. Because of restrictions placed on it by its congressional charter, early NP branches were often built by third parties with close ties to the railroad and then sold to the NP for a handsome profit. The first of these in Montana was the Rocky Mountain Railroad, which in the summer of 1883 built a line south from Livingston to the town of Cinnabar, about three miles north of Gardiner and the entrance to Yellowstone National Park. Named for a nearby mountain, the station at Cinnabar was a few miles south of an 1860s mining camp where prospectors mistakenly assumed the red-streaked sandstones and silts along the mountain front contained quicksilver, or mercury ore. NP purchased the line after its completion and designated it the Park Branch, notwithstanding a $50,000 lawsuit brought by Yankee Jim George for damage to his toll road. George had good reason to complain. Not only had the new rail line nearly put him out of business, but the tracks ran just a few feet from his front door. As his lawsuit dragged on, it is said that George often stood in the doorway of his cabin and swore and shook his fist whenever a train roared past.[10]

As soon as the Park Branch was in operation plans were made to extend the line through Yellowstone National Park to Cooke City and the New World Mining District. Although several plans were considered, the only practicable route for this extension was one that followed the Yellowstone River to the Lamar Valley and from there up Soda Butte Creek. In January 1884 Montana Territorial representative Martin Maginnis introduced a bill in the House of Representatives that proposed granting a right-of-way along this route to the Cinnabar & Clark's Fork Railroad, a surrogate of the NP. Because the proposed route crossed the

National Park boundary it required full congressional approval, and due to the objections of several members of Congress, Maginnis's proposal immediately ran into trouble.[11]

Shortly after Maginnis submitted the bill, a powerful lobbying effort, orchestrated in part by George Bird Grinnell, the editor of Forest and Stream magazine, mobilized opposition in both chambers of Congress. Grinnell, an anthropologist, naturalist, and writer, held a doctorate in zoology from Yale University and by the 1880s had attained prominence as a conservationist advocating for the preservation of Yellowstone National Park, especially its dwindling buffalo herd. Missouri senator George Vest allied himself with Grinnell and became a key leader of the opposition, rallying support in the Senate to prevent the NP, or any presumed surrogates, from defiling the park simply to advance its self-serving commercial interests. Although several bills were submitted in both the House and the Senate during the next few years, and several were passed out of committee, amended, and recommended for passage, each session of Congress ended without a vote being scheduled.[12]

In an effort to convince his colleagues that the railroad's goal was the development of Cooke City and not a land grab in the park destined to result in NP-owned hotels and tourist facilities, Senator Omar Conger of Michigan offered an amendment that reduced the width of the right-of-way from the usual two hundred to only one hundred feet. This change, he claimed, would reduce the railroad's impact on the environment and prevent the construction of anything but essential trackside structures. When this proposal failed to gain traction and attempts to bring the matter to a vote in the Senate during the summer of 1886 were unsuccessful, railroad proponents dropped their efforts at securing a right-of-way and decided to take a new approach.[13]

Having abandoned their plan for a right-of-way through the park, in late 1886 railroad proponents attempted to convince Congress to contract the park's northeastern boundary enough to allow a railroad to reach Cooke City without entering the park. The backers of this proposal, who again were presumed NP surrogates, asserted that the park's straight-line boundaries were completely arbitrary and the return of part of the northeast corner of the park to the public domain would have no impact on the natural wonders that required protection. This change would, therefore, cause no harm. They also argued that after encouraging development of the New World Mining District, Congress was now stifling economic activity by blocking construction of the railroad that was essential to its continued development. Although there was some truth to these statements, this proposal also met strong opposition. Grinnell claimed that the area proposed for withdrawal included critical wildlife habitat that should not be opened to hunters or commercial development.[14]

Although the idea of reducing the park's size was again proposed in 1890 by a company called the Montana Mineral Railway, when legislation was passed in 1892 forbidding railroad construction in National Parks, the NP and other advocates of a park-crossing railroad quietly abandoned their plans. In 1903, the NP managed to extend the Park Branch to Yellowstone's northern border at Gardiner, but there the tracks would end forever.[15]

Although much excitement accompanied the early development of the New World Mining District, production peaked in 1886 when 735,000 pounds of lead, 62,300 ounces of silver, and 438 ounces of gold were recovered with a value of about $105,000. This production was significant and attracted the attention of businessmen and promoters throughout the state. So, while the NP and its surrogates waged their battles in Congress, two new railroad companies were formed with the aim of tapping the district's developing potential. Both planned to avoid potential political complications by reaching the mining camp without crossing the park boundary. The schemes set forth by these new companies gave NP's congressional opponents additional justification for not bowing to pressure to allow a railroad construction in the park.[16]

The first plan originated with a group in Billings that included civil engineer Philip Gallaher and businessmen Thomas Hanlon and George Hulme, along with New Yorker George Sims and Henry Kelly of Philadelphia. Gallaher and his partners planned to build a railroad that would run west from Billings to the mouth of the Clarks Fork of the Yellowstone and then south and west along that drainage all the way to Cooke City. They also intended to build a branch line to the coalfield at Red Lodge

Philip M. Gallaher, visionary civil engineer and longtime proponent of a Bear Creek–Cooke City railroad. (Author's collection).

(Rocky Fork). The company they incorporated in March 1886 was called the Billings, Clark's Fork & Cooke City Railroad (the Clark's Fork).[17]

Strikingly handsome with deep-set eyes, dark hair, and a thick, manicured handlebar mustache, thirty-four-year-old Philip M. Gallaher was not new to the railroad business. Born in Jersey Shore, Pennsylvania, he graduated from the Polytechnic College of Pennsylvania in 1872 with a degree in engineering and spent the next eight years working on railroad construction projects in the east and Midwest. In 1880, he took a job as a mining engineer in Leadville, Colorado, and two years later relocated to Helena, Montana, where he and a partner opened a civil engineering office. Stoic and pragmatic, when his first wife, Frances, died in 1884, Gallaher elected to send his young daughter Ida away to be raised by her grandmother. Then, in early 1886, likely motivated by the prospect of returning to the railroad business, he moved to Billings. Although his partners would soon drop by the wayside, Gallaher would, for the next twenty years, remain a ceaseless advocate for a railroad up the Clarks Fork Valley.[18]

The other company that professed plans for a Cooke City railroad was the Rocky Fork & Cooke City Railway (the Rocky Fork). Coal mine developers James Platt and Hamilton Brown of Iowa; J. B. Hubbell of St. Paul, Minnesota; and Walter Cooper and Samuel Word of Montana incorporated the company in December 1886. Their plan was to branch off the NP near the station stop at Laurel, Montana; cross the Yellowstone River; and follow Rock Creek (Rocky Fork) to Red Lodge. A section of land called Tilden Junction was purchased near Laurel for the construction of a depot and other facilities. The prospectus issued by the company showed that from Red Lodge, it planned to reach Cooke City by either extending tracks west along the mountain front to the mining camp of Nye City and then south up the Stillwater River or by crossing the divide east of Red Lodge and following the mountain front south to the Clarks Fork River. Subsequent events would establish its preferred route as via Nye City, but time would prove that it was far easier to draw lines on a map than build a railroad.[19]

For the Rocky Fork, construction of a railroad up the Stillwater River valley to the New World Mining District would be a formidable task. The final few miles requiring an abrupt climb at a grade that might exceed 3 percent over a 9,800-foot mountain pass with the descent into Cooke City being equally steep and just as difficult. Confronted with this problem, the company revealed in its prospectus that it planned to avoid the issue by terminating the line in the Stillwater canyon some ten miles north of Cooke City and connect to the mines via a wagon road. For the Cooke City miners, this was better than no railroad at all but still not what they needed, as a wagon road would likely be serviceable only part of the year. Regardless of its stated intentions, it was widely known that Cooke City was not the Rocky Fork syndicate's real objective. The main goal of the Rocky Fork line was the development of coal properties the syndicate had acquired near Red Lodge, which were extensive and included a 640-acre tract recently purchased from Yankee Jim George and his three partners for $19,000.[20]

With their plans laid out and limited backing, both groups sent survey crews into the field during the summer of 1886. Philip Gallaher and his Clark's Fork party worked their way south along the Clarks Fork River through the mostly flat, largely uninhabited Crow tribal lands and then branched off on a line that followed Elbow Creek from near present-day Edgar over the low divide into the Red Lodge coalfield. With this task complete, they returned to the Clarks Fork Valley and continued south into the Wyoming Territory. Some fifteen miles south of the territorial boundary they followed the river west toward the sheer uplifted face of the Beartooth Mountains. After traversing a desolate windswept outwash plain and passing the upturned tan, gray, and rust-colored strata that flanked the mountain front, the survey party entered a broad glacial valley where the lazy Clarks Fork was transformed into a rushing mountain stream with white-water rapids and cascades. Within a few miles, the river curved northwestward and entered a narrow, six-hundred-foot-deep gorge sliced into the mountain's ancient granite core. This ten-mile-long canyon would be the most challenging portion of the route, a place where the roadbed would have to be blasted out of sheer granite cliffs. After working their way through the narrow confines alongside the often-roaring Clarks Fork River, the surveyors emerged onto a broad, forested, boulder-strewn high mountain valley surrounded by distant volcanic peaks highlighted with vestiges of late spring snow. This part of the survey traversed a largely unexplored wilderness that would require little rock work and only a few stream crossings, making construction of the final twenty-five miles of the line into Cooke City comparatively easy.

When Gallaher returned from the field in late June, he told the *Billings Gazette* that the proposed route was "more conspicuous for its natural scenery than its natural railroad grades." But despite this evaluation, Gallaher was not discouraged and he went on to note the need for three bridges and at least a half mile of tunnels. A congressional report written two years later that recommended approval of the route stated that it was "certainly a practicable one, and one of great utility to the entire country when constructed." The truth of this statement lay in the fact that although the climb from the mountain front to Cooke City required an ascent of some 3,250 feet, unlike the Rocky Fork line's route up the Stillwater, there were no high mountain passes to contend with and loaded ore trains would have a downhill run all the way to Billings. And yet the route remained controversial. A survey completed several years later by the NP noted that at least one section would require a grade of nearly 4 percent, something most locating engineers considered excessive. Gallaher, it seems, neglected to mention this problem in his report to Congress. Whether this was because he had located a superior alignment or did not view it as a problem is unknown. Certainly, some past mainline railroads had been built with grades that steep. Just a few years earlier, in 1878, the Spartanburg & Asheville Railroad in North Carolina built a section of mainline called the Saluda Grade that for three miles had an average gradient of more than 4 percent. But this type of construction was the exception, most locating engineers fiercely avoided grades this steep as they created myriad operational problems, such as the need for helper engines and runaway train safety tracks. If the NP was correct, despite Gallaher's optimism, a 4 percent grade in the Clarks Fork Canyon made this approach to Cooke City appear anything but "practicable."[21]

The other obstacle Gallaher's route faced was the need to blast several miles of roadbed out of the granite walls of the Clarks Fork Canyon. The *Billings Gazette*, an ardent supporter of any Cooke City line with a terminus in Billings, refused to acknowledge the potential problems and confidently proclaimed that "the line is remarkable for [its] cheapness of construction. . . . In the canyon there are several miles of heavy work, though much lighter than has been encountered on almost every division of the Northern Pacific." This optimistic assessment, likely written by a reporter with little knowledge of railroad construction, may have originated with Philip Gallaher who hoped to avoid negative publicity while he and his partners sought investors for their ambitious project. Regardless, the NP would conclude that the route was impractical due to both the "extremely heavy rock work" required and the steep grades. In later years, the NP would view the approach up the Stillwater River as the only practical route. Heavy rock work or not, if Gallaher had in fact located a superior alignment, the operational advantages of the Clark's Fork route were considerable.[22]

Beyond the technical challenges both railroads faced was the need to obtain both congressional and tribal approval to cross the Crow Indian Reservation, which encompassed much of the land south of the Yellowstone River as far west as Big Timber. This resulted in both companies initiating lobbying campaigns in Washington, DC, to secure their respective routes as soon as their initial surveys were completed. The

Rocky Fork line was the first to succeed. Congress approved its right-of-way in February 1887. Shortly thereafter, it negotiated an agreement with the Crow tribe that compensated it for the 888-acres removed from the reservation. As it was widely known the Rocky Fork's main objective was Red Lodge and not Cooke City, when news of the right-of-way approval was made public, James Platt was asked by Yankee Jim's partner M. M. Black what inducements would be necessary to get him to extend the line all the way to Cooke City. Platt replied that all he needed was for the mine owners to agree to give his road their business, "No bonus, no subsidies, nothing but patronage is requested." But a few days later, he admitted to NP president Robert Harris that "we have as yet made no survey from the coal mines to Cooke and only know of the nature of the route in a general way by passing over it." This was a telling admission as it likely explains how the Rocky Fork line was able to complete, submit, and get approval of its right-of-way ahead of Gallaher's group.[23]

With their route across the Crow Reservation approved, the Rocky Fork partners were poised to move forward, but they lacked the necessary capital. To solve this problem James Platt approached Samuel Hauser, a Helena banker, industrialist, and past Montana territorial governor with close ties to the NP and asked for his support. Hauser agreed to invest in the Rocky Fork line and because of his close ties to NP management his support came with the tacit understanding that the NP would soon be backing the project as well. Because their right-of-way approval stipulated that the railroad had to be completed within two years, the promoters decided to begin construction immediately. Grading began in August 1887 and by November construction of a bridge across the Yellowstone River was well underway. Then work came to an abrupt halt. The NP had not come forward with the anticipated support, and the Rocky Fork syndicate had exhausted the available funds.[24]

The unexpected shutdown had a ripple effect on the local community. A. J. Torreyson, who lived with his wife, Fannie, and young daughter on a 160-acre homestead five miles north of Red Lodge, had been hired by the Rocky Fork to cut ties for the railroad and needed the $300 he had been promised to get his family through the winter. With this incentive Torreyson spent much of the fall of 1887 with an ax in his hands cutting and shaping ties. But when he delivered the finished product to the railroad in early December, he was told that the promoter who had hired him was gone, having left town "between night and morning" to escape a possible lynching. It seems Torreyson wasn't the Rocky Fork's only victim. He returned home mad but managed to pull through a tough winter with little money thanks to his skill with a rifle and an abundance of wild game.[25]

With its cash reserves depleted and construction stalled, the Rocky Fork syndicate found itself in a precarious position: at risk of being supplanted by Gallaher's rival Clark's Fork line. Faced with the possible loss of its entire investment, the Rocky Fork syndicate began a campaign to thwart the Clark's Fork line's construction plans. In early 1888, stories and accusations began to circulate that bribes of flour and sugar had been given to Chief Plenty Coups, a key Crow tribal leader, in order to have him testify against the Clark's Fork line right-of-way. Walter Cooper, a principle in the Rocky Fork, was apparently one of the perpetrators as sworn testimony given by George Reed Davis placed him at the scene of the crime.[26]

When the skullduggery was revealed, the *Billings Gazette*, an ardent supporter of the Clark's Fork line, expressed the fervent opinion that the management of the Rocky Fork line would soon be shown, "in a very bad light," as they were "doing everything in their power, and asking every advantage over the other road." The bribes, if they were in fact made, probably weren't necessary, as Crow tribal leaders were already adamantly opposed to a second railroad crossing their reservation. But the Rocky Fork syndicate's efforts were not limited to the alleged bribery; they had also begun a lobbying campaign in Washington, DC, where they found more than one sympathetic ear in the House of Representatives. In a rebuttal to the proposed approval of the Clark's Fork right-of-way, Congressmen Knute Nelson of Minnesota, B. W. Perkins of Kansas, and John McShane of Nebraska argued that the Rocky Fork line's "work and enterprise should not be hampered and discouraged by Congress granting and encouraging a competing line to the same points and on nearly the same route." The congressmen went on to explain, "The undisputed fact is, that one road is badly needed, but there is not and will not be (the country being wild and unsettled) business for two roads for years to come." True as these arguments may have been, Philip Gallaher was persistent, and after spending two winters in Washington, DC, going over survey maps and lobbying key congressmen, his efforts were rewarded when the Clark's Fork syndicate was granted its right-of-way in June 1888. With this approval, there remained a major hurdle; the company still had to consummate an agreement with the Crow tribe, whose leaders continued to oppose it.[27]

With its right-of-way approved, as a counterstroke to the Rocky Fork syndicate's efforts to undermine them, in July 1888 Clark's Fork operatives made a deal with the NP for financial support by guaranteeing the railroad a minimum of fifty thousand tons of coal per year at a price below that being offered by the Rocky Fork syndicate. How exactly they expected to accomplish this is not clear, but because the need for high-quality coal was growing, the NP agreed to lend its support to the Clark's Fork line. This, no doubt, caused the Rocky Fork syndicate considerable distress, but without an agreement with the Crow tribe, the NP's backing was of little value and construction remained stalled.[28]

During the 1880s, Butte, Montana, had become one of the world's great copper mining districts. Marcus Daly, a savvy, self-taught geologist and mining engineer, controlled much of the production in Butte through his Anaconda Mining Company, which had developed huge mines and associated smelting and ore processing plants in Butte, Anaconda, and East Helena. All of these facilities relied on coal to keep them operating, and Anaconda Mining faced a constant struggle to maintain an adequate and reliable supply. The NP was in a similar position. Both Daly and NP's management knew that there was plenty of high-quality coal in Red Lodge, but they refused to finance its development until both the railroad and the coal mines were in friendly hands. To accomplish this, the NP turned to its longtime associate Samuel Hauser.[29]

With time about to expire on the two-year construction window, by September 1888, James Platt, leader of the Rocky Fork syndicate, knew the project was in trouble. So, when Hauser made him an offer and applied what has been described as "not-so-subtle pressure," Platt acquiesced and reluctantly sold Hauser controlling interest in both the railroad and the Rocky Fork Coal Company. Hauser reorganized the two companies into the Rocky Fork Railway and Coal Trust and secured additional funding by bringing in partners that included Marcus Daly and NP president Thomas Oakes. Their prearranged goal was to complete the line and then sell it to the NP for a profit. With his funding in place, Hauser managed to complete the railroad to Red Lodge on February 28, 1889, just a few days before the expiration of the two-year deadline. As the final work was being completed, A. J. Torreyson received the $300 he was owed for the ties he had cut more than a year earlier. While celebrations rang out in Red Lodge, the only activity on the Clark's Fork line was Philip Gallaher, acting as paymaster, settling the company's accounts for survey work that had been completed.[30]

Through much of 1889, the Clark's Fork project lay dormant, but this did not mean that Philip Gallaher had given up. In August, things began to change when it was announced that a group headed by Elijah Smith, a Boston capitalist with a long history in railroad and mining ventures had incorporated the Montana & Wyoming Railroad. Smith, who was born in New Bedford, Massachusetts, in April 1840, had entered the coal business in Boston as a young man. By the age of forty he was a well-established capitalist and soon became associated with German-born financier Henry Villard, who was working to dominate economic development in the Pacific Northwest. Smith's association with Villard soon expanded his business activities beyond finance and coal to include railroads. By 1880, Smith was involved in Villard's Oregon Improvement Company, a conglomerate that owned several railroads, the Franklin and Newcastle coal mines near Seattle, and the Pacific Coast Steamship line. In an effort to protect his existing railroad interests in Oregon and Washington, in 1881, Villard boldly seized control of the NP and pushed it through to completion. This achievement left Villard and the NP deep in debt, and in late 1883, his financial empire collapsed; Villard resigned as president of the NP in January 1884. His financial reverses caused him to lose control of his other holdings as well. Smith then stepped in and took over management of not only the Oregon Improvement Company but the Oregon Railway & Navigation (OR&N) and Oregon & Transcontinental companies too. Five years later, in mid-1889, after the OR&N had been sold and Smith lost a contentious battle with Villard for control of the Oregon & Transcontinental, Smith was ready to move on. His background in finance, railroads, and coal mining made him an obvious candidate to support Gallaher's Clarks Fork River railroad scheme. Due to his inability to attract investors, Gallaher probably sought out Smith in the hope he would be able to revitalize plans for a railroad to Cooke

City. When Smith became involved, Gallaher resigned from the Clark's Fork syndicate and worked to facilitate the transfer of its right-of-way approval to the newly created Montana & Wyoming Railroad. As a result, the route for Smith's new railroad was exactly the same as that of the Clark's Fork line: from Billings up the Clarks Fork Valley to Cooke City with a short branch line to Bear Creek. The only major change was the deletion of the now-redundant Red Lodge branch.[31]

In early December, in conjunction with their plans for a new railroad, Smith, Gallaher, and nine associates filed incorporation papers in Montana for the Montana Coal & Iron Company, an organization intent on the development of the coal deposits in the Bear Creek valley. Although their first coal patent was not filed with the federal government until December 4, the *Helena Independent* claimed that by August, Smith's company had invested $50,000 and controlled about three thousand acres of highly prospective coal lands. All of these steps had been carefully orchestrated in advance, as the original incorporation papers for the company had been filed in New York in April.[32]

Regardless of Smith's carefully laid plans, intransigence on the part of Crow tribal leaders continued to stymie efforts to build a railroad up the Clarks Fork Valley. But new hope was aroused in late 1890, when the tribe was cajoled into yet another treaty. This time it agreed to cede an additional 1.8 million acres on the west side of its reservation. This cession included the entire Clarks Fork Valley and obviated the need for further negotiations with the tribe. Unfortunately for Elijah Smith and his partners, the treaty was not ratified until October 1892, and before further action could be taken the Panic of 1893 destroyed all hope of raising capital for new construction. As the country slipped into a prolonged economic depression and plans for the Montana & Wyoming Railroad evaporated, Philip Gallaher, the ever-present proponent of a Clarks Fork–Cooke City railroad, reverted to his civil engineering background and took a job surveying the boundaries of Yellowstone National Park. At that point, it must have seemed that his seven-year struggle to build a railroad to the Red Lodge–Bear Creek coalfield and Cooke City had come to naught. But despite the frustration and repeated setbacks that had accompanied his early efforts he was not ready to give up.[33]

3

“We Can Control the Coal Trade of Montana”

IN THE LATE NINETEENTH CENTURY, COAL WAS NOT ONLY A ubiquitous transportation fuel powering ships and steam locomotives, but it was also the principal fuel used for everything from home heating and cooking to industrial purposes like smelting. Virtually everything used coal, and by the mid-1890s Montana’s appetite for the fuel was growing rapidly. Despite the completion of the Rocky Fork & Cooke City Railway—now owned by the NP and called the Rocky Fork Branch—and the opening of the massive East Side Mine in Red Lodge, there was an ever-growing need for more coal.

When Philip Gallaher returned from the National Park boundary survey, he once again began promoting a Bear Creek–Cooke City railroad. With NP’s Rocky Fork Branch now in operation Elijah Smith’s plan for the Montana & Wyoming Railroad, a line that would parallel the NP for its first thirty miles, had lost its appeal, and it was clear that a new approach was needed. Gallaher’s new plan envisioned a branch line that would start near Rockvale on NP’s Rocky Fork Branch and run south for thirty miles to Bear Creek. From there, he planned to extend the line another ninety miles into Wyoming’s Big Horn Basin with a forty-mile-long branch up the Clarks Fork Canyon to Cooke City. In proposing this new scheme, Gallaher reiterated his claim that he had “found it practicable to build a railroad up the Clarke’s Fork” and that it would not be “excessively expensive.” He went on to estimate the total cost for the 160-mile project at $2,540,000.[1]

By the time he made this new proposal Gallaher’s interests included not only Bear Creek coal and Cooke City but also the development of what he believed was a huge placer gold deposit in the gravel beds along the Clarks Fork River between Bennett Creek and Line Creek near present-day Clark, Wyoming. Gallaher informed the *Anaconda Standard* that the deposit covered between twelve thousand and fifteen thousand acres and claimed that prospectors had already recovered $200 worth of gold using only the "rudest appliances." In anticipation of developing this great resource, by late 1894 Gallaher and a partner named C. W. Chowning had bonded a number of placer claims along the route of his proposed railroad and brought in a dredging machine to begin mining operations.[2]

In an attempt to rally the support of local and out-of-state investors, in July 1894, Gallaher published a lengthy article in the *Billings Gazette* that described not only the value of the Bear Creek coalfield and the superiority of its coal but also the potential for extensive agricultural development in the Big Horn Basin and the absolute necessity of bringing a railroad to Cooke City. According to Gallaher, "there exists no doubt in the mind of anyone at all familiar with the camp, but what the Cooke City district could supply enough good ore to give a railroad a profitable business from the start, and that the region, encouraged by railroad connection, would rapidly develop and speedily become one of the most noted mining camps in the world." He went on to observe that because of Cooke City's proximity to Yellowstone National Park, "a railroad would obtain a large share of the travel to that Wonderland of America, for nowhere throughout the whole Park or Rocky Mountain Region is there more picturesque scenery to be found than that along the Clarke's Fork river."[3]

But eastern capitalists were still reeling from the prolonged effects of the depression brought on by the Panic of 1893, and despite Gallaher's enthusiasm, his project generated little interest. So, in early 1896, he headed east to spend two months in Boston and New York City meeting with investors from both Montana Coal & Iron and the moribund Montana & Wyoming Railroad. In May, Elijah Smith returned the favor and ventured out to Billings. While staying at the Gallaher residence the two men began to formulate a plan to entice the NP into building the rail line they needed. Since the NP had already shown some interest, the plan was simple, all they had to do was convince them that Bear Creek coal was superior to that mined in Red Lodge. With this in mind, in September

Gallaher opened a small mine and shipped the NP a one-hundred-ton sample for evaluation. Subsequent tests impressed the NP.[4]

With the test data in hand, NP engineers pondered the feasibility of extending the Rocky Fork line over the hill from Red Lodge to Bear Creek. Hearing of this, Gallaher felt compelled to send a letter to NP general manager John Kendrick wherein he extolled the virtues of a line up the Clarks Fork Valley and pointed out that it was impractical to extend the Rocky Fork Branch due to the elevation differences and the steep grades that would confront loaded trains. Being aware that his investment in Montana Coal & Iron was worthless without NP's support and wanting to encourage them in any way he could, he went on to suggest that "if we can combine our forces (and there is no reason why we should not) we can control the coal trade of Montana and the Dakotas, to our mutual benefit." Unfortunately, despite his blatant appeal to NP's monopolistic tendencies, Gallaher's logic and persuasion failed to generate the hoped-for response. Because the NP was still recovering from its 1893 collapse into receivership, regardless of what Kendrick may have thought of Gallaher's suggestion, the company was reluctant to invest in new construction. As 1896 came to a close, with the country still mired in the throes of a serious financial depression, both Gallaher and Elijah Smith must have felt a sense of despair as prospects for a railroad to their mining venture remained bleak.[5]

Despite the NP's failure to act on Gallaher's proposal, by 1897 the need for coal to fuel the state's economy was increasing and every possible source was being examined. By necessity this evaluation included not only the quality of the coal to be mined but also its proximity to transportation. Deposits of bituminous coal, suitable for coking, were known to exist about twenty-five miles north of Bear Creek in an outcrop belt that extended from the farming community of Joliet to the mountains just west of a place called Bridger's Crossing, the site of a town later called Bridger. This coal, which came from the same formation as the coal at Trail Creek and Bozeman Pass, was high quality, but the seams were thin and often difficult to mine. Regardless of these shortcomings, when these lands were returned to the public domain by the Crow cession of 1892, the coal rights were quickly claimed. William A. Clark, a hard-driven banker, financier, and soon-to-be US senator whose Butte mining and smelting operations rivaled those of Marcus Daly, acquired coal rights in the hills west of Bridger. Daly's Anaconda company needed this coal as well and acquired coal rights about twelve miles northwest of Clark's holdings.[6]

The advantage Daly seized was that his property lay adjacent to NP's Rocky Fork Branch about four miles west of Joliet. As a result, when Anaconda opened the Carbonado Mine in 1898, it was immediately served by a short spur track. The downside to the Carbonado Mine was the need to excavate a 980-foot vertical shaft to reach a disappointingly thin coal seam. Because the seam tilted (or dipped), three degrees to the west, this same coal cropped out at the surface on William A. Clark's holdings near Bridger. Clark was anxious to get this property into production, but he needed a railroad.[7]

Since the NP was reluctant to invest in new construction and Clark did not want to build and operate a railroad of his own, he made a deal with the NP. In a contract dated July 30, 1898, Clark agreed to pay for right-of-way acquisition, all grading, and the construction of bridges and trestles from a point near present-day Fromberg to his mine west of Bridger. A similar agreement was reached with the owners of the Clark's Fork Coal Company mine near Fromberg, who agreed to pay for the northern part of the line starting at Silesia. All of the work was to be done under the direction and supervision of NP's engineering department and once grading was complete the NP agreed to lay the track, operate, and maintain the line. Completed in December 1898, NP designated this new nineteen-and-a-half-mile line the Clarks Fork Branch with ownership of each section being proportional to each party's investment; NP retained the right to buy its partners out at any time.[8]

Having been informed of Clark's negotiations, Elijah Smith contacted NP president Charles Mellen in February 1898 with a proposition to extend the Clarks Fork Branch south from Bridger to the Montana Coal & Iron property on Bear Creek. In a proposal similar to Clark's, Smith offered to pay for everything except laying the rails. Not wanting to own the property, he stipulated that the NP rebate the cost of coal shipments until he had recovered his investment, at which point he would transfer ownership to the NP. Surprisingly, Mellen, who had been hired away from the New York, New Haven, and Hartford Railroad and

Despite having made a considerable investment, the Anaconda Copper Mining Company's Carbonado Mine near Joliet was abandoned after just four years due to its high operating costs. (Joliet Public Library).

appointed to his new position less than a year earlier, did not respond to Smith. This may have been a reflection of both his tough negotiating style and abrasive personality, traits that left him poorly regarded by many in the industry. A year later, after the Clarks Fork Branch was completed, Smith again wrote to Mellen. This time, in a most cordial and conciliatory fashion, he informed Mellen that he was ready to move forward if the NP would respond favorably. Again, he received no response. From an economic standpoint, Mellen's rejection of Smith's proposal makes little sense, but there were other factors in play, one of which may have been lingering animosity toward Smith due to his past interactions with the NP.[9]

When Henry Villard's financial empire collapsed in 1883, Elijah Smith and his Boston associates assumed control of the Oregon Railway

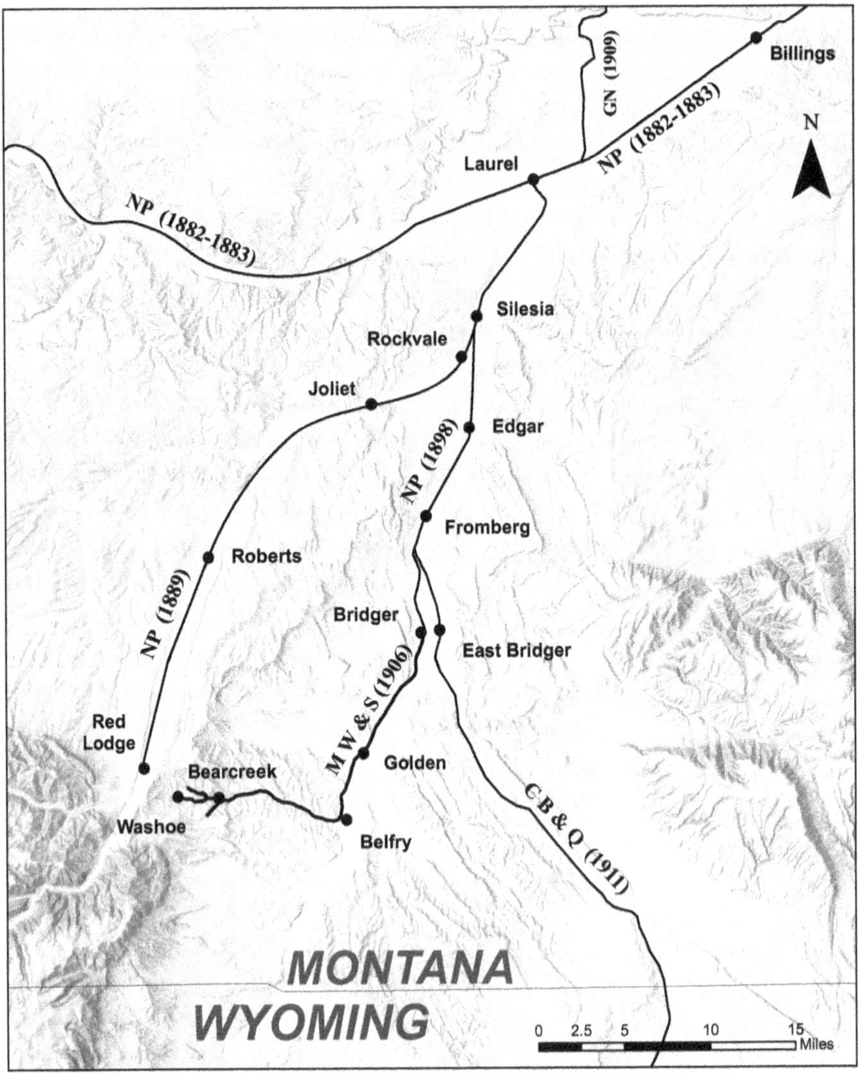

Map of railroad development southwest of Billings through 1920. NP (Northern Pacific); GN (Great Northern); CB&Q (Chicago, Burlington & Quincy); MW&S (Montana, Wyoming & Southern).

& Navigation Company (OR&N) and in 1884 Smith became the company president. Because the OR&N provided the NP with its only access to the West Coast, a contentious situation developed when the OR&N completed a line connecting it to NP's archrival, the Union Pacific. This connection allowed Smith to play the two companies against each other. A little over a year later, when a rate war dropped the tariff for freight between Chicago and the West Coast to sixty-five cents per hundred weight, Smith's OR&N refused to cooperate with the NP and continued to demand twenty-eight cents for their 213-mile haul from Wallula, Washington, to Portland. This left the NP with only twenty-eight cents for its 1,699-mile haul from St. Paul. The impact of this extortion on NP's bottom line was severe and immediate and was one of the reasons NP president Robert Harris felt compelled to complete their line over the Cascade Range into Tacoma with temporary switchbacks rather than await completion of the Stampede Tunnel. A year later Smith responded to Harris's diversion of NP traffic by leasing the OR&N line along the Columbia River in Oregon to the Oregon Short Line, a subsidiary of the Union Pacific. Then, in May 1888, OR&N further antagonized the NP when it formed a subsidiary called the Washington & Idaho Railroad, which began extending lines into NP territory in Idaho and eastern Washington. A connection with the Montana Central Railroad at Garrison, Montana, was also proposed that would have allowed the Great Northern Railway access to Washington and the west coast. Although the proposed connection was never completed, this and other fights over economic "zones of influence" in eastern Washington did little to improve Smith's relations with the NP. Smith left the OR&N in 1889, but his business dealings during the preceding five years must have left NP's management wary of him, to say the least.[10]

The NP's reluctance to work with Smith had a vindictive side as well. It seems that following the rejection of his offer to build a line to Bear Creek, NP management decided, based on the favorable coal test obtained in 1896, to take control of the coalfield and monopolize operations as they had done in Red Lodge. They, no doubt, reasoned that if they could force Smith to sell out by denying him the railroad he needed, the NP could secure the entire field for themselves. With this in mind, they surreptitiously began acquiring coal lands around Smith's holdings and soon had an agreement with their old ally Marcus Daly to acquire a position along Bear Creek as well. President Mellen claimed that he wanted "to assist Mr. Daly in every way with respect to his coal enterprise." Thus, two of Montana's most powerful corporations had aligned themselves to thwart Smith's mining ambitions.[11]

When NP's activities were revealed, sensing the futility of their situation, several of Montana Coal & Iron's major stockholders approached the NP with an offer to sell out. The NP responded favorably, but when a mutually agreeable price could not be reached, recently promoted second vice president John Kendrick informed the sellers that the NP was "willing to take the property off their hands; but . . . could get along for a great many years without it." This response was a calculated negotiating ploy, as their partner Marcus Daly was anxious to get his Bear Creek property into production, and on August 14, 1899, just two days after rejecting the stockholders offer, Kendrick told Daly, "I shall be very much disappointed if we do not succeed in securing the Bear Creek property in the near future." Daly's death just over a year later reduced the pressure to make a deal with Smith and his partners, and with the two sides still far apart on price, the NP seemed content to wait him out. Both Mellen and Kendrick knew that without a railroad, Smith's Montana Coal & Iron properties were of little value. But Smith was a fighter, and instead of capitulating, in 1900, he and his partners opened the mine and began hauling about six thousand tons per year over the hill to Red Lodge by wagon. Increasingly frustrated with Elijah Smith's obstinacy and perhaps feeling some pressure from Anaconda due to the closure of their Carbonado Mine in 1901, Mellen decided to move forward and ordered a survey from Bridger to Bear Creek in October 1902. But his plans progressed no further.[12]

James J. Hill, the founder of the Great Northern Railway, was an astute businessman who understood the railroad business and paid great attention to maximizing operating efficiency. He became involved with the NP in 1895 at the request of banker and financier J. P. Morgan, who had recently brought the company out of receivership. When Morgan appointed Charles Mellen to the NP presidency in 1897, Hill, a direct man who did not mince words complained that Mellen was one of Morgan's "overrated underachievers" who had "no business judgment more than a child" and "is unfit to occupy the position he does." To one of his associates Hill complained that prior to 1893, the NP had been financially wrecked by the "acquisition of a lot of worthless branches," and it appeared to him that Mellen was in the process of repeating that mistake. The construction of the Clarks Fork Branch and his decision to lease Frank Hall's Yellowstone Park Railway on Bozeman Pass being two examples. When Morgan finally gave Hill full control of the NP in 1901, Hill immediately ordered a halt to the construction and acquisition of branch lines. Having become a staunch Morgan man, Mellen probably resented the imposition of Hill's edict, and his decision to initiate a survey to Bear Creek in 1902 may have been an act of defiance. There can be little doubt that this was the sort of behavior that Hill would not tolerate. The survey to Bear Creek was canceled in July 1903; Charles Mellen resigned a few months later.[13]

The cancellation of NP's survey left Elijah Smith and his associates with but one option: build the railroad themselves. This was something they almost certainly had the wherewithal to do, but Smith, with prescient foresight understood that a privately held railroad with the NP as its sole outlet would exist at the mercy of its larger neighbor. Because of his past interactions with the NP, Smith knew that you did not encroach upon NP territory, especially where they had a vested interest like a potential fuel supply, without invoking their wrath and suffering the consequences. With this understanding, Smith wisely elected to avoid that trap and having abandoned his Montana & Wyoming Railroad project, would never again contemplate building a Bear Creek railroad of his own. Smith's hard-won knowledge was gained through experience, but in 1903, as plans for a railroad to his mine began to fade, a new, energetic, visionary player, unburdened by Smith's wisdom and insight, had already entered the scene.

Having tried his hand at wire manufacturing, distillery promotion, and the railroad business, when he was relieved of his obligations to the Yellowstone Park Railway Frank Hall wasted no time before diving into his next business venture. In November 1899, he joined a group of Bozeman-area businessmen to form the Trail Creek Coal and Land Company.

A month later, he sold the Hellinger mine on Trail Creek to this new company for $100,000, a property he had purchased for $22,500. The exact nature of this transaction is unclear, but it would appear he made a considerable profit, quite possibly at the expense of his partners. In December, Hall and Trail Creek Coal partners George Boyce and George Cox, moved in yet another direction and incorporated the Yellowstone Park Telephone and Telegraph Company headquartered in Bozeman. The company's Board of Directors consisted of company president Frank Hall, coal mine operator Charles W. Hoffman, and George J. Atkins, a banker and promoter from Chicago. Given his Chicago connection, Atkins may have become acquainted with Hall through the failed 1897 Montana whiskey distillery scheme. Whatever the origin of their relationship, it would come to an acrimonious conclusion within just a few years.[14]

As the year 1900 dawned, Frank Hall had a new company to run and his first task was to install a telephone line from Bozeman to the mines on Trail Creek. But as he worked to get the telephone company running, things began to go downhill for his mining interests. Just four months after buying the Hellinger property and investing considerable capital to develop the Kountz mine, the Trail Creek Coal and Land Company was forced to temporarily shut it down. The reason is unknown, but Hall, having made some money may have extricated himself from the company at this point, as he abruptly shifted his focus to the telephone company and began to concoct a plan for his next railroad.[15]

Having become enamored of the idea of a railroad to Yellowstone National Park, by early 1900 Hall had devised a new scheme. Because the NP had been forced to abandon the idea of extending the Park Branch to Cooke City, and there was no indication that their Rocky Fork Branch would ever progress beyond Red Lodge, Hall saw the opportunity for a new approach. Having realized that one of the problems with the Turner brother's Gallatin Railroad was the lack of online traffic, Hall elected to run his new railroad to the northeast corner of the park near Cooke City. This approach would allow him to capitalize on passenger service to and from the park as well as Cooke City's mining activity. Since railroad construction in the park was prohibited, Hall envisioned his new railroad as starting in Big Timber and following the Boulder River south into the

This view shows Cooke City's main street as it appeared around 1883. Little had probably changed by the time of Frank Hall's visit in 1900. (Yellowstone Gateway Museum of Park County 2006.045.525).

mountains. He probably believed this route would not only allow him to reach Cooke City but also would serve to revive old mining camps along the route. Copper-nickel ore had been mined for a time south of Big Timber at Hicks Park and a little farther south lay the moribund gold mining town of Independence. There were reports of coal deposits similar to those at Trail Creek along this route as well.[16]

The Boulder River route to Cooke City was essentially the same as the Stillwater route proposed by the Rocky Fork & Cooke City in 1886. But for all its commercial potential, the route up the Boulder had one serious drawback. Unlike the Stillwater drainage, the Boulder did not lead directly to Cooke City and, therefore, would require significantly more trackage in the high mountains. Nonetheless, with only a rudimentary knowledge of the terrain and construction difficulties he would face, in early 1900 Hall traveled to the East Coast and convinced a group of investors to support his plan. With this backing he returned to Bozeman on March 20 and as soon as trails were deemed passable, hired a guide to take him to Cooke City via the Boulder River.[17]

While his main goal was to investigate a route for his railroad, ever the promoter and entrepreneur, Hall had other plans as well. During his time in Cooke City, he met with representatives of several large mining companies and negotiated an agreement that promised him a half interest in their claims if he could bring a railroad to the district within four years. First reported in the *Big Timber Express* in June, this potentially huge windfall for Hall was later confirmed by the *Billings Gazette*, which stated that he had "secured options and deeds to half interests in many of the most promising mining properties of the district." For the miners, the agreement was an act of desperation. Although production records do not appear to exist for 1900, according to the US Bureau of Mines, production during 1901 for the entire New World Mining District amounted to less than forty-five ounces of gold and ten ounces of silver with a market value of not quite $1,000, meaning that the mines were, for the most part, shut down. Production during 1902 was even more dismal with less than $100 output reported. Offering Hall a half interest in what were effectively worthless properties in the hope he could get a railroad built was a risk the miners were willing to take; at that point, they really had nothing to lose.[18]

Having spent several days on horseback with his guide and a pack string making the sixty-plus mile journey through the wilderness to Cooke City, Hall's vision of using the Boulder drainage as a route for his railroad was probably short-lived. Given the rugged country, massive granite ledges, steep escarpments, and the nearly ten-thousand-foot mountain pass he had traversed, even a neophyte like Hall would have been impressed by the route's construction challenges. Although he was probably discouraged, he was not dissuaded. Due to the support of his East Coast backers and the deal he had with the mine owners, he was now more determined than ever to find a route to Cooke City and Yellowstone National Park.

While there is little doubt he accomplished much during his trip into the mountains, it did not end well. According to the *Bozeman Avant Courier*, Hall, who was described as a "railroad magnate," had a bit of trouble during his return. Near Lake Abundance, about six miles north of Cooke City, Hall's guide "fell by the wayside" after imbibing too much "Cooke City firewater." Annoyed, and anxious to get home, Hall saddled his horse, grabbed a pack animal and set off on his own, leaving the guide to fend for himself. But just two years removed from city life in Milwaukee, Hall was not well versed in the skills of wilderness navigation and was soon lost amid the monotonous rocky crags and pine forests of the high mountains. When he wandered into Yellowstone National Park, he was lucky to be discovered by two US Army scouts, who took him into custody and cited him for having a pack outfit in the national park without the requisite permit. According to the newspaper, despite his smooth talk he was unable to convince the soldiers of his innocence and was escorted to the Soda Butte station, where, after further interrogation, he was released with instructions to find his way back to Bozeman via Cinnabar.[19]

The story of Hall's misadventures suggests that he was well-known at the *Courier* and liked seeing his name in the paper. Their description of him as a "railroad magnate" was pure hyperbole, as having built a seven-mile branch line to a coal mine hardly established those credentials. The fact that he shared what might be considered an embarrassing story, tried to "smooth talk" the army scouts, and later attributed his navigational failure to a faulty compass show that despite having lost his way, he had not lost his bravado. His failure to locate an acceptable route up the Boulder was a major setback and because the clock was now ticking on his deal with the mine owners, when he returned to Bozeman he immediately set to work on a new plan.

Having become acquainted with Philip Gallaher at the Cook and Woldson hearing a year earlier, Hall must have been aware of Gallaher's water-level route up the Clarks Fork River to Cooke City. Thus, his next move was to contact Gallaher and seek his insights on the 1886 survey. Gallaher, the longtime advocate of a Bear Creek–Cooke City railroad, having become frustrated with Elijah Smith and the NP's reluctance to undertake the project, was probably happy to assist. And so, Hall, the ambitious, sometimes irresponsible entrepreneur, and Gallaher, the highly respected engineer and surveyor, were drawn together in the pursuit of a common goal.

In early August 1900, accompanied by a crew numbering a dozen or more, Hall and Gallaher arrived in Red Lodge in the company of George Lamport, a surveyor, Red Lodge businessman, and rancher with interests in the Bear Creek coalfield. Although they were loath to discuss their plans, by then it was well known that Hall had made a deal with several Cooke City mine owners. Observers in Red Lodge rightfully concluded that the purpose of the expedition was to survey a railroad line from the NP terminus at Bridger to the mines at Cooke City following Gallaher's 1886 route up the Clarks Fork River.[20]

Although the Cook and Woldson hearing would have alerted Gallaher to Hall's questionable reputation, it appears he was willing to set those concerns aside in the hope of seeing the railroad he had envisioned fourteen years earlier finally get built. The several weeks he spent with Hall hustling chains, stadia rods, and transits through the mountains with the survey crew would have allowed them to become well acquainted. Gallaher probably spent evenings around the campfire reviewing the day's survey notes while instructing Hall in the intricacies of surveying and railroad construction. Hall, on the other hand, likely waxed eloquent about his experience building the Yellowstone Park Railway and his vision for a railroad to the National Park. Despite what Gallaher must have known about Hall's past business activities, when the survey was finished in late September, they parted company on good terms.

Upon their return to Billings both Gallaher and Hall soon found their names in the newspaper. Gallaher with a report on the survey results and Hall for a less auspicious event. The report that Gallaher shared with the *Billings Gazette* at the end of September revealed that the route to Cooke City was one hundred miles long and would cost an estimated $1.5 million. He also reiterated his 1886 observation that it passed through country with unsurpassed scenery and stipulated that the future of the project lay entirely in the hands of "the moneyed powers" in the east who had authorized the survey.[21]

Two weeks prior to Gallaher's announcement, Frank Hall, who seemed forever destined for trouble, also had his name in the newspaper. According to the *Butte Miner*, on September 19, Hall was assaulted and punched in the face by a barber named C. T. Hart, who discovered

Hall walking with his estranged wife. Enraged, Hart had to be restrained and arrested. A scandalous sensation for the day, the page-two story began with the headline, "FALL OF A WOMAN—Pronounced blonde, Beautiful to look upon, but inclined to flirt with horrid men." The article that followed referred to Hall as "a prominent railroad promoter" and portrayed him in a most disparaging light, noting that his behavior was a bit "too gay." But the story's veracity was put to question that evening when Mrs. Hart arrived at the offices of the *Butte Miner* and let it be known that Frank Hall was a perfect gentleman whom she had only just met on the train from Red Lodge. Stylishly gowned, clutching a small satchel, the pretty blonde dressmaker with a sweet smile explained that Hall had helped her and a lady friend from the train—"as is often done by gentlemen"—and then assisted her by carrying her grip. Mrs. Hart claimed that she was the one confronted and struck by her husband and went on to state, "I do not think he could get up the courage to strike a man." She made clear that her reason for coming forward was to set the record straight. "Mr. Hall," she said, "is an entirely innocent party in the matter." In the end, the truth of Hall's alleged dalliance will never be known, but there is little doubt he returned home, a wiser, if not a better, man.[22]

With the survey complete and East Coast money backing him Hall was optimistic. Seldom failing to include the name of the National Park in his business ventures, in October 1900, along with investors from New Jersey, New York, and Indiana, he incorporated the Yellowstone Park Railroad in Trenton, New Jersey, capitalized at $2,500,000. Curiously, despite his involvement in the latest survey and two earlier Cooke City railroad schemes, Philip Gallaher did not participate in Hall's new company.[23]

Once the incorporation papers were filed, Hall remained in the New York City area trying to interest additional eastern capitalists in his project, but after several months, it was obvious that his initial optimism was misplaced. There was little interest in his Cooke City railroad scheme. Having all but given up, Hall returned to Montana in late May. During a brief stop in Billings, a reporter sought Hall out and inquired about the status his Cooke City line. Remarkably, and quite possibly for the first time in his life, Hall had nothing to say. This was probably no great surprise to the reporter. In February, months before his return, the *Billings Gazette* had forecast the project's demise, claiming that plans for Hall's railroad had fallen through and that "no one seems to be seriously disappointed from the fact that no great amount of confidence was ever placed in the scheme from the beginning."[24]

At the same time, Gallaher's construction plans and cost estimate were also being questioned. A January 1901 story in the *Big Timber Pioneer* reported that rather than build the line up the Clarks Fork Canyon, as originally planned, the latest survey showed that it would be necessary to divert south over Dead Indian Summit, a climb of some 1500 feet. This diversion, if truly necessary, would add operational difficulties and eliminate the line's advantage of being a downhill or a water-level run from the mines all the way to Bridger. Whether the story was accurate or not, it was evident that either route would present serious engineering and construction challenges. The nagging question behind these issues was whether it was even feasible to profitably operate a railroad through the mountains to Cooke City.[25]

Because of its elevation of around 7,600 feet and annual snowfall totals over two hundred inches, during winter months railroad operations around Cooke City would be extremely difficult, if not impossible. In April 1887, the *Billings Gazette* claimed that during the winter there was ten feet of snow on the ground in Cooke City and unscrupulous hucksters were pushing stovepipes into the snow and selling unwitting greenhorns the fine cabin that was promised to exist underneath. Spring thaws revealed nothing more than a rusty stovepipe, the erstwhile salesman long gone. The *Bozeman Weekly Chronicle*, a great champion of the mining camp, took exception to this story saying it was a "downright falsehood and deserves only the contempt of the readers of that paper." The *Chronicle* asserted that there had never been more than six feet of snow on the ground that winter and that by April it had already settled down to about three feet. While the editors of these fine papers felt it necessary to quibble over the snow's true depth, the fact remained that Cooke City got a lot of snow.[26]

Investors who evaluated both the traffic potential and the cost to build and operate a line that might battle snow for half the year, were likely unimpressed with the potential returns. This conclusion seems to have been reached by the Chicago, Burlington & Quincy (CB&Q), which in 1900 was contemplating a branch line from Toluca, Montana, to Cody, Wyoming. At one point, the CB&Q announced that it would extend the line all the way to Cooke City and possibly beyond. But it appears that after an economic review the idea was dropped; CB&Q's line never progressed beyond Cody. It is impossible to know if Hall appreciated the importance of this type of analysis, but ever the promoter, he was persistent. Despite having returned to work at his telephone company, in December 1901 he told the *Big Timber Pioneer* that he felt "confident that it will not be a great while until the road is built." This was just wishful thinking, and Hall knew it.[27]

Having refocused his energy on the telephone company, in July 1901 he completed a line to the mining camp of Independence and the next month connected Livingston to the town of Fridley, near present-day Emigrant. Seeing the need for a new base of operations, in late September he moved his company headquarters to Livingston and rented office space at the corner of West Park and North Second Street directly across from the NP depot. Following the move, he was back at work extending the telephone line from Fridley south to Jardine and Mammoth Hot Springs.[28]

Since its inception in late 1899, the Yellowstone Park Telephone and Telegraph Company had developed into a going concern. In early July 1901, Hall told a reporter from the *Butte Inter-Mountain* that the company had over one hundred miles of line operating in Park, Gallatin, and Sweet Grass Counties and was regarded as a great success by the communities it served. From there, it continued to expand. Two years after completing the line to Mammoth Hot Springs, Hall connected Livingston with the town of Cokedale, a few miles to the west. In October 1903, he formed a syndicate and acquired the Southern Montana Telegraph Company of Virginia City. A year after that, he appeared before the Butte City Council to get permission to run a telephone line through downtown Butte. Clearly, despite the frustrations that accompanied his railroad plans,

Hall remained a busy man. But as with his earlier business ventures, all of this activity was digging his company deeper and deeper in debt. The extension of phone lines to places like Cokedale and Independence was ill-advised as both soon became ghost towns. Seemingly oblivious to these sorts of miscalculations Hall forged ahead.[29]

While he plowed more and more money into the telephone company, in keeping with his characteristic flamboyance and desire to be "a man about town," he acquired one of the first automobiles in Park County. In June 1902, while in Washington, DC, on official business with the Department of the Interior, he applied for a permit to drive his new machine through Yellowstone National Park. Much to his surprise, his application was denied. Government officials cited a rule that forbid the use of motor vehicles in national parks, as it was feared they would frighten the horses used by the tourist coaching services. Disappointed, but seldom lacking in witty repartee, Hall commented that "anything that would frighten some speed into the horses of the Yellowstone Park service would gladly be welcomed by the tourists."[30]

Another contraption Hall possessed was a jointed fishing pole rigged with a wire that allowed him to tap his phone lines anywhere along the road and send messages without grounding the wires. When a group of tourists spied the pole stashed in a corner of the Mammoth Hot Springs Hotel, they asked Hall if it was an electric fishing pole. Seeing the opportunity for some fun, he assured them that it was, noting that it was one of the latest models and in widespread use in the area. Hall explained that with a battery attached to the handle, when thrust into the water it would kill all the fish within "several rods" leaving the fisherman to collect his catch as they came to the surface. Whether his attentive audience was taken in by his nonsense is open to conjecture.[31]

While Hall devoted more and more time to his telephone company, he never abandoned his railroad ambitions and presumably stayed in close contact with Philip Gallaher. The *Butte Miner* noted that Hall spent Christmas 1901 in Billings. Since he was not a resident and probably had few acquaintances there, it seems likely that Philip Gallaher was the one who extended the invitation. If this was the case, among the topics they undoubtedly discussed during his visit was how to get East Coast investors interested in his Cooke City railroad. Future events suggest that these discussions prompted Gallaher to begin to ruminate on other possible sources of funding.[32]

In June 1902, while Hall was in Washington, DC, and the Yellowstone Park Railroad languished for lack of financial support, Philip Gallaher took a job with Amalgamated Copper (Anaconda) and moved to the newly established town of Storrs on the west side of Bozeman Pass to supervise the construction of a new coal plant at Chestnut. Located on the NP-operated Yellowstone Park Railway, Storrs was the site of a coal mine and coke ovens that produced fuel for the furnaces in Anaconda. A model company town, every home had running water and electric lights. Its existence was owed in part to Frank Hall, who was instrumental in building both the railroad and telephone line that made its development possible, a fact that was probably not lost on Philip Gallaher.[33]

Almost a year later, in April 1903, while Hall and Gallaher were both otherwise occupied, as a precursor to President Mellen's planned survey, the NP sent an assistant engineer from their St. Paul headquarters to inspect possible routes from Bridger to the Bear Creek coalfield. This visit generated a great deal of speculation in and around Billings, but of course, nothing came of it. The survey, part of Mellen's plan to control the Bear Creek coalfield, was canceled in July. In October, Elijah Smith arrived in Billings in his private railcar to visit with local associates involved in the Montana Coal & Iron Company and do some trout fishing before moving on to Oregon for a tour of the West Coast and Mexico. When asked about the possibility of a railroad to Bear Creek, Smith indicated that "as far as he could see the prospects for it were not of the brightest, at least so far as any immediate move in that direction was concerned." While this assessment was correct in regard to the NP, unbeknownst to Smith there were local forces at work, and all of that was about to change.[34]

4

"A Railroad Will Be Built"

ELIJAH SMITH'S PESSIMISTIC OUTLOOK IN OCTOBER 1903 might have been all that was needed to convince Philip Gallaher to give up on the Montana Coal & Iron Company. James J. Hill's edict against branch line construction and Smith's refusal to build a railroad of his own made it seem unlikely that the transportation issue would ever be solved. Still believing there were fortunes to be made in the commercial coal business in Montana and North Dakota, shortly after Smith's visit Gallaher contacted prominent Billings businessman Christian Yegen and convinced him to join in a new venture.

Christian Yegen and his brother Peter were highly successful Swiss immigrants who had built an extensive mercantile empire in the Billings area. Their commercial interests included retail sales, real estate, warehousing, and banking. Christian's influence extended to state and local politics, having served in the state legislature, the Billings City Council, and as mayor of Billings. Impetuous by nature, Christian's dark eyes, receding hairline, and unruly mustache conveyed the look of a man determined to succeed. By contrast, his younger brother Peter's gentle features and neatly trimmed beard projected a calm, staid personality. Unobtrusive and disinclined to take risks, Peter preferred slow steady growth. It is said that Peter often smoothed the furrows that his brother Christian left behind.[1]

Swayed by Gallaher's knowledge of the Bear Creek coalfield and hoping to cash in on the next big opportunity, in November 1903 Chris Yegen, Philip Gallaher, and four others incorporated the Bear Creek Coal Company. Within six months, the company had acquired a highly

Christian Yegen, businessman, entrepreneur, and president of the Bear Creek Coal Company. Energetic and driven, he was always on the lookout for the next big opportunity. (PAc 99-36.79, Senator Christian Yegen, Montana Historical Society Photograph Archives).

Peter Yegen, businessman and entrepreneur. Calm and thoughtful, his personality served to counterbalance his older brother's ambitious nature. (Courtesy Western Heritage Center, Billings, Montana).

prospective 480-acre block of patented coal land just east of Montana Coal & Iron's holdings. Bear Creek's position soon expanded to about eight hundred acres. With their coal rights secure, the partners were anxious to get a mine in production and immediately announced plans for a wagon road, but what they really needed was a railroad. Since the NP had shown little interest in the project, Gallaher knew that someone else would have to build it, and he now believed he knew just the man for the job.[2]

A few days after the incorporation papers were filed, Chris Yegen, who had no prior railroad experience, informed the *Anaconda Standard* that

> a railroad will be built from Bridger to the Bear Creek coal mines next year. There is no doubt about it. In case the Northern Pacific does not take the matter up we have the capital guaranteed by a man who commands it to build and equip the road. . . . It will require only $200,000 to build and equip the road in good condition to handle the business. . . . It is not a matter of speculation or guess work in regard to obtaining the money to build the railroad. It is guaranteed by a man who lives right here in Billings and who knows what these coalfields are.[3]

Although Philip Gallaher was currently employed at Storrs, his background as both a surveyor and engineer made him the only person with enough credibility to induce Yegen to make his sweeping proclamation and must, therefore, have been the person Yegen referred to as "a man who lives right here in Billings." A longtime advocate for a Bear Creek–Cooke City railroad, Gallaher knew the coalfields well and when he returned to Billings at the end of January 1904, he immediately set to work planning a railroad up the Clarks Fork Valley. Among the first things he needed was a manager, and due to their past association, he turned to Frank Hall. Gallaher was aware of Hall's passion for a railroad to Yellowstone National Park and the two had probably stayed in contact during the preceding two years, as Storrs was only a short train ride from Hall's Livingston headquarters. A January 19, 1904, letter from NP's acting chief engineer to newly elected NP president Howard Elliott supports this assumption by revealing that before Gallaher had returned to Billings, Hall had already submitted some sort of "proposition" to the NP regarding a new railroad. The nature of Hall's proposition is unknown, but it may have been a request for the type of support he had received from the NP when he built the Yellowstone Park Railway. Whatever the nature of his request, it alerted the NP to his plans and was summarily rejected.[4]

The "guaranteed" funding Gallaher promised Chris Yegen would come from a group of investors in southeastern Pennsylvania led by Philadelphia physician Oran M. Belfry and an attorney from Marietta named George Heisey. Having grown up near Williamsport, just north of Lancaster, and gone to college in Philadelphia, Gallaher must have maintained some contacts in the area and been familiar with the area's prominent businessmen. The guarantee he gave Chris Yegen indicates that he had already been in contact with these individuals, discussed his railroad plans, and received some assurance of their support. All of this was likely the result of Gallaher's ruminations about possible new sources of funding following Hall's unsuccessful attempts to raise money on the East Coast during 1900 and 1901.

Despite Chris Yegen's bold prediction that a railroad would be built in 1904, more than a year passed before there was any further activity. Finally, in January 1905, three men "from the east" arrived in Bridger and visited the coalfield. These three men were not identified, but four months later, Oran Belfry and George Heisey arrived in Red Lodge and checked into the stylish Pollard Hotel. Belfry and Heisey were soon joined by Hall and Gallaher and the four of them spent the next week touring the Bear Creek mines and Clarks Fork Valley. When finished, Belfry and Heisey were sufficiently impressed to agree to fund both a survey and the acquisition of necessary right-of-way for a railroad from Bridger to the Bear Creek mines. With this backing in place, the Bear Creek Coal Company offered Hall free use of their mine lands for the construction of sidings and yards and a reduced price for the coal used in locomotives. So, by late spring, the pieces for the long-awaited railroad to the Bear Creek mines were slowly falling into place.[5]

Although the main goal of the railroad was the shipment of coal from Bear Creek, an additional incentive for investors like Dr. Belfry was the resumption of activity in the New World Mining District. After nearly twenty years of slumber, and just as Frank Hall's four-year deal with the miners was about to expire, mining activity around Cooke City was on the cusp of revival. In 1904 high-grade copper ore had been discovered in the northern part of the district near Goose Lake and a road was built to exploit the deposit. That same year Gottwerth L. Tanzer, a German mining engineer, organized the Precious Metals Company (later called Western Smelting & Power Co.) and began amassing a claim block with the aim of large-scale development of gold-copper deposits on Henderson Mountain. If these projects proved to be successful, there might be justification for a rail line to Cooke City after all, and Frank Hall's dream of a railroad to Yellowstone National Park would finally be realized.[6]

The near-term promise of lucrative coal contracts coupled with the future potential of tapping the New World Mining District prompted Frank Hall and his Pennsylvania investors to incorporate a new Yellowstone Park Railroad (YPRR) in Augusta, Maine, on May 17, 1905. Although the incorporation papers show I. L. Fairbanks as both the president and treasurer, there being no vice president or secretary listed, it appears this was a short-term expedient as Frank Hall soon replaced Fairbanks as president. Samuel Mumma, a wealthy tobacco farmer from Landisville, Pennsylvania, became the company's vice president, and Hall's old Chicago acquaintance George Atkins, the secretary-treasurer. Atkins's connections to Chicago area bankers and investors made him a logical addition to the company's leadership hierarchy. The company was capitalized at $3 million in common and preferred stock with an equal amount of forty-year first mortgage gold bonds bearing 5 percent interest, Farmer's Trust Company of Lancaster, Pennsylvania, being the trustee. Despite Philip Gallaher's involvement in putting the deal together, as with Hall's previous Cooke City railroad venture, he once again declined participation. His reasoning is not clear, but it may be that lingering doubts about Frank Hall's managerial skills influenced his decision.[7]

Howard Elliott, a graduate of Harvard College, was elected to the presidency of the NP in October 1903, replacing Charles S. Mellen. Elliott, a competent railroad man with twenty-two years' experience, was the type of hardheaded manager James J. Hill liked. Armed with a degree in civil engineering, Elliott knew the theory and practice of railroading thoroughly, having worked his way up through various jobs with a succession of midwestern railroads before becoming second vice president of the CB&Q in May 1902. Naturally reserved, his chiseled features and receding hairline projected his sincere, honest, and determined personality. Unlike his predecessor, he was said to be incapable of making enemies. But despite his outwardly pleasant demeanor, when it came to business, he could be a steadfast and ruthless adversary.[8]

In early 1905, as plans for the Yellowstone Park Railroad began to coalesce, Frank Hall traveled to NP headquarters in St. Paul on several occasions to meet with Elliott and discuss his plans. Although his interactions with Charles Mellen and John Kendrick six years earlier left much to be desired, Hall now hoped to establish friendly relations with NP's new management. Among other things, Hall proposed that the NP and YPRR establish through rates on freight traffic and a shared depot in Bridger with joint agency. But Elliott, having heard that Hall was "discredited pretty generally all through Montana," was suspicious from the start. The negative outcome of the recent Cook and Woldson settlement would have given him an additional reason to be wary of Hall. Rumors of Yellowstone Park Telephone's mounting financial troubles would only have added to his concerns. After politely listening to Hall's proposals Elliott refused to make any agreements or cooperate with him in any way. Having initiated the meeting full of youthful optimism, Hall departed St. Paul frustrated. A short time later, he further aggravated Elliott by telling potential investors that the NP had promised "friendly relations," something Elliott vehemently denied.[9]

Elliott's opinion was that there was no need for a railroad to Bear Creek, as it appeared to him that existing coal production in Montana was completely adequate. He admitted privately, however, that given the opportunity NP should increase its holdings in the area, as one day there would be a need for more coal. He also acknowledged that the railroad's dependence on Red Lodge coal made them vulnerable to a supply disruption should there be a serious accident or fire at the mine, but because the NP still had its Rocky Canyon and Mountain Side mines on Bozeman Pass, he was not overly concerned. Elliott viewed the Bear Creek coalfield as effectively belonging to the NP, and when the NP needed the coal, it would build a railroad to get it. This attitude was in

Northern Pacific president Howard Elliott (*on right*), with cigar in hand, is seen here conversing with James J. Hill. Known as the "Empire Builder," by 1901 Hill controlled not only the Northern Pacific but the Great Northern and Chicago, Burlington & Quincy railroads as well. Hill considered Elliott the right man for the job when he was elected president of the NP in 1903. (Minnesota Historical Society).

keeping with both James J. Hill's directive on branch lines and a corporate philosophy first articulated in 1883 by Thomas Oakes, then the company's general manager, who explained to an associate, "Our policy is to oppose the building of any lines connecting with our mainline unless we have control thereof and absolute ownership." This long-standing corporate philosophy concerning connecting railroads was still in place when Frank Hall's plans came to light in January 1904. The NP's acting chief engineer E. J. Pearson informed Howard Elliott at that time, "The past history of the short connecting road under foreign ownership has not been entirely satisfactory . . . in view of which it is suggested when the traffic south of Bridger is such as to justify the construction and operation of a railway line that it should be exclusively a Northern Pacific proposition."[10]

Given NP's prior unsatisfactory experience with "foreign ownership," having an interloper like Frank Hall announce plans for a railroad that NP management considered theirs alone to build caused them some consternation. The decision to oppose him was thus preordained. When confronted with the problem, Howard Elliott expressed his concerns to the company's general counsel, C. W. Bunn, and asked if the NP could refuse to connect with Hall's railroad. He also wondered if they did connect, would they be forced to interchange cars. Bunn likely advised him that the connection was mandatory, but his response to the car interchange question, as will be seen, was a bit more nuanced.[11]

To add to Hall's problems, Elliott logically assumed that this new railroad was somehow associated with Elijah Smith, another individual who was not in good standing with NP management. Elliott further suspected that Hall's real goal was "to build something that will have a nuisance value" and then force the NP to buy him out. This type of conjecture was repeated by other NP officials who claimed to have heard rumors to that affect. But there is no direct evidence to support this conclusion. Frank Hall was a man with a vision and whereas some of his investors might have been looking for a buyout and quick profits, Hall, it seems, had long-term plans. He wanted to make his mark: to be someone, a railroad magnate. This was his chance. But being suspicious of Hall from the start, Howard Elliott viewed his project as both unneeded and an annoyance. It was, therefore, inevitable that Elliott would do everything in his power to undermine Hall, hoping he would either give up or be coerced into selling out cheap.[12]

In the spring of 1905, the Clarks Fork Valley south of Bridger was mostly uninhabited sage-covered cattle country. The only break in the monotony of the flat valley floor were the thickets of willows and tall cottonwoods that populated the banks of the Clarks Fork River and its tributaries. Steep sandstone bluffs and low hills rimmed the valley to the west while rounded grass-covered cuestas and low jagged knolls defined its eastern boundary. On a clear day, to the southwest, the dramatic snowcapped peaks of the Beartooth Mountains were visible in the distance. Having traversed the valley a number of times, the panorama created by the varied terrain and distant mountains was by now familiar to both Gallaher and Hall. In April, when they boarded NP's triweekly mixed train in Billings for the six-hour ride to Bridger, the *Billings Gazette* eagerly predicted that trains would be running to the Bear Creek mines by December 1; the extension to Cooke City would soon follow.[13]

Gallaher, who was in charge of surveying, chose an economical route that stayed close to the west side of the valley, bypassed agricultural lands in the valley center, and avoided the need to bridge the Clarks Fork River. Except for some minor rock work and excavation along the river bluffs, the first twelve miles of construction would be relatively easy. Grades would be variable but generally less than half a percent. The only negatives were the curves needed to follow the river, and the trestles and fills required to span the numerous ravines, gullies, and small streams that descended from the western escarpment. Just north of the point where Bear Creek flows into the Clarks Fork River, a branch would veer off the mainline to the west and follow the Bear Creek Valley for about nine miles to the mines. Grades along the branch line steepened and increased to 2.5 percent or more as the road ascended the ever-narrowing valley flanked by rounded hills of gently tilted buff and light gray siltstone covered in grass, sage, and scattered junipers. Occasional blocky outcrops of dull yellow sandstone crowned by sparse stands of pinyon and lodgepole pines were the only accents in the otherwise bleak repetitive terrain. Bear Creek, which carried little more than a trickle of water most of the year, was confined to deeply incised meanders cut into the sage-covered valley floor. As Frank Hall would soon learn, despite its innocuous appearance, this stream and its tributaries could wreak havoc during heavy rains.[14]

When Gallaher completed the survey to Bear Creek in late May, Hall headed east to discuss the start of construction with his Pennsylvania investors. On May 29, a dinner meeting was held at the Wild Cat Resort, a posh getaway near York, Pennsylvania, that overlooked the farmlands of the Susquehanna River valley. Attendees included Dr. Oran Belfry, George Heisey, YPRR vice president Samuel Mumma, and seven local investors, mostly businessmen and tobacco farmers from southeastern Pennsylvania. An air of anticipation likely pervaded the proceedings. For these small-time investors the idea of building a railroad in a far-flung state like Montana must have seemed both exciting and risky. Although Oran Belfry and George Heisey had visited the area, Frank Hall was the only one present with actual railroad experience, and he was, no doubt, the center of attention as the group anxiously crowded around maps of the recently completed survey. While answering a multitude of questions, Hall probably employed his well-practiced salesman's charm to assure them there was little to worry about. They would build a railroad to Bear Creek and immediately begin making money hauling coal. Once that line was established, they would begin the extension to Cooke City and Yellowstone National Park, where the combination of freight and passenger traffic would ensure a steady profitable income. There is no doubt that Frank Hall was excited. His dream of a railroad to the park seemed at last to be within his grasp.[15]

Based on Gallaher's latest survey, the total cost of the line to Bear Creek was estimated to be $528,000. So, with this number in mind, after an evening of discussion, fine dining, and libation, the group gave Hall authorization to begin work. Their reasoning is unknown as the YPRR appears to have had little in the way of cash assets. The company's July 1905 annual statement shows that capital stock paid for in cash amounted to only $25,000, and further stipulated that "the amount of its capital stock paid in, in any other way and the way and the manner in which paid, is as follows: ($)503,000 issued for construction work." The exact meaning of the phrase "issued for construction work" is unclear, but it may refer to shares of common stock that Hall would soon begin to freely distribute to purchasers of YPRR construction bonds. While much of the railroad's early financing remains a mystery, one thing is clear, construction was begun before adequate funding was in place. The decision to move forward was a fateful one, the consequences of which would haunt the company for many years to come.[16]

With the support and backing of his Pennsylvania investors secured, Hall returned to Montana to finalize construction plans, but before construction could begin, he had to disentangle himself from the Yellowstone Park Telephone and Telegraph Company. Due to his poor business decisions and profligate spending, the telephone company was deep in debt and being sued by numerous creditors. But Hall found a way out and deftly sidestepped his financial obligations by making a quick sale of the company to Rocky Mountain Bell Telephone. This allowed him to walk away from the phone company and leave his numerous unsecured creditors with nothing. NP president Howard Elliott was aware of Hall's legal problems and questionable business dealings and was mystified by his ability to raise money and find new investors. What kind of people would go into business with someone like Hall, he wondered. In a July 10, 1905, letter to NP's second vice president Jule Hannaford, written just as construction on the YPRR was about to begin, Elliott expressed the opinion that it was, "inconceivable that any reputable businessman would go into his [Hall's] enterprise without finding out the real facts." Elliott asked Hannaford to have someone unaffiliated with the NP look into Hall's business, find out where his money was coming from and who his investors were. He also wanted to learn more about ongoing merger talks between the Bear Creek mine owners and instructed Hannaford to look into the whole thing without drawing undue attention because "such a move might indicate too great anxiety on our part." A month and a half later, an operative for J. P. Morgan reported to Elliott that little had been discovered except that one of Hall's investors was a Pennsylvania attorney named George Heisey, who "doesn't seem to cut very much ice" or "command any very great amount of capital." This information may have put to rest Elliott's belief that Elijah Smith was behind the whole scheme and since it appeared that Hall did not have any consequential backers, Elliott may have also concluded that Hall's plans had only a slim chance of success. Nonetheless, because NP had its own plans for the Bear Creek coalfield, Hall and the activity at the mines continued to be a source of anxiety and irritation for Elliott.[17]

In June, while Howard Elliott fretted over the news from Bear Creek, Frank Hall awarded a grading contract to the Weast brothers of Red Lodge, and by the end of July 1905, the first five miles of roadbed were finished. As construction got underway Hall contacted a representative of William A. Clark's organization to explore the possibility of buying his interest in the Clarks Fork Branch between Fromberg and Bridger. News of this negotiation prompted the NP to immediately exercise its option on Clark's interest to prevent any possible encroachment by Hall. An internal NP company memo described Hall's activities as "not in the interest of this company."[18]

Although Hall had initially planned to establish his headquarters in Bridger, when his overtures to Howard Elliott were rejected and the deal with William Clark fell through, Hall, along with James Rich, a real estate speculator, and Bert Viall, treasurer of the Bear Creek Coal Company, formed the Belfry Townsite Company, and purchased a forty-acre tract of irrigated farmland near where the line turned west to follow Bear Creek. This would be the site of the railroad's main offices, shops, and yard, as well as the location of a new town. Hall named the place Belfry, in honor of Dr. Belfry, to acknowledge his role in getting the project started and perhaps in the hope that a little flattery would entice him and his associates to continue their financial support.[19]

From the beginning, Frank Hall had big plans for his railroad. Having been strongly influenced by Philip Gallaher's undying enthusiasm for the project, Hall envisioned, among other things, the eventual construction of a smelting complex in Belfry where, because of its proximity to ample coal and water, the ores from Cooke City could be cheaply reduced and processed. He told all who would listen that Belfry would soon rival Anaconda as the center of smelting and ore processing in Montana. He even talked about damming the Clarks Fork Canyon to create a vast irrigation project in the upper Clarks Fork Valley and building a hydroelectric power plant that would allow electrification of YPRR's line to Cooke City. Despite his limited financing, as NP president Charles Mellen had observed some years earlier, Frank Hall liked to talk.[20]

By the time the Weast brothers finished the first five miles of grade, Hall was out of money. So, in August 1905, he headed east and spent time in Boston and New York seeking investors before moving on to Pennsylvania. The trip must have resulted in some success, for he returned to Montana and informed the *Billings Gazette* that he was "unable to say when the road to the coalfield will be in operation" but claimed that "we are ready for steel, but there is a delay in getting our orders filled." The first part of his statement was undoubtedly true, but the rest was fabrication—more of Hall's fanciful talk. The line was not "ready for steel," as there were no ties on the ground. In fact, no ties had even been cut, and the "delay" in getting his orders filled was likely due to his limited credit with suppliers. In his usual manner, he also stated that there was "nothing in the way of sufficient financial backing to complete the road through to Cooke City." He went on to say that he believed that tracks would reach the mining camp by April 1, 1906. Later that month, he also claimed to have ordered 150 cars and 2 locomotives, but as with his other announcements this statement would soon prove to be a fabrication. Lacking the funds or credit to complete the railroad, Hall found himself in an unenviable position. Fearing that the company's financial plight would discourage new investment, he continually attempted to mislead anxious reporters and investors in an effort to obfuscate the company's tenuous situation. Although he clearly did not have enough money to complete the line to Cooke City, there was some progress being made on the line to Bear Creek.[21]

In September, George Towne of Bridger was awarded a contract to supply ties for the railroad, and he immediately went to Billings to assemble a crew. With the help of a local judge, who apparently cleared out the city jail, Towne headed south to the Pryor Mountains with a dozen men on September 25. But it was mid-November before the Weast brothers had enough rail and ties on hand for the first eight miles of track. Along with weather delays, the work was slowed by a lack of horses. J. P. Weast complained that he was willing to pay up to $225 per team but was not finding many. To add to Hall's difficulties, in late November, Russell Kimball, the railroad's chief engineer, tendered his resignation after he and Hall suffered some sort of "misunderstanding." The nature of their disagreement is unknown, but it might have had something to do with cost-cutting measures Hall was enforcing. In sympathy, Kimball's entire engineering staff went out on strike.[22]

While Hall wrestled with myriad construction issues, investors George Heisey and John Monk, both of whom were on the board of directors, announced that the railroad had secured haulage contracts with three mines guaranteeing annual revenue of $180,000. This guarantee, along with potential future expansion in both mining and agriculture made the railroad's future appear secure and there is no indication that either of them were contemplating a quick sale. At the end of November, Frank Hall, George Atkins, and an investor named Harry S. Wiest traveled to Butte. Their goal was to gain an understanding of the copper industry in order to assess the advisability of extending the YPRR to Cooke City. While in Butte they met with O. P. Chisholm, a mining man from Bozeman who had recently inspected the Cooke City mines. Chisholm's opinion was that Cooke City had incredible potential. "There are mountains of ore at Cooke . . . mountains of it," Chisholm reported with unrestrained enthusiasm, "and the average of the ore is higher than that taken out in Butte." Chisholm went on to assert that all the district needed to become, "an immediate producer of high-grade copper ore" was a railroad, and having evaluated the area himself, he was confident that one would soon be built. That decision, of course, was in the hands of Hall, Atkins and the other members of YPRR's board of directors.[23]

In late November, while Hall, Atkins, and Wiest learned about copper mining and Cooke City, Philip Gallaher, seemingly unaware of the company's financial struggles, optimistically informed the *Billings Gazette* that "track laying will be commenced next week and when that is begun we are ready to lay one mile a day. At that rate, the road will be ready for use at Christmas time." He went on to note that "arrangements are being made to continue the road on to Cooke City and if the weather permits, grading will be continued well along to the state line this winter. The rest of the road is assured and the project will not be allowed to rest until the entire line is completed." Gallaher's statement was reminiscent of Chris Yegen's confident declaration made two years earlier. It exuded both unwarranted optimism and a less than complete understanding of the company's financial limitations. Detached as he was from the company's day-to-day operations, the source of Gallaher's misleading information may have been Frank Hall, who reigned supreme in the dissemination of inaccurate reports.[24]

In late 1905, following his announcement in the *Billings Gazette*, either convinced that the railroad he had been planning and promoting for nearly twenty years was about to become a reality or sensing that trouble lay ahead, Gallaher removed himself from further involvement in the YPRR. At the same time, he also resigned from his position as Yellowstone County Surveyor, a job he had won in a close election less than a year earlier. Having recently been elected to the Bear Creek Coal Company Board of Directors and assumed the position of secretary and general manager, he left Frank Hall behind and began preparing the Bear Creek mine for full production. A year and a half later, as trouble began to simmer for Frank Hall, Gallaher and his second wife, Helen, moved to their cattle ranch on Shell Creek near Basin, Wyoming. After diligently pursuing his goal of a railroad to the Bear Creek coalfield, this move signaled the end of Gallaher's involvement in both the railroad and the mines it served.[25]

As the trials and travails of 1905 wore on, one bright spot for Frank Hall was the arrival of Miss Laura S. Solberg, whom Hall had convinced to come to Montana from Milwaukee to serve as his personal secretary. Born in Minnesota to Norwegian immigrants, she and her parents had moved to Milwaukee where her father worked as an insurance agent. Given her Milwaukee connection, it must be assumed that she and Hall were more than casual acquaintances. A pretty thirty-year-old city girl, it must have been some combination of love and Hall's salesman's wit and charm that persuaded her to leave home and move out to a frontier mining town like Bridger. In any case, she was soon an admired and well-liked member of the local community. By October, she was working alongside Hall in her new job with the YPRR.[26]

Philip Gallaher's prediction that the railroad would be finished by Christmas 1905 proved to be totally unrealistic. It was late December, or perhaps early January, before a track crew composed mostly of Japanese immigrants began laying the first sections of new sixty-pound rail on the roadbed south of Bridger. Remarkably, with actual track laying just getting underway, Hall, whom the *Butte Inter-Mountain* heralded as "the head of one of the largest enterprises in Montana," claimed that the grading was complete and that tracks had already reached Belfry. Hall embellished this transparent fiction by announcing that the Bear Creek mines "will be tapped by our road and by a branch line, but the destination of the main line is Cooke City, via the Clark's Fork route." Having traversed the route with Philip Gallaher in 1900, Hall elaborated with some authority, saying, "Work will be pushed on this main line as rapidly as possible and when it is complete, we shall have a scenic route that will present views and vistas grander than those of the world-famous Rio Grande, Grand Canyon or Royal Gorge. . . . Our road will afford a new gateway to the park, and owing to the attractive features of this 125-mile ride, we expect it will become one of the most popular routes for tourists to that natural wonderland."[27]

Thus stated, it is clear that during the past several years Hall's passion for a railroad to the park had not diminished. As proof of those intentions, the *Butte Miner* reported in late January that engineers in the field had already completed cross-sectioning forty-five miles of that route. Later that year P. J. Wilson of Belfry claimed he had received the contract to build the necessary bridges and in October, Wilson asserted that contracts had been let for the construction of the first eighteen miles of line south of Belfry.[28]

As initial track laying finally got underway, Hall attempted to lease a locomotive from the NP, but in keeping with its efforts to thwart his progress, the NP refused to help, claiming it had none to spare. So, in mid-January, he traveled to Anaconda to arrange the purchase of the YPRR's first locomotive from the Butte, Anaconda & Pacific Railway (BA&P), a subsidiary of Amalgamated Copper. The engine Hall acquired was an ornate American-standard type (4-4-0) built in 1882. It was Number 15 on the BA&P roster, and although it was officially Number 1 on the YPRR roster, Hall must have been remiss in having it repainted as locals referred to it as "Little Fifteen" for years to come. Although Little Fifteen was needed for construction, it was not the ideal locomotive for the work it would soon be called on to do. Its sixty-four-inch drivers being more

Known as "Little Fifteen," Yellowstone Park Railroad's first locomotive was purchased from the Butte, Anaconda & Pacific in 1906. It is seen here in Anaconda, Montana, in 1900. (PAc 97-93.14069, BAP 15, Montana Historical Society Photograph Archives).

suited for fast passenger service than hauling heavily loaded coal cars on steep mine spurs. But for now, it would have to do.[29]

Despite Hall's earlier claims, grading to the Bear Creek Coal Company mine was not completed until mid-February 1906, at which point the end of the track was still four miles north of Belfry on Golden Flat near Dry Creek. With just one-third of the line complete, Hall was again out of money, and the project was stalled. Unwilling to admit defeat, in early 1906 he once again headed east to New York City and Philadelphia. When, shortly after his departure, eight carloads of new rail destined for the YPRR arrived in Billings from the Colorado Fuel & Iron Company, the vendor seized the shipment and sold it to the NP, claiming that the rails had not been paid for. When questioned about this turn of events, Hall, in typical manner, denied that the bill had not been paid and asserted that he had refused the shipment because he already had enough rail to reach Cooke City. This was nonsense. The NP, of course, may have been a party to this escapade, using its influence to ensure that the delivery was not made—one more way to stifle Hall's progress.[30]

When Hall returned to Montana in mid-March, he maintained that the project was amply funded. But this could not have been the case, as he turned around and headed east again in April. Some of Hall's money-raising troubles may have originated with NP president Elliott, who had advised major East Coast banking houses to beware of him. Quite probably frustrated in his efforts to get his bonds placed, and seeking relief in any way possible, on his return trip to Montana in late April, Hall made a point of taking NP's flagship train the *North Coast Limited*. This just happened to be the same train that Chicago, Milwaukee, and St. Paul Railroad (Milwaukee Road) president A. J. Earling was taking to Butte. There is little doubt, given his chilly relationship with the NP, that Hall hoped to meet with Earling and elicit the support and backing of NP's newest rival.[31]

In 1906, the Milwaukee Road had just begun construction of its Pacific Extension, a transcontinental line to be built across Montana in direct competition with both the NP and Great Northern. According to newspaper reports, Hall and Earling had a lengthy meeting on the train. Hall, no doubt, regaled Earling with his plans for Belfry and the Cooke City extension and extolled the benefits of a Milwaukee Road connection with the YPRR. When Hall disembarked in Billings, rumors quickly spread that he had made a deal with Earling for either a friendly connection or a complete buyout, but neither rumor proved to be true. Nevertheless, the story illustrates that with only eight miles of track on the ground, Hall was well aware of his predicament: limited funding and an adversarial relationship with his only outside connection, the latter being a problem that Elijah Smith had recognized years earlier. Because James J. Hill now controlled not only the NP but also the Great Northern and CB&Q, Hall's only chance for a friendly outlet was via the Milwaukee Road. Despite the fact that its mainline lay eighty miles to the north, out of necessity this unlikely connection became an escape route that would be pursued for years to come.

Notwithstanding the problems he faced, Hall refused to publicly acknowledge his difficulties. When questioned by a reporter sometime in

April, he claimed to have purchased forty miles of used rail and was ready to complete the railroad. But in May 1906, with grading completed to the mines, the rails he supposedly purchased failed to materialize. The end of the line was still north of Belfry and the mine operators were becoming increasingly irritated. As he had done in the past, Hall was stalling for time, but time was running out. Both the Bear Creek Coal Company and Elijah Smith's Montana Coal & Iron Company had invested heavily in their properties during 1905, and their patience was running thin. At the end of May, Chris and Peter Yegen met with Hall in Billings to discuss the completion of the railroad. During the meeting Hall must have confessed that despite his best efforts he needed more money, likely adding that he expected that his investors would soon provide the necessary funds. After they listened to his explanations and plans, with few options available, the Yegens agreed to provide a six-month loan for the purchase of 1,200 tons of used sixty-pound rail from a firm in Chicago; this being enough rail to allow completion of the line to their Bear Creek mine. The loan was secured by a lien against the railroad and all its property. Not fully trusting him, the Yegens made sure that Hall placed the order before leaving town.[32]

During April and May, Hall was a busy man. In addition to ordering the rail to finish his line, he had depots, an engine house, coaling tower, water tanks, and other facilities designed and built. In May, it was reported that he had ordered one hundred boxcars to be painted yellow, to distinguish them from NP's rolling stock, and had once again placed an order for two new locomotives. Although the trackside structures were eventually completed, this new order for boxcars was either never placed or canceled because as late as 1910, the railroad still owned no interchange rolling stock. And just like the forty miles of rail he claimed to have ordered in April, the two locomotives he supposedly ordered failed to materialize as well. These events emphasize Hall's tendency to promulgate stories designed to conceal the company's desperate situation. In reality the YPRR was in deep financial trouble, and things were about to get even worse.[33]

5

"In Its Utilitarian Advantages the New Station Is Unsurpassed"

THE ARRIVAL OF THE RAILS PURCHASED WITH THE YEGEN loan allowed completion of the line into Belfry in June 1906. To celebrate this event Hall decided to stage a huge Fourth of July celebration in Belfry with a special chartered train hired to carry passengers from Billings. Meant to showcase his new depot and up-and-coming town that now boasted a number of new businesses, posters displayed in Billings announced: "Last year a wheat field, this year a city with sidewalks." Round-trip tickets sold for two dollars with the train departing the Billings Depot at 8:00 a.m. on Wednesday, July 4, with a return scheduled for 10:00 p.m.[1]

Frank Hall was up early Wednesday morning and, according to the *Billings Gazette*, "superintended" the start of the excursion. Having gained a level of celebrity, the flamboyant, gregarious Hall likely spent the early morning hours greeting passengers as he roamed up and down the platform between the depot and the five dark green NP coaches reserved for the trip. A second train pulled by Little Fifteen left from Bridger with local "excursionists" who endured smoke, dust, and cinders while riding on three open air flat cars. A few hours later, under a bright summer sky, the trains announced their arrival in Belfry with clanking bells and blasts from their whistles. As red, white, and blue bunting and flags with forty-five stars fluttered in the soft morning breeze, ladies in flared Edwardian ankle-length skirts escorted by gentlemen wearing morning coats and dapper straw boater hats, strolled down Broadway Avenue arm in arm to join the day's festivities. By all accounts the celebration, which included a carnival and street dance, was a great success with more than one thousand people in attendance. It was a party locals would never forget, and it solidified Belfry's place on the map as the newest town in Carbon County.[2]

Laid out in a simple north–south, east–west grid, Belfry was probably Hall's vision of a model town. Bert Vaill's role in its founding was recognized by naming the street that ran through the middle of town Vaill Avenue. Frank Hall acknowledged his adopted home state by naming the north–south lane, where the town's school would be built, Wisconsin Street. Other streets were given names like Yellowstone and Carbon. Despite its new sidewalks, Belfry was a typical western town with dusty unpaved thoroughfares that were reduced to rutted mud after a heavy rain or rapid spring thaw. Convinced that his new town had a bright future, Hall persuaded Colonel Charles K. Lush, a well-known Wisconsin newspaperman and journalist, to move down soon after its founding and help him start the town's newspaper. As with so many of Hall's plans, things did not work out. After just six weeks, Lush moved back to Wisconsin, claiming Belfry was a bit too isolated and primitive for him.[3]

But not everyone shared Colonel Lush's harsh opinion of Hall's new town. According to the *Carbon County News*, in 1910, a doctor named Chilcott established his practice in Belfry. The story about Dr. Chilcott claims that he nearly went broke as no one in Belfry ever got sick, the main cause of mortality being old age. The explanation for this rare phenomenon was said to be the area's "pure mountain air, excellent water, a salubrious climate and the choicest of fruits of the earth." With all of these factors working against him, after nine years with little to do, the good doctor moved on.[4]

Whereas the town's purported healthful environment may have been detrimental to Dr. Chilcott's practice, the town still needed a doctor. According to local historian Jetta Regan, in 1908, a man named Elza Ogden got into a disagreement in one of the town's drinking establishments and ended up with a serious gunshot wound to his abdomen. There being no doctor in town, a phone call to Bridger summoned Dr. Arthur Movius, who arrived sometime later after a dusty twelve-mile ride in his horse drawn buggy. While helpful bystanders held Elza down on a table, the doctor sorted out his damaged "innards" and stitched him

A view to the west down rutted, unpaved Vaill Avenue in Belfry. The Occident grain elevator, visible in the distance on the left, was built in 1919 and dates this photo as probably having been taken in the early 1920s. A lone dairy cow can be seen next to the house on the right. (Author's collection).

Downtown Belfry as it appeared around 1920. The flagpole in the middle of Broadway Avenue was installed in 1918 to support the war effort. The railroad depot is just out of sight to the left. (Author's collection).

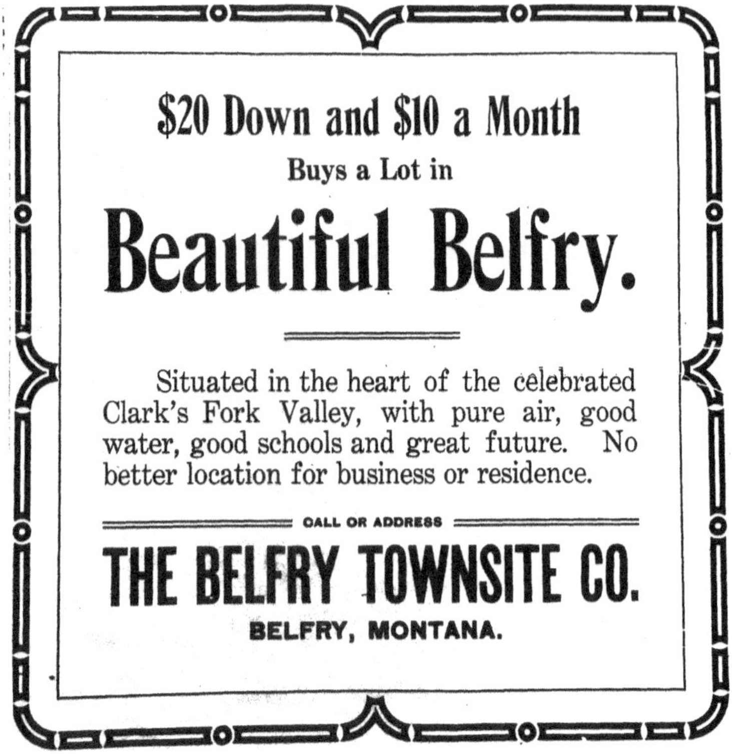

An advertisement from the October 22, 1908, Belfry edition of the *Carbon County News* extolled the virtues of Frank Hall's new town.

back together. The wounded man recovered and lived to be eighty-eight, quite possibly an early beneficiary of the "pure mountain air" and "salubrious climate" that contributed to Dr. Chilcott's financial downfall.[5]

The Belfry Depot, which would serve as both the railroad's headquarters and the centerpiece of Hall's new town, was the embodiment of his bold vision for the future. Designed by Billings architect John Mitchell and completed in June 1906 at a cost of $18,000, the depot was perched on the north-facing slope of Bear Creek at the west end of Broadway Avenue. Architecturally distinct, the 4,650-square-foot building was a craftsman-style structure divided into four sections. The west end housed a freight/baggage room, the midsection a passenger waiting room and business office, and the east end living quarters for the company president or other company official; a walkout basement

The Belfry Depot, Frank Hall's lasting monument to his new railroad, is seen here as it appeared shortly after its completion in June 1906. (Carbon County Historical Society and Museum).

that opened onto Bear Creek included two additional apartments. The depot's hip roof was adorned by eyebrow dormers on each side and four prominent ridge chimneys. The overhanging eaves displayed scrolled rafters and beveled soffits. Exterior walls were decoratively clad in square butt shingles at the base, octagonal in the middle, and a diamond pattern in the friezes.[6]

The depot grounds included a six-acre park, complete with cobblestone-lined Koi ponds, a white gazebo surrounded by flowerbeds and lush green lawns that terraced down to the rippling creek. Shortly after its completion, the *Red Lodge Picket* described the depot as "second, from an artistic viewpoint, only to the one in Livingston." This was high praise indeed. NP's Livingston Depot was an impressive red and yellow brick structure with a trackside colonnade and architectural details such as ornate terra cotta lions' heads and floral figures. The *Picket* went on to describe the virtues of Belfry's new station by claiming "In its utilitarian advantages the new station is unsurpassed . . . let it suffice to say that it is up to the highest standard both as to design and execution." The depot was clearly an edifice that Frank Hall could be proud of.[7]

In addition to the depot and the various businesses that soon sprang up, Belfry was home to the YPRR's shops and engine servicing facilities. Located just northwest of the depot on a broad plain at the base of the

The architectural details of the Belfry Depot are evident in this view from 1931, which include three types of decorative shingles on the walls, scrolled rafters, and beveled soffits. (CCHS&M).

hills on the north side of Bear Creek, these structures included a two-stall engine house with a machine shop and a distinctive coaling tower. The coaling tower's unique appearance, similar in many respects to a CB&Q branch line design, was accentuated by an array of large external sheaves and cables used for hoisting coal. There was a water tank next to the engine house and a second one on the mainline about a mile and half to the north where a steam jet was used to pump water from the Clarks Fork River. There were no yard tracks as such, only a house track or two for storing and repairing equipment. The mainline to Cooke City ran north–south along the east side of the engine house crossing Bear Creek on a short trestle to reach the depot. As forecast by Philip Gallaher at the start of construction, it was anticipated that this line would soon be pushed south into Wyoming and one day see heavily loaded ore trains rolling into town destined for the massive smelting complex that Hall visualized along the Clarks Fork River.

This view of the engine house and yard facilities in Belfry is to the north. The water tank and the top of the coaling tower are visible just beyond the engine house. The tracks in the foreground connect the mainline to the Bear Creek branch and form the wye used for turning locomotives. (General Photograph Collection, Railroad Museum of Pennsylvania, PHMC).

The branch line to the Bear Creek mines diverged from the Cooke City mainline north of the engine house and after a half mile of tangent, swept through a broad curve to enter the Bear Creek valley. A curved connecting track between these two lines created a "wye" for turning locomotives. Until the Cooke City extension was complete the mainline would remain a stub track extending about a quarter mile past the depot. This track would be used for loading sugar beets, livestock and other agricultural products. A lonely section of graded roadbed extended a short distance into the sage brush flats beyond the end of tracks. In 1909, a siding and sugar beet loading ramp were built about a half mile north of the depot and in 1919 the stub south of the depot became the site of the Occident grain elevator and the Walruth bean processing plant. At some later date a second grain elevator was built about a mile north of Belfry.[8]

This 1954 view of the north end of the engine house reveals the railroad's unique coaling tower with its numerous external cables and sheaves. A drop-bottom gondola is visible on the unloading ramp at the base of the structure. (PAc 97-93.14416 MWS Shop-Coal Dock Belfry 5/1954. TTT, Montana Historical Society Photograph Archives).

Following the festivities of July 4, the nine miles of track to the recently platted town of Bearcreek were quickly completed. Incorporated in 1905 by George Lamport and his son-in-law Robert Leavens, the town was laid out in a narrow part of the valley about a mile east of the Bear Creek mine. For reasons unknown, Lamport and Leavens christened their town Bearcreek, one word rather than two, and by January 1906, its population justified a post office. By the time the railroad arrived in late July, the population had swelled to around five hundred. In excited anticipation of all the activity just over the hill, the *Red Lodge Picket* picturesquely reported: "The future of the little city of Bearcreek may not be written until some other day. Its location is not the most desirable, topographically speaking, for a city of extensive magnitude. That it is

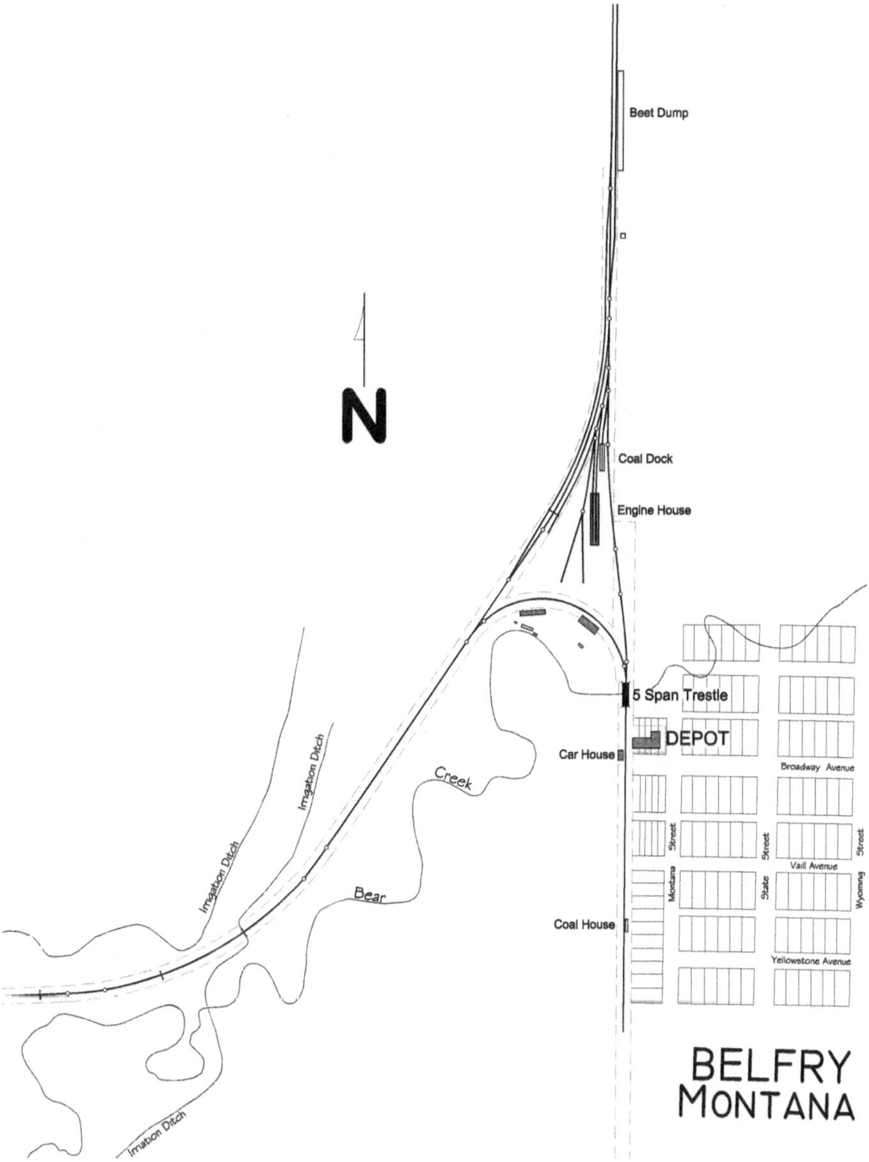

Map showing the layout of Belfry yard in 1917.

This northwesterly view of Bearcreek taken in 1918 shows the recently completed Foster Gulch wye in the bottom of the valley, one leg of which departs the mainline to the right of the short trestle visible in the lower right. The other half of the wye can be seen cutting across the hillside in the center left. The MW&S depot is located trackside just to the left of the trestle at the corner of Fourth Street and First Avenue South. Virtue Gulch is visible in the upper left. (CCHS&M).

destined to become one of the greatest coal mining camps in the entire western country, is an assured fact. . . . At present the town is growing rapidly, no less than ten buildings being in [the] course of construction. Among these are a building that is being erected by B. E. Vaill in which a bank will be established."

During its early years, about half of Bearcreek's population consisted of miners, many of whom were recent immigrants from Scotland, Montenegro, Serbia, Italy, and elsewhere. Due to it being located in an area where flat land was at a premium, residential housing quickly spread westward up the valley toward the mines. As a result, neighborhoods were created that eventually coalesced to fill much of the valley, each an ethnic enclave with its own name. Just west of Bearcreek one of the earliest was Stringtown, but soon there were others named Chickentown, Caledonia, Cousin Row, and Horseshoe Bend.[9]

Because most of the town's population consisted of miners who, for the most part were young single men, life in Bearcreek could, from time-to-time, get a bit rough. One afternoon in late 1906, while work was still progressing on spur tracks to the mines, Riley Fredericks, a grading contractor from Joliet, was enjoying a beer at Bearcreek's only saloon. Inexplicably, but possibly due to some political disagreement, Fredericks suddenly grabbed a beer bottle, broke it on the bar and confronted a group of Italian miners. One against many, Fredericks didn't stand a chance and was soon beaten senseless. When the proprietor intervened and ejected the assailants, they responded with a barrage of rocks, breaking glass and damaging furniture. Because the town lacked its own constabulary, a desperate panicked call to Sheriff Potter in Red Lodge precipitated a wild horseback ride over the hill in the company of Undersheriff Vaughn. Although things had calmed down by the time the sheriff arrived, when he and Vaughn attempted to round up the ringleaders shots rang out. The lawmen took cover, and after a short stand-off, the perpetrator surrendered. He and two others were subsequently hauled off to jail. Fredericks recovered, but if he ever returned to Bearcreek, he probably took care to keep his political views to himself.

Bar fights were one thing, but on November 26, 1906, Bearcreek was the site of a cold-blooded murder. The tragedy occurred when Slavonian miners, Gabriel Sedlak and Stephen Novota were pulling buckets of water from a well behind their boardinghouse. Sedlak, a twenty-one-year-old, had teased and ridiculed the older Novota about his strength for several days. When he began to tease him again, while lifting water from the well, Novota, a small, exceedingly repulsive-looking man, became enraged. Muttering, "I will kill you like a jackrabbit," Novota stomped off to his room, grabbed a shotgun, leaned out a second-floor window, and shouted "Gabriel, look up!" When Sedlak turned, Novota pulled the trigger and blew part of Sedlak's head off. As the sound of the gunshot echoed up and down the valley, news of the incident quickly spread and an angry mob soon formed. Had it not been for the timely intervention of local peace officers, Novota might have been the guest of honor at Bearcreek's first lynching. When he was hustled out of town and safely installed in the Red Lodge jail, threats of violence subsided.[10]

In addition to the main valley where Bearcreek and residential enclaves occupied much of the open ground, there were two important side valleys. Foster Gulch, a narrow, treeless, rounded valley with a small incised intermittent stream at its base, branched off to the southwest immediately south of the Bearcreek town site. A half mile upstream, Virtue Gulch, home to another minor tributary, joined the Bear Creek Valley from the northwest. Following a winding trace, Bear Creek continued westward beyond Virtue Gulch into a narrow canyon called Scotch Coulee. Here Bear Creek branched off to the south while the railroad continued up Scotch Coulee along a minor drainage called Keucking Creek. One of the few flat spots just west of Virtue Gulch was selected as the terminus of the Bear Creek branch and the site of a small yard called International Junction.

Nestled between the base of a steep hillside and the abrupt drop into the brush-covered ravine carved by Bear Creek, facilities at International Junction included an aboveground turntable, section house, and water tank. No coaling tower was needed as fuel for the locomotives was taken directly from nearby mine tipples. During the early years of operation all trains were assembled and disassembled at this point and cars were shunted up one of three spur tracks to the various mines. One spur followed the main drainage a short distance up Scotch Coulee to the Bear Creek mine and then continued about another mile to Montana Coal & Iron's mine, which was now referred to as the Smith mine. In the spring of 1907, another spur was extended the opposite direction. This spur ran from International Junction to the northeast and then swung around a sharp curve to the northwest hugging the south side of Virtue Gulch for a one-and-a-half-mile assent up a steep 4.5 percent grade to the Smokeless & Sootless mine. A second spur branched off in the same direction, crossed to the north side of Virtue Gulch and climbed steeply for a short distance to the International Mine. These spur lines were referred to as the McCarthy and International branches, the first being named for one of the original owners of the Smokeless & Sootless mine. While nearly all the freight handled by the YPRR would be outbound coal, agricultural products were also shipped on a seasonal basis. Incoming freight

A view of International Junction looking northeast. The mainline to Bearcreek diverges to the right just before the water tank visible in the distance. The turntable is located just to the left of the water tank. Virtue Gulch forms the valley on the left. (CCHS&M-Kidwell Collection).

was predominantly machinery and lumber for the mines. Crews who worked at International Junction were instructed to keep the switch to the mainline closed at all times to prevent runaway cars, which were not infrequent, from careening through Bearcreek and down the line toward Belfry.[11]

Upon completion, the railroad's trackage, including spurs and mainline, totaled about twenty-three and a half miles. A little more than a year later, in September 1907, the line was extended one and a half miles up Scotch Coulee to Anaconda's new mine and company town of Washoe. According to historian D. B. Robertson, the YPRR's total construction cost came to $401,305 with an additional expenditure of $149,427 for equipment. This was slightly more than the estimate given in the company's July 1905 annual statement, but it is unclear whether Robertson's total included the various mine spurs, sidings, and the extension to Washoe or referred only to the cost of the mainline to International Junction. If all twenty-five miles are included, the cost to build the YPRR was about $16,000 per mile, or double Chris Yegen's 1903 estimate.[12]

Prior to 1917, the turntable at International Junction was the only means to turn locomotives. The track curving off to the right is the mainline to Bearcreek. The track that passes behind the water tank is the McCarthy Branch that extends up Virtue Gulch. The bare rails in this winter photo taken around 1924 suggest that despite the completion of the Foster Gulch wye, the turntable may still be in use. (CCHS&M-Kidwell Collection).

The steep grade to the International Mine is apparent in this view. The Bearcreek mainline is visible on the left while the McCarthy Branch to the Smokeless & Sootless Mine is visible in front of the section house on the extreme right. The snow-covered Beartooth Mountains can be seen in the distance. (CCHS&M-Kidwell Collection).

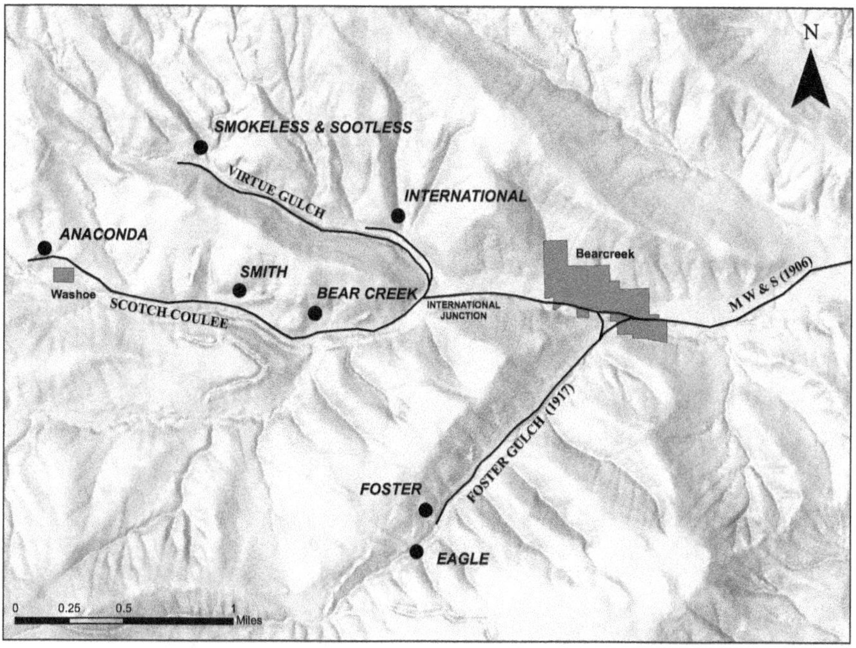

Map showing the location of the principal mines and main trackage between Bearcreek and Washoe.

Because construction was begun without adequate funding, Hall had been continuously strapped for cash and was forced to implement substandard engineering practices and cut corners where he could. Although NP engineers would later acknowledge that the trestles were generally well-built and some rip-rap had been used along stream banks, in most places the roadbed was narrow and poorly drained. In one section called Jenning's Sway, about three miles south of Bridger, northbound trains running downgrade from the mines were forced to negotiate a short adverse grade. This problem could have been solved with deeper cuts and an earthen fill, but Hall, in an effort to economize, apparently rejected that expenditure. This was the type of decision that could have precipitated the November 1905 resignation of his chief engineer, Russell Kimball.[13]

When grading was complete, the track was laid using relatively light sixty-pound rail (only the first five miles of which was new), spiked to untreated fir ties placed directly on the dirt roadbed. A latter-day report by

During the district's early years, the Bear Creek Coal Company operated the largest and most important mine; the boiler house and tipple are seen here as they appeared around 1917. The inclined tramway visible on the hillside behind the boiler house provides access to the mine's main portal. (CCHS&M).

the Montana Railroad Commission would derisively describe the YPRR as having "mud ballast," pointedly suggesting that there was nothing more than loose dirt between the ties. Due to its shoddy construction, during periods of heavy rain or melting snow the roadbed would become so soggy that the track would often "squish out" under the weight of passing trains. If the resulting dip was severe enough, cars would uncouple and the train would be thrown into emergency braking. In some sections, slack coal was used as ballast, but this proved to be of little value as it did not provide adequate drainage or stabilize the track. Due to its light construction, during summer months heat expansion would sometimes cause the track to kink or buckle. This was just one of many issues that contributed to the frequent derailments the railroad would suffer in ensuing years. Until improvements were made, operating the YPRR would be a risky and challenging business.[14]

Regardless of the line's inadequate funding and poor construction, on a cool Saturday in mid-September 1906 under a slate-gray sky, as

An eight-car train pulled by an unidentified locomotive barely visible behind the brush in the lower left has just arrived at the Bear Creek mine. Note the massive piles of slack and waste rock on the hillside. The mine tipple is just out of sight to the left. (CCHS&M-Kidwell Collection).

periodic rain showers swept the valley, YPRR's aged locomotive Little Fifteen cautiously made its way up the spur to the Bear Creek Coal Company mine. Following hand signals from his brakeman, the engineer eased the locomotive back until, with a heavy, dull metallic clunk, it coupled onto the waiting string of loaded cars. As hot steam and coal smoke lingered in the misty autumn air, the rumble from the engine's firebox was punctuated by rhythmic percussive exhausts from the single-stage air pump as it labored to fill the train's brake lines and reservoirs. Moments later a waved signal from the caboose was answered by two blasts from the engine's whistle and with a slight slip of the locomotive's drivers, the first train load of Bear Creek coal began its downhill journey to Bridger and coal vendors across the state. As significant as this milestone was, this was not the first revenue train to grace the company's rails. Financial records reveal that during the fiscal year ending June 30, 1906, with only twelve miles of track in place, the railroad had already generated net earnings from operations of almost eighty dollars! Not much, but for Frank Hall it was a start. But NP's management was not pleased with Hall's success, and in November, it announced that the NP would haul Bear Creek coal no further than Billings. This was just the beginning of operational interference by the NP, there was much more to come.[15]

Having promised that the railroad would be in operation before the end of 1905, by the time the first train left Bearcreek, Hall was almost a year behind schedule, and the mine owners were not pleased. This was especially true of Elijah Smith who had met with Hall in August 1905 and, no doubt, been assured that the YPRR would soon be in operation. Well-known in the area, the sixty-six-year-old Smith was a bearish, determined-looking man. His receding hairline, broad forehead, slightly bulbous nose, and white untamed beard gave him the look of a not too jolly Saint Nicholas. Considered an "eccentric old man" by the *Red Lodge Picket*, a little over a year after meeting with Hall, in a demonstration of both his eccentricity and frustration, Smith blocked construction of a spur line up Foster Gulch to one of his company's more promising properties. Smith claimed he preferred to leave the coal in the ground for his grandchildren, an interesting comment for a bachelor. His erratic behavior was presumably an expression of both his irritation with Hall and a harbinger of mental health issues that would land him in a sanatorium less than five years later. Due to Smith's obduracy, despite having completed the grading and tie placement, Hall was forced to abandon the spur and salvage the ties for use elsewhere.[16]

With the railroad finally in operation, it is easy to imagine Frank Hall at work, ensconced in his well-appointed office in the Belfry depot. While a Regulator clock likely ticked reassuringly on the wall near his desk and a coal fire burned in the midroom stove to ward off the late November chill, Hall began the process of sending out annual passes to railroad presidents and dignitaries across the country. Included with these passes, which offered free transit across the entire system, was a list of the line's stations and an advertisement that proclaimed the YPRR was open for business. Annual passes were both a courtesy and an announcement. So, while Miss Solberg sat poised at her typewriter, Hall probably

Yellowstone Park Railroad

F. A. HALL, President

General Offices, Belfry, Mont.

SHORT LINE

Between Clark Fork Valley Points and Red Lodge.

CONNECTS

At Bridger with Northern Pacific Railroad.

At Belfry with Stage for Chance and all Upper Valley Points.

At Bearcreek with Stage for Red Lodge.

The Only Line to the Famous Bear Creek Coal Fields

On October 15, 1908, two years after the first coal was shipped, Frank Hall proudly advertised his railroad as "The Only Line to the Famous Bear Creek Coal Fields" (*Carbon County News*, Belfry edition).

thumbed through the pages of the most recent edition of *Poor's Manual of Railroads* deciding who should receive the honor of an annual pass. At Hall's prompting Miss Solberg would have inserted a beige wallet-size card with the words "YELLOWSTONE PARK RAILROAD Co." emblazoned across the top into the typewriter's carriage. Rolling the card down to the first blank line next to the word "PASS," on card number 490, she typed "Mr. R. J. Camp, President." Advancing the return to the next line she continued with "Florida & Georgia Railway Co." Handing the card to Hall, he then signed "F A Hall" in neat flowing cursive in the card's lower right corner, finishing with an angled slash through the first letter. The fine print on each card informed the recipient that it was good "until December 31st 1907, unless otherwise ordered" and must be signed on the back in ink by the person accepting it.[17]

While it seems unlikely that President R. J. Camp of the Florida & Georgia Railway ever signed his pass, or felt compelled to visit Bearcreek or Belfry, for Frank Hall the distribution of annual passes was confirmation of his accomplishment. At age thirty-eight, as he sat in his new depot his thoughts might have been interrupted by Little Fifteen whistling a warning at the grade crossing west of town. Rising to peer up the valley, he would have known it wasn't just any whistle, it was his whistle. Although he was undoubtedly proud of what he had accomplished, he may not have fully appreciated the significance of his achievement, the importance of which would be evident for the next forty-seven years as the railroad he struggled to build formed a critical link in supplying coal to domestic vendors, businesses, and factories across Montana and beyond. For many years, its importance would manifest itself in the staccato exhaust of steam locomotives hammering up the steep grades to the mines with strings of empties; followed by the creak and groan of heavily loaded coal drags cautiously drifting down the valley toward Belfry with retainers set, brake shoes smoking. Although Hall had accomplished much since his arrival in Montana, as he gazed out the windows of the Belfry depot at the sage brush flats and distant mountains south of Broadway Avenue during the winter of 1906, he would have known that his biggest challenge still lay ahead. He had completed the branch line to the mines, but the fabulous tourist railway he envisioned winding its way up the Clarks Fork Canyon to Yellowstone National Park and the mines at Cooke City, remained an unfulfilled dream.[18]

Although trains were now running, 1907 did not start well for Frank Hall. During the first week of January, the district court forced him to pay a settlement of $3,856 owed to two ranchers who had not received payment for the right-of-way through their properties north and west of Belfry. This was followed by a damage suit for $1,800 filed by another rancher. The following day the Yegen Brothers Savings Bank instituted foreclosure proceedings against the railroad for failure to repay the loan made the previous May. According to the filing, the YPRR owed the Yegens $32,302.11, the company having repaid only $20,000 of the original loan. In addition, the Yegens were demanding 12 percent interest and $5,000 in attorney's fees. Their suit asked that the railroad be sold and the proceeds applied in payment of the amount sued for. Hall and his attorney, C. F. Merrill of Bridger, argued that the Yegens had not fulfilled their part of the contract in delivering the required number of rails; this appeared a specious defense at best. Whether he knew it or not, Hall was playing with fire. The Yegens were not men to be trifled with. Now that they had the railroad they needed for their mining venture, as NP president Charles Mellen had once said, what they wanted from Hall was "some money and not so much talk."[19]

To add to his ongoing problems, in March, with two lawsuits already pending, a group of bondholders in Massachusetts brought suit in Federal Court against the YPRR and the Farmer's Trust Company for nonpayment of interest on the bonds they held. As with the Yegen brothers, they too were demanding foreclosure and sale of the railroad. In this case, Hall claimed that the bonds had not been properly issued, but when they were shown to be legitimate the interest payments were made and the suit was dropped. Nonetheless, with the Yegen foreclosure hanging over him, Hall and his railroad were in a precarious position.[20]

Hall headed east in March 1907 determined to find a way to save his struggling enterprise. While in Indianapolis, he purchased a derelict gasoline-powered trolley car to use for passenger service (see chapter 9), and on April 16, while still in the Indianapolis area, Hall and his secretary, Laura Solberg, were married. But Hall, perhaps enjoying an extended honeymoon, or traveling to Montana incommunicado in his new railcar, neglected to inform his associates in Montana of his whereabouts. In late June, a Bridger newspaper commented that he had left town about two months earlier, and with the foreclosure suit about to go to court, his attorney and others had been unable to locate him. On June 27, with Hall still out of town, Judge Frank Henry awarded judgment to the Yegen Brothers Savings Bank for $36,055.73 and $5,000 in attorney fees. Judge Henry ordered that the YPRR be sold at a sheriff's auction in

Red Lodge a month later, but the proposed July 23 sale never took place. Sometime before the sale date, Hall returned from his midwest sojourn and met with the Yegens. During this meeting, Hall likely used a bit of smooth talk and persuasion to assure them that given a little more time he would make good on the loan. Convinced or not, given the turmoil that a change in ownership might cause, it is likely that brother Peter counseled against foreclosure reminding his older sibling that keeping their mine in operation was their primary concern. Whatever their rationale, the Yegens agreed to a six-month extension, but Hall's problems were far from over.[21]

With foreclosure still threatening their investment, Hall's bond and stockholders had become disillusioned with his financial management and brinksmanship with the Yegen brothers. Because of the delays in construction and Hall's adversarial relationship with the NP, none of the investors, except those who had sued, had received interest payments on their bonds. The railroad's finances were so shaky that Hall was even deferring his rather generous salary. From the investors' vantage point in Pennsylvania, it was easy to assign blame for the company's woes to Hall's fiscal mismanagement. Because of this, George Atkins and George Heisey decided that it was time for Hall to go. Atkins and Heisey planned to replace Hall with Chris Yegen who had indicated he was willing to take on the job. Yegen's ownership in the Bear Creek Coal Company, the railroad's biggest customer, made him a logical choice for the position. A simple majority vote by the board of directors was needed to replace Hall, but he apparently still had supporters and Atkins and Heisey were unable to muster the necessary votes. Being frustrated in their attempt to remove him via the board, Atkins and Heisey decided to approach Hall with a buyout offer. The nature and extent of their negotiations are unknown but they likely focused on the value of the stock Hall had been awarded as company president. At par these shares were worth $50,000, the equivalent of more than $1 million in 2020. Hall presumably insisted on a full payout, something Atkins and Heisey were unwilling to consider, and as a result, Hall remained in charge. As can be imagined, this outcome did nothing to mollify Atkins who was now more determined than ever to get rid of Hall. Feeling fully justified in his position, Hall probably did not appreciate the extent of Atkins's animus. But in the coming months, with the complicity of Heisey and other bondholders, Atkins would work diligently to develop a scheme designed to remove Hall from office without compensation.[22]

While his investors plotted against him, and having postponed foreclosure, Hall now faced a new set of challenges from the NP. In August, in an apparent attempt at intimidation, the NP once again sent a surveying crew to Bridger, generating rumors that a line paralleling the YPRR was about to be built. Shortly after the surveyors were dispatched, Howard Elliott, feeling the need to investigate the situation firsthand, ventured out of his St. Paul headquarters and headed to Montana. He arrived in Red Lodge on September 15 in the company of Chris Yegen, Frank Hall, and NP division superintendent Dan Boyle. Now that the YPRR was in full operation, Hall probably hoped to convince Elliott that friendly relations would be beneficial to both companies. At the same time, with his investors breathing down his neck and the Yegen's foreclosure suit still hanging over him, Hall probably would not have been averse to a buyout offer from Elliott, if the price was right. That is to say, a price that assured Hall a sizeable profit. Although his motives differed, Chris Yegen probably would have been happy to see the NP buy the YPRR as well.[23]

When they arrived in Red Lodge, the group disembarked and made the bumpy ride over the hill to Bear Creek. After spending several hours inspecting the mines, they boarded a YPRR train, which took them to Bridger, where Elliott's special train was now waiting. This visit, short as it was, gave Elliott a clear picture of the area's potential as well as an appreciation for the YPRR's flawed construction and financial vulnerability. Rather than being enticed into making a buyout offer, Elliott decided to stick with an approach he had just begun to implement. About a month after Elliott returned to St. Paul, James J. Hill's eldest son, James N. Hill, who now had oversight of the NP, wrote to Elliott and expressed his interest in buying Hall's railroad at "panic prices." Because NP management had not expected Hall to complete the YPRR, much less put it into operation, Hill perceived it to be the sort of nuisance that Elliott had predicted, and Hill now felt something must to be done.[24]

Since the NP was the YPRR's only source for cars, Hill suggested that Elliott induce the desired panic sale by arranging the car supply so there would be no chance of the YPRR ever making a profit. In making this suggestion, Hill emphasized the need for certain people to keep their mouths shut. Elliott responded by informing Hill that during his trip to Montana he had given "the people in Livingston instructions to keep down the supply of cars for Mr. Hall's road to the very lowest point possible." Elliott went on to explain, "The only reason that any cars were given at all to the Hall road during the last few months was so as to keep quiet as possible the Billings and Montana people, who were apt to go to the Montana Commission and make a disturbance." Unfortunately for both Hill and Elliott, despite their efforts at secrecy, the mine owners were already aware of their chicanery. In late August, when asked about a looming coal shortage in Billings that winter, Peter Yegen informed the *Billings Gazette* that his mine could supply one thousand tons per day if the NP would simply furnish the needed cars. While this may have been true, the YPRR's ability to handle that volume of traffic was an open question.[25]

6

"Physically . . . A Broken-Down Man"

WITH ONLY LITTLE FIFTEEN AVAILABLE TO HANDLE ALL OF the switching and mainline operations, trouble plagued the YPRR from the start. To cope with the increasing traffic load, in February 1907, the railroad acquired a badly needed second locomotive. This engine, a Consolidation-type (2-8-0) built by the Rhode Island Works of the American Locomotive Company, had been ordered by the Duluth, Rainy Lake & Winnipeg Railroad and became available when the Duluth road canceled its order. Given the number 3 on the YPRR roster and affectionately referred to as "Old Three Spot," it was said to be capable of handling fifteen to eighteen empty cars up the grade to International Junction and as many as forty loads on the downhill run to Bridger, a considerable improvement over Little Fifteen.[1]

The acquisition of the new engine gave the railroad the chance to provide adequate service, if and when the NP chose to provide cars, but the YPRR was still taxed to its limits. With four mines in operation, in addition to hauling trains to and from Bridger, there was the constant need for switching cars at each of the mines. This involved not only replacing loads with empties, but also moving cars across the mine scales so bills of lading could be prepared prior to shipping. But with the railroad being poorly constructed and owning no cars suitable for coal shipment, trouble of one sort or another was never far off. The first major washout occurred in July 1907 when, less than a year after the road's completion, fifty feet of roadbed disappeared about six miles north of Belfry at Golden Flat. Then, on September 7, after the NP released a few extra cars to quiet complaints from vendors in Billings, the YPRR

Yellowstone Park Railroad's second locomotive known as "Old Three Spot" was a December 1906 product of the Rhode Island Locomotive Works. It provided critically needed support as coal traffic began to increase during 1907. (Museum of the Rockies, RVN19268, W. R. Swanson).

set a record by hauling fifty-six loads to the yard in Bridger. This was a significant achievement, but just as things seemed to be getting better, the railroad suffered a major accident and its first fatality.[2]

Patrick F. Dolan, who had previously worked as yardmaster for the NP in Billings, was hired by the YPRR in July 1906. A little over a year later, he was promoted to superintendent of construction. On September 25, 1907, three days after his promotion, he was supervising the unloading of telephone poles from a flat car on the McCarthy Branch when a runaway train with five loaded cars careened down-grade from the Smokeless & Sootless mine and slammed into the car he was on. The collision, which barely slowed the runaway, knocked Dolan from his feet and, with its brakes locked tight, skidded the flat car down the track like a sled at forty miles per hour before it was hurled from the rails on the curve near the bottom of Virtue Gulch. Thrown under the car during the derailment, Dolan suffered serious injuries. Two employees of the Mutual Telephone Company working with Dolan were injured by flying debris. All three were rushed to the hospital in Red Lodge, where Dolan soon succumbed to his injuries. The runaway's engineer, Charles Burns, and his fireman were uninjured, having jumped from the engine when the train's brakes failed and it began to gain speed. A wrongful death lawsuit was soon filed by Dolan's widow naming Frank Hall and the YPRR as defendants. The suit was later amended, Hall's name was dropped and replaced by engineer Burns. A year later Charles Cyr, one of the Mutual Telephone Company employees, also filed suit against the railroad for his injuries. The outcome of this litigation is unknown.[3]

Operations returned to normal shortly after Dolan's tragic death, but in November, the car shortage arranged by the NP became acute, causing layoffs and a partial shutdown of the mines. With winter approaching and the need for coal becoming critical, the mine owners appealed to the Railroad Commission to force the NP to deliver the needed cars. The appeal ended up on the desk of the Montana attorney general, who ruled that the commission had no authority over this issue as there was no contract in force that required delivery of more than fifteen cars per day. A lengthy article in the *Butte Inter-Mountain* reported that Frank Hall then accused the NP of deliberately trying to force him out of business by refusing to supply the cars he needed. NP's assistant general manager denied the allegation, but of course, Hall was right. This was exactly what NP was doing. In sympathy with Hall, the *Inter-Mountain* expressed outrage that with winter coming on, the NP would use the people of Montana, who relied on coal to heat their homes, as pawns in their petty game to control the upstart YPRR.[4]

For reasons unknown, ten days after Hall's accusations were published, he retracted them. In a letter to the newspaper's editor, Hall claimed that he had been "quoted without warrant and made to express beliefs which I have never entertained." He went on to explain: "it is absurd to assume that the officials of that company [NP] would impose suffering upon the public and financial loses [*sic*] upon itself deliberately with no better purpose than to injure a smaller company which serves all the use of a profitable feeder to the Northern Pacific system without any expense whatever." Whether Hall believed what he was saying or was attempting to heal a rift he had created by antagonizing his powerful neighbor is impossible to ascertain. Whatever his true feelings, Hall was unwilling to submit to NP's abuse and his pugnacious side was revealed when he negotiated the lease of one hundred thirty-ton-capacity ore cars from the Butte, Anaconda & Pacific. Having just opened their mine in Washoe, Anaconda (BA&P's parent) had a vested interest in maintaining YPRR's car supply. While not the ideal conveyance for the coal being shipped, these cars happened to be available due to a slowdown in Butte caused by the Panic of 1907. The cars alleviated the heating fuel crisis in the Billings area that winter and provided Hall with a small victory over the NP's persistent and carefully coordinated plan to drive him out of business.[5]

While Hall struggled to provide the cars needed by the mines, interference by the NP was relentless. In December, President Elliott complained to James N. Hill that despite their plan, he was forced to send occasional cars to the YPRR because it was well known that the NP had empty cars sitting idle in Montana, especially in their yard in Livingston. At about the same time, Hill forwarded a letter to Elliott that had been received from Russell Harrison, son of the late US president and an investor in the YPRR, regarding the possible value of his investment. Elliott responded by telling him that Montana had plenty of coal and that the YPRR was of "light construction" and not likely to do much business. While implying that the YPRR was not a good investment, Elliott refused to offer an opinion concerning its possible value. His aim, it would seem, was to discourage Harrison from considering any further investment in the YPRR while reducing his expectations, should the NP decide to buy him out. Elliott's broader hope might have been that Harrison would share this disquieting appraisal with other investors and further impede Hall's efforts.[6]

Despite the NP's constant interference, by January 1908, Hall had raised enough money to reach a settlement with the Yegens and the foreclosure suit was dropped. With the lawsuit behind him and claiming to have secured additional backing from Philadelphia capitalists, Hall once again began to talk about building the extension to Cooke City. But his ambitious plans would have to wait. His exhausting travel schedule and the constant stress of seeking new investors while fending off bondholders, lenders, ranchers, and the NP had taken its toll. Hall's health had begun to fail. Said to be seriously impaired (some sources claimed that he eventually lost the use of his legs), on February 1, Frank and Laura Hall packed up and headed to New York City to seek medical advice and treatment. The Halls appear to have remained in the east for about four months while Frank convalesced and worked to regain his health. When he returned to Montana in June, he was a changed man. He no longer talked about the extension to Cooke City but began to think instead of extracting himself from the debilitating quagmire the YPRR had become.[7]

By September 1908, the railroad was operating reasonably well. Trains were routinely handling twenty-five to forty loads per day, and there were one thousand tons of sugar beets sitting on the ramp in Belfry awaiting transport. Despite this, the coal mine operators were not happy. With five mines now in operation even forty cars per day was limiting production. The constant switching needed to service the five mines and the time required to haul the trains over the poorly constructed track to Bridger were beyond the capabilities of the railroad's two locomotives. To add to this, the YPRR continued to be beleaguered by frequent derailments, wrecks, and periodic washouts that often forced the mines to close for days at a time.[8]

In an effort to improve service, in mid-November 1908, the YPRR acquired its third locomotive, a three-truck class "C" Shay from the Lima Locomotive Works in Lima, Ohio. Unique to southern Montana, the Shay was a perceptive and potentially significant addition to the YPRR roster. Shay locomotives were conceived and developed in the late 1870s by Michigan logger and sawmill operator Ephraim Shay. His design arranged the locomotive's cylinders vertically and connected them to the wheels through a series of drive shafts and gears. This arrangement eliminated the dynamic forces created by conventional side-rod engines and delivered equal torque to both sides of the locomotive at the same time. Because of this, Shay locomotives were able to operate efficiently not only on poorly constructed track but also on steep grades and tight curves, attributes that fit the needs of the YPRR perfectly. The Shay's top speed of twenty-eight miles per hour would not be a detriment as YPRR trains seldom achieved half that speed. Given the number 5, it was hoped that the new engine would double the number of cars taken up to the mines at one time. Unfortunately, the railroad's sanguine expectations went unfulfilled.[9]

Called "Maud" by the engine and shop crews, Number 5 never lived up to its promise. Shortly after its arrival, a test run to the mines was

The boxcars in this photo are being loaded with agricultural products from horse-drawn wagons on the stub track south of the Belfry Depot. For many years, the YPRR and MW&S served as a critical link for farmers in the upper Clarks Fork Valley. (CCHS&M-Kidwell Collection).

successfully completed with twenty cars, but by December, there was trouble. The problem stemmed from firemen not being able to maintain steam pressure while working up the grade to Bearcreek. Whether it was the engineer's lack of experience operating a geared locomotive or a problem with maintenance, remains a mystery. Maud was soon sidelined and the YPRR returned to having only two viable locomotives. This again left the YPRR with no margin for error, and when either engine was involved in an accident or needed maintenance, service to the mines inevitably lapsed.[10]

Balky engines, runaway trains, and washouts weren't the only problems YPRR crews faced. On the afternoon of November 21, 1908, engineer George Garver had just opened the throttle for the uphill run out of Belfry with a few loaded cars and a string of empties when he spotted a body on the tracks. Garver applied the brakes while fireman Anton Ludwigson swung down from his perch on the left side of the locomotive cab. As squealing brakes slowly brought the train to a stop, Ludwigson sprinted ahead and dragged the man to safety. It seems the miscreant

Yellowstone Park Railroad's Number 5, delivered in November 1908, was a class "C" Shay. Dubbed "Maud" by shop and engine crews, it never lived up to expectations. Retired in April 1910, it was sold a few months later. (Allen County [OH] Historical Society).

had been drinking in Belfry and decided to stagger his way home by following the railroad tracks. After a short distance, he needed to rest and found a suitable spot between the rails using one of them as a pillow. A sage at the local Belfry newspaper humorously observed, "It's certainly a foolish trick to fill up on tanglefoot and attempt to steal a nap on the railroad track, even if YP trains are not noted for speed."[11]

From the start of construction Hall had difficulty raising money. In order to entice investors, he was forced to offer the company's First Mortgage bonds at an original issue discount of 25 percent. As an additional incentive, he awarded bond purchasers shares of company stock equal to the amount of their investment. This policy led to the stockholders and bondholders being the same people. Because the bonds had been sold at a steep discount, even though the total cost of the line was only about $550,000, by September 1906 the company's funded debt stood at $696,000. Had Howard Elliott elected to cooperate with Hall and not been determined to drive him out of business, the YPRR might have been able to generate enough cash flow to fund improvements and attain profitability, but because of his interference, Hall was forced to constantly seek new investors. Although the bonds he sold were ostensibly for the construction of the Cooke City extension, the railroad's financial condition required that he apply the money to ongoing operating expenses. This caused funded debt to grow ever larger, and as the railroad's precarious financial situation became more apparent Hall may have been forced to discount company bonds even more deeply in order to keep desperately needed cash coming in. None of this was his fault; its origins lay in the decision to begin construction without adequate funding and the NP's persistent refusal to cooperate with him.[12]

During 1908, while day-to-day operations on the railroad rolled on, and Hall dealt with his illness and pondered the future, his investors grew increasingly restless. The bondholder's concerns and lack of confidence in Hall's plans and management were reinforced when an August 25 auction resulted in a bid of only $6,500 for $10,000 of YPRR first mortgage bonds. This sale may have been a test, as it revealed how deeply YPRR bonds were discounted on the open market just three years after issue. In an apparent response to the declining asset value and the fact that interest payments were being deferred, the bondholders held a meeting in York, Pennsylvania, on October 12. The meeting resulted in a five-person committee being formed to prepare an agreement designed to protect the bondholders' property and prevent adverse proceedings. On October 27, in preparation for the company's annual board of directors meeting, nearly forty stockholders gathered at the prestigious Colonial Hotel in York to discuss the selection of a new board. If Atkins was going to remove Hall from office, he needed a board sympathetic to his views; a board that would vote Hall out. There can be little doubt that this was the point of the meeting and that no small amount of energy was expended to make sure that when the time came, the votes went the right way.[13]

When the annual meeting was convened in Lancaster about two weeks later, the stockholders voted to replace board members, Oran Belfry, George Heisey, Louis Rosenfeld, and John Monk with four new members, all of whom hailed from York, Pennsylvania. According to the *York Dispatch*, Frank Hall was removed from office, and Henry W. Heffener, the owner of a local cigar box manufacturing plant, was elected company president. Heffener's election was a meaningless gesture as Hall not only retained his seat on the board but also his position as company agent. Because of this, Hall remained in control of the company's affairs. As for Heffener, lacking any railroad experience or qualifications for the job, it is doubtful he ever exerted any control over the company. He did, however, inform the *Dispatch* that he felt "the responsibility of his new office" and even though he was a great distance from the company's operations, he claimed to be "familiar with the territory having hunted through it upon different occasions." While Heffener's election made little sense, it may reflect the level of internal turmoil the company was suffering, all of which was likely due to George Atkins's continuing efforts to undermine Hall's authority.[14]

Following what must have been a fractious board meeting, Hall knew he was in trouble. His only hope now was to sell the company and make some money, if he could, while he retained control. With few options available to him, shortly after the Lancaster meeting, Hall traveled to New York City to meet with John D. Ryan, president of the Anaconda Copper Mining Company. Cognizant of the fact that he could not deal with the NP and having unsuccessfully courted the Milwaukee Road, Hall saw Anaconda as the only remaining potential buyer for the YPRR. Hall hoped that Ryan would be receptive to a buyout because Anaconda already operated a railroad in Montana and had just opened a mine at Washoe that was now served by the YPRR. The meeting in Ryan's office at 42 Broadway in lower Manhattan was cordial and, according to Ryan, covered a number of topics, one of which was Hall's interest in selling the YPRR. Hall told Ryan that he could deliver the YPRR to Anaconda free and clear of all debt for $775,000. The price indicated that the company's indebtedness had increased by nearly $80,000 during the past two years. Hall's proposal came with the caveat that he would receive 49 percent of the new company's stock. When Ryan indicated that Hall's stock ownership might not be acceptable, Hall allowed that he would forgo the stock interest for a cash payment of $112,500. Not surprisingly, Hall's proposal was entirely self-serving. The sale price would allow him to redeem the outstanding bonds at par, pay the accrued interest, retire his other debts, and secure a large cash payment for himself. Although paying off his bondholders was all he was legally obligated to do, the stockholders had a completely different view. They expected to make a profit.[15]

A keen negotiator, Ryan, who had only recently assumed the presidency of Anaconda after successfully consolidating the company's position in Butte with the takeover of the United Copper Company and the properties of William A. Clark, was now focused on expanding copper production. Even though Anaconda owned the Butte, Anaconda & Pacific, a railroad that hauled ore from the Butte mines to the smelters in Anaconda, Ryan had little interest in owning another railroad in Montana, even if it did service an Anaconda-owned mine. Despite his lack of interest, he told Hall that he would consider his proposal. But when the meeting was over, instead of going to Anaconda's board of directors, Ryan relayed the pertinent details to Howard Elliott. While admitting to Elliott that he was not sure he was at liberty to share the information, Ryan went on to say that he felt a takeover of the YPRR by the NP "would be for the best interest of everybody, including Hall." Elliott responded by asking Ryan to forward the information to James N. Hill and promised that the NP would make a prompt decision.[16]

Shortly after the Hall-Ryan meeting, the *Billings Gazette* reported that the Milwaukee Road had decided to build a branch line south from Roundup, Montana, through Billings, to a connection with the YPRR and then continue on to Cooke City and Yellowstone National Park. The story achieved an air of legitimacy by giving a rather detailed description of the Milwaukee Road's proposed route. The newspaper went on to say that there were rumors the Milwaukee Road had already purchased the YPRR, and that Frank Hall had retired and been replaced by George Atkins; Henry Heffener, the supposed president of the company, was never mentioned. This narrative likely came as a shock to Hall who immediately denied both the sale and his retirement. But these rumors indicate that Atkins was still working behind the scenes to circumvent Hall's authority and make his own deal. Determined to rid himself of Hall, Atkins's insubordination may have been motivated by reports of Hall's meeting with John Ryan as well as his frustration with Hall's perceived mismanagement, failing health, and long absences. Although rumors of a Milwaukee Road buyout persisted for some time, nothing further transpired.[17]

Having survived the coup d'état attempted by Atkins and his other investors and having received no response from John Ryan, by mid-December Hall was desperate and must have felt the walls were closing in. So, while on a holiday trip to Milwaukee with his wife, Hall stopped at NP headquarters in St. Paul to once again meet with Howard Elliott. The two being well acquainted, the meeting was no doubt affable. Elliott later noted that he felt sorry for Hall, who appeared to be "physically . . . a broken-down man." But when Hall proposed that the NP buy the YPRR, having no idea that John Ryan had already supplied Elliott with all the pertinent details, he must have been stunned when Elliott, regardless of his personal feelings, dismissed his proposal out of hand.[18]

While Hall searched for a buyer and a way out, the shop crew in Belfry continued to struggle with the new Shay locomotive. Notwithstanding the mines' demands for better service, with only two viable locomotives, the YPRR simply did not have the resources to move cars efficiently. This was especially true during the winter when coal demand was highest and snow often blocked the tracks. Despite NP's continuing efforts to keep the car supply at a minimum, in December 1908 the yard in Bridger was crammed with nearly 150 empty cars awaiting delivery. Periodic derailments continued to plague the railroad as well.[19]

On Christmas Eve 1908, Number 3's tender jumped the track while switching near Bearcreek, slightly damaging the locomotive. After several hours' work, and an assist from Maud, the engine limped back to Belfry under its own power. Old Three Spot was soon back in service, but a month later, on a chilly, partly cloudy Sunday in late January, the engine's performance left much to be desired. Returning from their holiday trip to Milwaukee, Frank and Laura Hall boarded the train awaiting them in Bridger. As the train headed south on the twelve-mile run to Belfry, Old Three Spot crept along at not quite five miles per hour leaving the Halls confined to the hard wooden seats of the combine for two and half hours. The local newspaper headlined the story of Hall's return with "All Records Broken" and sarcastically claimed that knowing the Halls were anxious to get home, the engineer "threw the throttle wide open soon after leaving Bridger." The engine's dismal performance was attributed to "leaky flues" caused by a spell of bad weather. A more plausible explanation was poor or perhaps deferred maintenance. As historian Charles Mutschler described in his book *Wired for Success*, turn-of-the-century steam locomotives were labor-intensive machines, typically requiring up to six hours a day for servicing and minor repairs. They also needed monthly boiler washing and inspections that could remove them from service for days at a time. With coal production increasing and only two locomotives available, the YPRR was pushing its engines to their limits and hard-pressed shop crews probably had a difficult time keeping them in top mechanical condition.[20]

While Hall was in Milwaukee following his December meeting with Howard Elliott, a group of bondholders, again probably led by George Atkins, hired well-known Butte attorney William Scallon to reopen negotiations with the NP. Their proposed sale price was $1.5 million, or nearly twice what Hall had put forward just a few weeks earlier. The bondholder's proposal was totally unrealistic and exemplified their complete ignorance of the current situation. Having estimated the value of the YPRR at less than $250,000, Howard Elliott responded to Scallon's proposal as would be expected, letting him know that their ideas of a price were "beyond all reason." Although Elliott indicated that he was willing to negotiate concerning the price, the Pennsylvania bondholders refused to budge. Realizing there was no point in further discussions with either Hall or the Scallon group, in May, Elliott had decided to put the issue to rest by having the NP build its own branch line to the Bear Creek mines, with the estimated cost being $750,000.[21]

Incorporated on June 2, 1909, the new branch line was set up as an NP subsidiary called the Bear Creek & Western Railroad. Its stated goal was the construction of a line from Bridger to Bear Creek and Cooke City. Prior to incorporating the new company, Elliott had investigated possible conflicts involved in crossing the YPRR's tracks and gaining access to the various mines. Discussions with the mine operators revealed that they were anxious to have the NP build the new line and would help in any way possible. This included the possibility of the NP gaining exclusive access to Montana Coal & Iron's as yet untapped Foster Gulch property.[22]

The route chosen for the Bear Creek & Western was a near straight line up the middle of the Clarks Fork Valley with grades of 0.4 percent or less. At Belfry the proposed line turned westward and paralleled the YPRR by following Bear Creek to the mines. This route required two bridge crossings of the Clarks Fork River but avoided the curvature, cuts and fills, and variable grades encountered on the YPRR. Following incorporation, preliminary surveys were completed to Belfry and south to the vicinity of Clark, Wyoming. Despite their charter, having evaluated and rejected the Clarks Fork Canyon route, the NP never seriously considered extending the line beyond Clark.[23]

How Frank Hall spent the early part of 1909 is unknown, but his deteriorating health made it unlikely that he was able to travel and seek new investors. This lack of funding made it impossible for him to address the critical need for rolling stock, locomotives, or improvements to the track and roadbed. Meanwhile, George Atkins and the other bondholders, seeing the value of their asset declining and the chance of making a profit slipping away, clung to the hope of making a deal with the Milwaukee Road or some other buyer. Failing this, they believed the railroad could, at a minimum, be more efficiently and possibly even profitably run under new management. Rightfully or not, from the earliest days of construction their disillusionment with Frank Hall had grown. Having identified Hall as the main impediment to profitably exploiting their investment and having carefully laid the groundwork months in advance, Atkins was now ready to make his move. The final showdown took place in May 1909 at a special stockholder's meeting held in Augusta, Maine.[24]

At the Augusta meeting, the company's new board of directors corrected their earlier oversight and voted unanimously to remove Frank Hall as the company agent. According to the *Lancaster Intelligencer*, despite his poor health, Hall made the multiday cross-country journey to plead his case. Given all that had transpired during the past two years, he could not have been surprised by the meeting's outcome, but he likely did not anticipate the malicious fight that was about to ensue. Having been voted out, he affixed his signature to the document removing himself from office and was given some assurance that he would receive $50,000 for the company stock he held. But the board of directors had no intention of honoring that commitment. Although the exact sequence of subsequent events is uncertain, following the meeting George Atkins headed to Montana with a group of private investors that he hoped would buy the railroad. At about the same time ownership of the YPRR was transferred to Langley & Company, a New York bonding house that had agreed to pay $900,000 for it; this being the exact amount of its current funded debt. Since funded debt is senior to all other claims, this carefully coordinated transaction invalidated Hall's stock ownership. When the board's duplicity became apparent, Hall sued the YPRR by filing a bill in equity in Pennsylvania, Maine, and Montana in an attempt to stay the sale, but it was too late; Atkins's plan had worked. Hall was out; his stock, worthless. But Atkins had underestimated Hall. This was, after all, "his railroad," and it would not be taken from him without a fight. He had invested both his health and energy into its construction and was undoubtedly stunned by the board of directors' arrogance. Feeling he had been skillfully manipulated and swindled, Hall felt compelled to respond.[25]

On June 2, 1909, in an attempt to regain control, Hall filed an attachment against the railroad and its real property for $36,347.78 in uncollected back salary. Surprised and angered by this unexpected maneuver, the board responded on June 28 with a countersuit claiming that Hall had misappropriated $80,801 in company funds and refused to release the company's financial records. This move played into Hall's hands. With two lawsuits pending and the company in turmoil, on June 29, Hall requested that the federal court in Helena appoint a receiver, asserting in his application, "a conspiracy on the part of the Pennsylvania stock and bondholders." The judge in Helena agreed and the next day appointed YPRR superintendent Harry R. French and General Manager Michael W. Maguire the company's receivers, each man representing one side in the dispute. With the railroad in receivership the bondholders had been backed into a corner and were now compelled to act. In an effort to salvage the situation, in the following days they reached an undisclosed but reportedly "amicable" settlement with Hall that ended his lawsuit and removed him from any further connection with the railroad.[26]

No longer a party to the railroad he had long dreamed of and struggled to build, Frank and Laura Hall departed Montana for the last time in early August 1909 enroute to the spas at Baden Baden, Germany, where Frank hoped to recuperate and regain his health. They returned to the United States in 1910 and took up residence with Laura's parents in Milwaukee while Frank continued his recovery. In 1911, the Halls moved to Fullerton, California, and Frank purchased a ten-acre orange orchard in nearby Anaheim. Reputed to be one of the best groves in the district, it served Hall well, and in June 1913, he sent a crate of oranges to the patrons of the Bank of Belfry as a gift. In 1920, he sold the orchard for $60,000, a notable sum at the time, and bought a five-acre tract at the corner of Cherry Avenue and Hill Street on Signal Hill near Long Beach. There, he and Laura built a lavish, two-story Italian-style home with birch and pine trim, oak floors, and tiled bathrooms. The Halls joined the nearby Virginia Country Club and enjoyed the "good life." Laura became an avid golfer, tended the gardens around their home, and hosted afternoon tea parties.[27]

Just one year after moving into their new house, Frank's world was shattered when, having exhibited no signs of illness, Hall's devoted and loving wife, Laura, suddenly collapsed into unconsciousness at their home and died a few hours later. Heartbroken, early the next year Frank made a sizeable donation to the Hi-Tri Girls Club of Long Beach, a YWCA affiliate that Laura was very fond of. The money funded the construction of an activities building christened the Laura Hall Clubhouse.[28]

Despite his crushing personal loss and the continued debilitating effects of the illness that had overtaken him in 1908 and left him wheelchair bound, with the support of numerous friends and a niece who lived nearby, Frank Hall persevered. About a year after Laura's passing, his luck began to change. In June 1921, Royal Dutch Shell had struck oil half a mile east of Hall's home. Shell's well was a gusher that blasted oil over one hundred feet into the air and marked the discovery of one of the largest oil fields in the United States. Excited promoters soon leased Hall's property, and on August 13, 1922, they began drilling a well. Wearing a white shirt and dapper straw boater hat like the one he wore to celebrate the completion of the Yellowstone Park Railway twenty-three years earlier, Hall, and his partner Herbert Webber, christened the start of drilling by smashing a bottle of champagne on the drill bit.[29]

The well was a success and royalty checks poured in. This newfound wealth guaranteed Hall a secure financial future. He spent the ensuing years quietly and died at his home on Signal Hill on September 20, 1929. In May 1931, the memories of Frank and Laura were honored by the mothers of the Hi-Tri Girls Club at a reception in the Laura Hall Clubhouse. From there Frank Avery Hall, the smooth-talking entrepreneur and visionary railroad promoter from Milwaukee passed into history. Although never a swindler, Hall was often guilty of overreaching himself. The *Long Beach Sun* eulogized him as a "retired capitalist" and "philanthropist." But Hall's true legacy was the three towns he helped create and the railroad he built that for nearly fifty years would support the economy and serve people of the upper Clarks Fork and Bear Creek valleys.[30]

7

"The Track-Bed Is in Fierce Condition"

AFTER FRANK HALL WAS FORCED TO RESIGN, GEORGE ATKINS and the other bondholders were anxious to divest their interest in the YPRR in the hope of making a quick profit. There being little chance that the Milwaukee Road would step in and extend a line to Bridger, and having abandoned the idea of selling the railroad to either the NP or Anaconda, the only remaining option was to find private investors. To this end, in late May 1909, Atkins arrived in Billings aboard the private railcar Alcazar. He was accompanied by a group of bankers and financiers from New York and Pennsylvania that included Edwin G. Baker, president of the Buffalo (New York) Savings Bank; E. S. McGurdy, another Buffalo area banker; George W. Chase from the Masonic Life Insurance Company; and G. M. Young, who represented English capitalists. Several wealthy private investors from Pittsburgh were included in the group as well. In an effort to impress these potential investors with the asset he had for sale, Atkins had arranged a tour of the railroad and its surroundings in the hope that they would form a syndicate to buy the YPRR.[1]

On May 24, a pleasant but partly cloudy Monday morning, Atkins and his guests climbed aboard the special train hired for the occasion and departed Billings. After navigating the interchange at Laurel, the train crossed the three-span steel truss bridge over the Yellowstone River, rounded a broad curve and climbed a short grade into the Clarks Fork Valley. Lush green pastures interspersed with fields of wheat, beans, corn, and sugar beets swept past on both sides as the train quickly accelerated to twenty miles per hour. Thirty minutes later the train bumped through the turnout at Silesia and hastened south rocking along at a prosaic twelve miles per hour while the passengers enjoyed periodic views of the Clarks Fork River. The train rolled past the small stations at Edgar and Fromberg and finally eased to a stop in front of NP's two-story Bridger depot. Here a YPRR locomotive took over.

As the train whistled its way out of Bridger, its passengers might have noticed a slight change in tempo when they rounded the sandstone bluffs south of town and negotiated Jenning's Sway. From there, the engineer opened the throttle up for the six-mile, thirty-minute run across Golden Flat. After rumbling over the short trestle at Dry Creek, distant views of the Beartooth Mountains were obstructed by the steep sandstone bluffs along the Clarks Fork River. Just north of Belfry, the train once again entered open fields and was soon creeping past the YPRR's coaling tower, engine house, and shops. After easing its way across the trestle over Bear Creek, the train squealed to a stop next to the Belfry depot and its remarkable creekside park, terraced gardens, and gazebo.

Atkins's eastern financiers spent two days "roughing it" in the coalfields. At the end of the excursion the group expressed considerable excitement about the area's potential and the possibility of a Cooke City extension. When they returned to Billings, Atkins ventured into town to retrieve his laundry and along the way was intercepted by a reporter from the *Billings Gazette*. "No," he told the reporter, "the Yellowstone Park railroad has not been sold, at least the party which I had in charge has not as yet purchased it." He then cryptically added, "I am not saying that the road will not be sold, and that the people with me are not a trifle more than mildly interested. The fact is there is nothing to give out for publication, but there may be something doing, there may be, and something that will do Billings no small amount of good. But I'm not going to talk anymore." Atkins then snatched up his laundry bundle and made a dash for the Alcazar. His cryptic interview and hurried departure suggest that he knew he was grasping at more than just his laundry. He knew he was grasping at straws, burdened with the knowledge that if he could not close a deal with the current group of investors there was little chance the railroad could be sold at a profit.[2]

Whereas Atkins's bankers and financiers may have been intrigued by what they had seen, what they may have overlooked was that the NP still controlled the YPRR's fortunes. This was something that even

Atkins may not have fully appreciated, but Frank Hall knew all too well. When the NP announced its plans for a railroad to the Bear Creek mines on June 2 and Frank Hall filed his lawsuit against the YPRR the same day, Atkins's highly touted buyers must have quickly lost interest. The YPRR's poor financial performance during the past year would have caused them some concern as well. Due to the lack of equipment, washouts, wrecks, limited car supply, and political turmoil that had roiled the company, coal shipments were on the decline. A later review would show that the YPRR hauled only 264,680 tons of coal between September 1, 1908, and August 31, 1909, or an average of twenty loads per day (six-day workweek). This amounted to less than half the potential output of the five mines and defined the railroad's most serious deficiencies. If Atkins's asking price was still $1.5 million, the fact that he could not find a buyer is not surprising. His inability to close the deal with the banker group left the YPRR's new owners with no way out. Instead of turning a quick profit, by July it was obvious they had to come up with a new plan.[3]

With few other options available, the company's owners decided to reorganize, and on July 30, 1909, they formed the Montana, Wyoming & Southern Railroad (MW&S). Incorporated in New Jersey, corporate headquarters were located at 15 Exchange Place in Jersey City, but the company's main office was situated across the Hudson River in lower Manhattan at 2 Rector Street. How they settled on the company name is unknown; perhaps they felt it encapsulated Frank Hall's vision of a regional carrier with branch lines to Cooke City, Yellowstone National Park, and beyond. Regardless of their reasons, just as Hall had created historical confusion by repeatedly using the name Yellowstone Park in his various business ventures, the new owners of the YPRR added to the problem by selecting a name that was already in use.[4]

The first Montana, Wyoming & Southern Railroad had been incorporated almost a year earlier. Conceived by a group of Sheridan, Wyoming businessmen, their plan was to build a bridge line along the Tongue River between Sheridan and Miles City, Montana, that would connect the NP with the CB&Q. A preliminary survey had been completed in late 1908, and in February 1909, the US Senate granted the company a right-of-way through the Fort Keogh Military Reservation. When the decision was made to reorganize the YPRR as the Montana, Wyoming &

Southern, the Sheridan group voluntarily changed the name of its company to the Yellowstone, Montana & Wyoming Railroad. Following the name change nothing further happened, but interestingly one hundred years later, there was once again serious talk of building a railroad along the same route.[5]

The sale of the YPRR to Langley & Company may have been intended as a short-term expedient to avoid having to compensate Frank Hall for his stock, but when George Atkins failed to find a buyer for the railroad, the bonding house was left to deal with the problem. As a result, new 5 percent thirty-year gold bonds were issued through the Empire Trust Company and the assets of the Yellowstone Park Railroad were conveyed to the Montana, Wyoming & Southern Railroad on September 1, 1909. The new bondholders were mostly New Yorkers, as were six of the eight members of the board of directors. The other two were from Pennsylvania, but neither had held a seat on the YPRR board. Langley & Company's prominence in the new organization was reflected in William H. Langley being elected vice-president, and both he and W. C. Langley having seats on the board. This change suggests that early investors like Oran Belfry, George Heisey, and George Atkins, having recouped their investment, were now gone.[6]

If the new owners expected big changes now that the railroad was under new management, they were in for a rude awakening. The name change and reincorporation had little effect on the company's circumstances. NP president Howard Elliott remained persistent in his efforts to undermine their operation and problems like washouts and derailments were unrelenting as well. The only substantive change was in the company's top management. Newly elected president Frank S. Gannon and ex-YPRR general manager Michael W. Maguire were both career railroad men having started out in the late 1870s as clerks and telegraphers on the Erie Railroad. Gannon went on to work for the Long Island Rail Road and Baltimore & Ohio, eventually becoming third vice-president and general manager of the Southern Railway, and later, president of the Norfolk & Southern. He was well respected and had a reputation as one of the most efficient and practical railroad men in the country. Maguire had also worked his way up through various positions with the Erie and eventually became general superintendent of the Norfolk

At least ten horse teams and more than a dozen men are hard at work repairing damage to the line about three and a half miles west of Belfry. This undated photo looking east down the Bear Creek valley illustrates one of the railroad's recurring problems: washouts that were a direct result of its narrow, poorly drained, unballasted roadbed. (CCHS&M-Kidwell Collection).

& Southern before moving to Montana. Besides having similar career paths, the two men were brothers-in-law. Over the next ten years, this familial connection would help them in their struggles with both the NP and day-to-day operations.[7]

As if to emphasize the railroad's unchanged situation, a few days after the transfer of ownership, a cloud burst at Dry Creek washed away two hundred feet of track. Once repaired, with only two locomotives, the MW&S struggled to maintain service and was soon forced to lease "a small engine" from the NP. Later that month one of the engines derailed between Bearcreek and Washoe. While the crew struggled to get it back on the tracks, two young men on a moonlit stroll with their girlfriends happened by. Despite not being dressed for the dirty work at hand, they pulled off their coats and joined in. The engine was soon back on the rails and the grateful crew gave the group a ride "on the cushions" up to Washoe in appreciation. This sort of occurrence was part of normal operations on the MW&S, just as it had been on the YPRR.[8]

Railroad accidents were common during the early twentieth century and October 1909 proved that these often-deadly mishaps were not confined to the YPRR or MW&S. On the cool clear night of October 7, around 8:00 p.m., an NP coal train from Red Lodge rounded the big curve at Rockvale heading north. In anticipation of the straight run down the valley past the station at Silesia, engineer Teeters opened the throttle and sparks briefly flew from the stack as the train gained speed. Teeters and the rest of the crew were from Livingston and their train was running as an "extra" on the Rocky Fork Branch, so they may not have been well versed in that line's operating rules. Unbeknownst to them, a northbound train off the Clarks Fork Branch, which had the right-of-way, had pulled forward onto the Rocky Fork mainline at Silesia and stopped. As the Red Lodge train emerged from the deep cut south of Silesia and approached the station, Teeters must have assumed the other train had stopped short of the switch as he made no effort to slow down. When the locomotive's headlight suddenly brought the Clarks Fork train into focus, Teeters slammed the throttle shut, reached for the brake handle, hauled down on the whistle cord, and instinctively braced for impact; there was little else he could do. Teeter's train sideswiped a car or two and then collided with the other engine from behind. The collision toppled both locomotives. Amid the screech of brakes and splintering wood, loaded coal cars jackknifed and piled up on the locomotives. Fifteen cars were damaged or destroyed in the wreck leaving a scene of shattered cars lying among heaps of spilled coal. Fireman Martin and head brakeman McKeefrey on the Red Lodge train were killed in the collision, engineer Teeters had both legs severed and died a short time later at a Billings hospital. There were no injuries to the Clarks Fork crew, but both the NP and MW&S were shut down for several days while the wreck was cleared and the tracks repaired.[9]

Just a week or so after the Silesia wreck, the MW&S suffered a much less serious accident of its own, when poor track caused a derailment not

On October 7, 1909, a northbound NP train from Red Lodge collided with a stationary train off the Clarks Fork Branch at Silesia. The wreck resulted in the deaths of three crewmen and disrupted operations on the NP and MW&S for several days. (L. G. Webber photo, Joliet Public Library).

far from Bearcreek. The train, pulled by Old Three Spot, with engineer Garver and fireman Ludwigson at the controls, was cautiously drifting downgrade toward Belfry. While traversing a curve with some questionable looking roadbed, the crew realized there was trouble. Moving at no more than ten miles an hour with twenty to twenty-five loads and a passenger car, the rails suddenly spread under the weight of the loaded cars. When the derailment snapped the air brake line and threw the train into emergency braking, passengers were tossed from their seats while hatboxes and gripsacks flew from the overhead luggage racks. According to the *Billings Gazette*, the passengers got "a good shake up and were pretty badly frightened." Once the train ground to a halt, one of the less shaken up passengers was instructed to hike back toward Bearcreek and alert the crew of a train that was following close behind. Because the derailment occurred near the middle of the train there were no serious injuries, but one car was completely demolished and several others were damaged along with a section of track. After taking a quick look at the situation, Garver and his crew hastily uncoupled Number 3 and headed to Belfry to get help. The wreck was cleared by the next morning, but the track remained unsafe for several days. The *Gazette* made a point of noting that this was the third wreck on the MW&S in the past two weeks.[10]

Despite the repeated wrecks, in the hope of improving service, one of Frank Gannon's priorities was to negotiate a truce with the NP. After repeated overtures, Howard Elliott finally agreed to meet with him in New York on October 12, 1909. At that meeting Gannon expressed his desire for the MW&S to have amicable relations with the NP and for the two railroads to work in harmony. Gannon also let it be known that the MW&S was still for sale, and although the new owners believed that the property was worth $1.5 million, they were now willing to sell it to the NP for $1 million. As he had been with Frank Hall, Elliott was polite but dismissive. He gave Gannon no encouragement and reminded him that the NP still intended to build its own line to the Bear Creek mines, implying that once this was accomplished, the MW&S would be irrelevant regardless of price.[11]

If the corporate reorganization did nothing to improve the railroad's rapport with the NP, it also had no effect on its relationship with the mine operators, who continued to complain about the lack of cars, sporadic service, and the railroad's inadequate equipment. Due to these complaints the Montana Railroad Commission held a hearing in Billings on January 30, 1910. Because the MW&S's poor service was having a huge impact on Montana Coal & Iron's profitability, Elijah Smith came west to attend. Having been involved in both coal mining and railroads for a number of years, when interviewed by the *Billings Gazette*, Smith was quite outspoken and asserted:

> The service which the road has been given [*sic*], and which it has always given since it was put in operation some four years ago, is by no means adequate and it ought to either be improved or abandoned.
>
> The failure was due entirely to the inability of the road to furnish enough cars to meet our demand. Since the charges were brought before the commissioners and the date of the hearing set the road has done a

A much smaller operation than it would one day become, Montana Coal & Iron Company's Smith Mine is seen here as it appeared in October 1916. (CCHS&M).

> little better and we have been able to work the mines about half of the time. But at no time since the road was put in operation has it been able to supply the mines with enough cars.

When asked about rumors that the NP was about to build a line to Bear Creek, Smith claimed: "I know nothing positive about the Northern Pacific building from Bridger to Bearcreek. . . . The nearest approach to the truth on the question that I have ever received was a statement from Jim Hill himself. I have known Mr. Hill well for a number of years and a few months ago while in New York he intimated very broadly that it would a matter of but a few months before the road is into Bearcreek." Smith went on to divulge that he knew the NP had sent a surveying crew to the area, but he wasn't sure if this meant they were ready to build or were just trying to "bluff out the original road."

At the conclusion of the hearing, Smith expressed some frustration and informed a reporter from the *Billings Gazette*:

> The Yellowstone Park Railroad company turned over to the present owners, the Montana, Wyoming and Southern Railroad company, a line that had no rolling stock and insufficient and worn-out motive power. . . . The operators of the district pay a good round sum for the transportation of their product and the railroad commission should see to it that we get service, which I believe it will . . . had the railroad company furnished even a fair amount of equipment, the business would have been of a magnitude, even at the rate complained of, or less, that would easily provided the interest on the excessive capitalization.[12]

Elijah Smith's assessment of the situation was completely accurate, but his optimistic expectations were only partially fulfilled. The commission responded to the hearing by issuing a reprimand to the MW&S for failing to perform its duties as a common carrier. They also ordered that the railroad be equipped to provide "reasonable service." The exact meaning of which was left to interpretation. Testimony had revealed that the MW&S had no interchange rolling stock and lacked snow removal equipment such as plows or flangers, making coal shipments during critical winter months at times impossible. The mine operators claimed that they could load fifty to sixty cars per day and increase that to seventy-five a day in short order if assured by the MW&S that the necessary cars would be delivered. For its part, the NP professed innocence and stated that there was a standing order for only forty cars per day, and when delivered, these cars were often not picked up.[13]

Having made the decision to build their own line to Bear Creek and not wanting to injure their future customers, the NP was no longer attempting to deny an adequate car supply but, at the same time, was making no effort to ensure one either. This was especially true for coal being shipped off the NP system. NP's position was that if the customer was located on the Milwaukee Road, Great Northern, or CB&Q, then those railroads should be the ones supplying the cars. But the local populace was aware of the NP's complicity in the car shortage issue. In this regard, the *Bridger Times* editorialized that "the Northern Pacific engineered the deal from start to finish and brought on this remarkable commission inquiry. . . . It appears to the average person that the Northern Pacific wants Bearcreek territory for its own . . . that it maneuvered things in such a way as to force the railroad commission to call a hearing, thus

NP S-2c class Ten-wheeler Number 115 was leased by the MW&S for several months in early 1910. It is seen here seven years later after it was involved in a sideswipe accident with a passenger train a few miles west of Miles City, Montana. (Museum of the Rockies, RVN03553, Ron V. Nixon).

placing the Montana, Wyoming & Southern in the position of defendant on trial for its life."[14]

With Maud sidelined and Number 3 once again in the shop for repairs, the mine operators repeated complaints forced the MW&S to lease another locomotive from the NP. This time they acquired a more capable engine in the form of a S-2c class "Ten-wheeler" (4-6-0). With this addition, things began to improve and a daily train of twenty-five to forty cars was routinely hauled to Bridger with some expectation that a second train might soon be added. A further improvement was made in January 1910 when, after borrowing an additional $50,000, the MW&S received its first interchange rolling stock in the form of fifty-seven new thirty-six-foot, forty-ton capacity boxcars.[15]

At the next railroad commission hearing held in March 1910, the five Bear Creek mining companies filed another complaint against the

Built in January 1910 by Mt. Vernon Car Manufacturing Company, Mount Vernon, Illinois, boxcar number 516 is representative of the first fifty-seven cars purchased by the MW&S. (Yellowstone Gateway Museum of Park County 2006.045.0841).

MW&S, this time regarding grain doors. Grain doors are temporary walls installed inside boxcars that block the lower part of the doorway to allow the shipment of bulk commodities like grain and coal. Since most of the coal shipped out of Bear Creek was hauled in boxcars, in order to properly load the cars grain doors were necessary, but in an effort to cut costs, the MW&S refused to install them. Since the NP would not accept loaded cars without grain doors, the mines were forced to complete the installation themselves. After review, the railroad commission determined that cars had to be delivered to customers ready for loading and stipulated that as of June 1, 1910, the MW&S would be required to install grain doors. If the railroad neglected this requirement and forced the mines to do it, the mines could assess the MW&S up to two dollars per car (about fifty dollars in 2020). Surprisingly, the installation of grain doors would remain an issue, and ten years after the initial hearing, it would be the railroad that was complaining about the work being done by the mines.[16]

In an effort to calm things down after the acrimonious testimony at the commission hearings, on April 28, 1910, Gannon and Maguire invited the mine owners to a banquet at the well-appointed Northern Hotel in downtown Billings. Officials from four of the mines, including at least

A Northern Pacific work train and wrecker have been hired to clear yet another derailment. Part of a grain door, or slab, is visible in the derailed boxcar's open door. (CCHS&M-Kidwell Collection).

one of the Yegen brothers, attended. Notably absent was a representative from Elijah Smith's Montana Coal & Iron Company. The purpose of the meeting was for the coal operators to become acquainted with the railroad's new management and establish a better working relationship. During their dinner Frank Gannon probably assured them that with the arrival of the new boxcars and the locomotive leased from the NP, he would soon have the MW&S operating smoothly and capable of handling increased production. For their part, the mine operators likely enjoyed the sumptuous repast while reserving judgment about the MW&S's future.[17]

In an effort to continue improving service, during April the balky class "C" Shay Maud was sold to a lumber company in Pennsylvania. Fireman Freebury accompanied Maud on its trip east with the intention of returning with a conventional side-rod replacement locomotive. Surprisingly, Maud worked out well for its new and subsequent owners as it labored away for another thirty-two years before being scrapped in 1940. Its troubles on the YPRR would forever remain a mystery.[18]

Despite the company's efforts to mitigate operational problems, employment on the MW&S remained dangerous. On May 9, 1910, five loaded cars got away from a crew switching at Anaconda's Washoe no. 2 mine. The cars quickly gained speed as they rumbled down the 4 percent

This undated photo shows an all-too-common occurrence during the early years of operation. A runaway boxcar has left the rails on a curve somewhere in the Bear Creek Valley. Although the ties appear to be in good shape, the railroad's "mud ballast" is clearly evident. (CCHS&M-Kidwell Collection).

grade in Scotch Coulee. Brakemen clinging to the cars worked frantically with their wooden clubs to tighten the hand brakes but were forced to jump as the cars sped down the valley out of control. After about a mile, four cars left the rails on the curve just below the Smith mine while the remaining car continued on to the upper switch at the Bear

As soon as the insurance claim was settled, a new engine house was built to replace the one destroyed in the July 3, 1910 fire. This building would endure into the early twenty-first century before falling victim to a state highway project. (Courtesy of Montana Department of Transportation).

Creek mine before it too hit the ground. The brakemen were uninjured except for Hugh Ray, a sturdy rancher from the Clarks Fork Valley who had signed on with the railroad to earn some extra money. Ray suffered a sprained ankle and was said to have been "shook up considerably" by his wild ride. Three of the five cars were completely destroyed; the remaining two required extensive repairs. It took almost three days to remove the wrecks, clean up the mess, and put the track back in service. This event may have also marked the end of Hugh Ray's brief career as a railroad brakeman.[19]

Disaster struck the railroad again just two months later in the form of a fire. On the night of July 3, coal cinders from one of the locomotives somehow ignited materials in the engine house and before anyone knew what was happening, the entire structure was ablaze. Engineer Charles Burns and fireman Jimmy Powell rushed to the scene and attempted to save the locomotives, which had their fires banked, but the intense heat forced them back. Along with the engine house, a pump house, water tank, the motor car "Sunny Brook," a tool car, and one loaded coal car were destroyed. Old Three Spot and Little Fifteen were extensively damaged but deemed repairable. Luckily the two leased NP engines were no longer on the property.[20]

Construction of a new engine house was begun almost immediately, and by mid-August, both engines were repaired and back in service; however, Old Three Spot's resurrection was short-lived. On August 26, a runaway boxcar moving at high speed collided with Old Three Spot while switching at the Bear Creek mine. The collision destroyed the errant boxcar, knocked the cab completely off the locomotive, and caused critical damage to its running gear. No injuries were reported, but fireman Holland was trapped in the locomotive cab for a time after the accident. A wrecking train and replacement locomotive were immediately requested from the NP and service to the mines once again suffered.[21]

The many vicissitudes that afflicted the MW&S during its first year (September 1, 1909, to August 31, 1910) were reflected in a 5 percent drop in coal haulage to 251,163 tons. But the arrival of a replacement for Maud in late October 1910 was a critical step toward improving service. The new engine, built by the Lima Locomotive Works, was another Consolidation-type (2-8-0) and was given the number 5, the same as the retired Shay. This addition to the locomotive roster was soon followed by the completion of the new Belfry engine house. These improvements and the establishment of scheduled passenger and mail service in January 1910 gave the MW&S the potential for profitability but its financial situation did not immediately improve.[22]

In order to comply with demands for better and more reliable service, the MW&S needed to make improvements to both its track and equipment, but due to an April 1909 railroad commission decision, the company did not have the money to do so. In May 1909, just before control of the YPRR was assumed by its bondholders, the Montana Railroad Commission had yielded to complaints from the mine operators and reduced the allowable freight tariff. The original rate granted the YPRR was $0.45 per ton for haulage from the mines to the NP interchange at Bridger. The miners claimed this rate was excessive and did not allow them to compete with coal being mined elsewhere in Montana or Wyoming. After lengthy testimony, the commission agreed to cut the rate to

Delivered in October 1910, Consolidation Number 5 was a replacement for Maud, the class "C" Shay that had carried the same number. (Allen County [OH] Historical Society).

$0.35 per ton effective August 1, 1909. Soon after the new rate went into effect, it was clear that the MW&S was losing money, and its management asked for a rehearing in the hope of restoring the original tariff. The MW&S cited negligence on the part of the YPRR and Frank Hall for not being present at the April 1909 hearing, Hall having been distracted at the time by the pending stockholders meeting in Maine. After a rehearing in December, the commission reasserted its original findings and denied the MW&S's application. The $0.35 per ton rate would stand.[23]

Following the rate decision, the MW&S suffered another ten months of losses. Then, in desperation, on October 3, 1910, the railroad filed a Bill of Complaint with the Circuit Court of the United States that alleged that its business had been impaired and confiscated by the commission's order in contravention of the Fourteenth Amendment of the Constitution of the United States. Testimony given at the subsequent inquiry showed that during the twelve months ending August 31, 1910, the MW&S had generated a gross corporate income of $32,474 but, after interest charges, showed a loss of $14,609. The court determined, however, that the company was "well and economically managed" and that operating expenses were "no greater than reasonably necessary." As a result, an injunction was issued against the commission's rate reduction order and the $0.45 per ton rate was reinstated. The impact of this decision was not immediately felt as the rate order would not be made permanent until a final ruling in March 1912. During the interim, the mines were charged the higher rate, but the additional revenue was held in escrow awaiting the court's final decision. The outcome of this ruling left the mine operators not at all pleased.[24]

If this were not enough, the mine owners were further aggravated by the railroad's repeated refusal to switch loaded cars to scale tracks when needed. Although most of the mines had scales near their main tipples, cars were sometimes loaded on other tracks and needed to be moved to the tipple track for weighing. Because the MW&S had no scales of its own and refused to do the necessary switching, the mines were forced to have these cars weighed by the NP. This practice cost the mines money as it resulted in delayed invoicing. When the mine owners complained, the MW&S responded by petitioning the railroad commission for permission to assess a $1.00 per car surcharge when these switching moves were required. The commission investigated and denied the railroad's request, and the bickering between the mine owners and the railroad continued.[25]

By the spring of 1911, the mine operators had had enough and let it be known that if the NP did not move ahead with its branch line, they were ready to build a railroad of their own. According to Chris Yegen, they planned to mortgage their properties and use the money to build a line connecting the mines to the recently completed CB&Q line running from Warren to Fromberg. This proposal was little more than an idle threat. Due to the intervening mountains, there was no practical way to tie into the CB&Q without following the MW&S nearly all the way to Bridger. But the announcement got the NP's attention. Not wanting to risk the CB&Q having access to Bear Creek, where the NP still planned to develop their own coal properties, they no doubt tried to defuse the situation with assurances that there would soon be NP tracks to the mines. This must have appeased the mine operators as nothing further was heard from them in this regard.[26]

With the higher tariff in place, it soon became apparent that the MW&S still did not have the cash-flow to fund the necessary capital improvements. Washouts, derailments, wrecks, and an inadequate car supply continued to plague the railroad and complaints from the mines

During its early years, the MW&S was plagued by numerous washouts like this one that occurred just east of Bearcreek near Mile Post 19 on September 4, 1912. (General Photograph Collection, Railroad Museum of Pennsylvania, PHMC).

continued unabated. In August 1912, a serious washout about one mile north of Belfry took out a section of track on a steep hillside near the Clarks Fork River. About a month later another washout removed one hundred feet of roadbed and embankment just east of Bearcreek, leaving the tracks suspended in midair. As usual, these events forced the mines to suspend operations and prompted four of them (Anaconda did not join) to file a report with the railroad commission that solicited assistance in remedying the poor service afforded by the MW&S. The report read in part: "The track-bed is in fierce condition. . . . There is hardly a week passes but what there is a wreck of some kind, and consequently the mines have to remain idle. The yards in various mines are nearly always congested with loads, and this does not help the present car situation. They have only two engines in operation, and at the present time we understand only one is in use, the other being under repairs. The ties are out of shape and broken, and something should be done at once, and we are asking for your kind co-operation."[27]

The mine operators' complaints prompted an inspection tour by the commissioners, who looked into the condition of both the mines and the

Drop-bottom gondola number 204 is representative of those built for the MW&S by Mt. Vernon Car Manufacturing Company, Mount Vernon, Illinois, in 1912. Many of these cars remained in service until the railroad's abandonment. (Yellowstone Gateway Museum of Park County 2006.045.0870).

railroad. The commissioners' observations included the poor condition of the unballasted roadbed and the fact that many of the ties, which had only been in place for about six years, were "in a decayed condition" and often broke under the weight of passing trains. They also noted that about one thousand ties had recently been replaced and that another eight hundred to one thousand were ready for installation. These they felt would put the line in "fair condition" for the winter. The commissioners also ascertained that because of the inadequate rail service, the five mines had been idle about one-third of the time between October 20 and December 7, 1912, loading an average of only thirty-nine cars per day. The miners assured the commissioners that they could ship eighty cars per day, and MW&S management asserted that it could handle that many, if the NP would supply the cars. It was also noted that the intermittent rail service caused by washouts and wrecks made it difficult for the mines to maintain an adequate and experienced workforce. The commission concluded that despite all of the MW&S's shortcomings, its problems were due, in large part, to the NP's reluctance, or inability, to ensure an adequate car supply. The commission appealed to the NP in this regard, and the company promised to "exert every effort to this end." Regardless of NP's stated intentions, immediately following the investigation, using what little money it had available, the MW&S ordered an additional fifteen boxcars and twenty-five new fifty-ton capacity drop-bottom gondolas.[28]

If things were not bad enough already, tragedy struck the MW&S again on December 5, 1912, when eight-year-old Emma Nixon was killed near Bearcreek. Emma, along with other schoolchildren, routinely walked the tracks on their way to and from school. As Emma made her way home on that December day, a particularly slow-moving train with two empty cars trailing the caboose, enticed her to try to get a free ride home. Her attempt to climb onto the moving train proved fatal and her father responded by suing the railroad for failing to adequately fence the right-of-way. At times like this, it must have seemed there would be no end to MW&S's misery.[29]

8

"In the Interest of Economy and Efficiency"

DESPITE ASSURANCES GIVEN TO THE MINE OWNERS IN THE spring of 1911, the NP made no immediate move toward building a branch line to the mines. But a year later, closure of the NP's coal mining operation at Chestnut on Bozeman Pass and persistent rumors about the Milwaukee Road making a move toward Bear Creek caused Howard Elliott to begin to worry. With the company's future coal supply in question, he felt he could not risk having a competitor build into Bear Creek. Therefore, something had to be done to secure his company's position. Elliott realized that the simplest solution was to buy the MW&S.[1]

For reasons unknown, negotiations did not begin until October 1912 and once started did not progress far. Estimating that it would cost $750,000 to build their own line, Elliott was willing to pay no more than $500,000 for the MW&S, given the costs involved in bringing that line up to NP operating standards. Having grown somewhat desperate themselves, by now the MW&S stockholders had dropped their asking price to $900,000, or approximately the amount of their total investment but still well above what Elliott was willing to pay. In December, in an attempt at intimidation, Elliott authorized survey crews to begin work. He wrote to J. E. Spurling, the NP's general agent in Billings, and suggested hopefully that "active work toward building the line will perhaps result in the other people being willing to sell out." He told Spurling that he was "not very keen about buying them out, but if they are willing to make a fair price, it will probably be better to buy them, rather than duplicate railroad facilities."[2]

Unfortunately for Elliott the presence of NP survey crews working their way up the valley toward Bear Creek failed to elicit the hoped-for response. So, in March 1913, the NP executive committee authorized Elliott to begin purchasing right-of-way. Still far apart on a sale price, in a letter written on April 4, Elliott broke off negotiations and informed Frank Gannon in his usual cordial manner that "we have no feeling whatsoever that you and your associates desire to be disagreeable in any way, but there is a difference between the views of those who represent you and ourselves as to the best way to handle the coal business in that field." An April 29 story in the *Great Falls Tribune* brought news that all but a few farmers had agreed to terms for the right-of-way and that "practically all" of the mine owners had signed a tentative agreement to ship their production via the new NP branch.[3]

Given the financial and operational issues that plagued the MW&S from the start, it is astonishing that the stockholders held firm to their price and position. They had everything to lose and little to gain. Recouping part of their investment should have appeared preferable to losing all of it, which is exactly what would happen once the NP line reached Bear Creek. Whether they perceived the NP's activities as a bluff, which they were not, or believed that the railroad was truly worth their asking price since it had finally begun to show a profit is impossible to know. Whatever their reasoning, they held firm and risked it all. Their obstinacy was remarkable, but equally so was the NP's sudden abandonment of the Bear Creek & Western. Having secured a land position in the coalfield early on and planned a railroad to Bear Creek for more than ten years, the Bear Creek & Western never progressed beyond the expenditure of about $120,000 for surveys and the acquisition of two-thirds of the needed right-of-way. Howard Elliott's resignation and departure from the NP in August 1913 may have been a factor, along with the realization that the Milwaukee Road had no plans for a Bear Creek extension.[4]

In December, an assistant to newly elected NP president Jule M. Hannaford, assured the Billings Chamber of Commerce that the NP was still planning to build the Bear Creek & Western, but this seems to have been the NP's last gasp. At some point, Hannaford probably reevaluated the situation and felt no immediate need for action. With the mines in Red Lodge producing around 1 million tons per year, the NP had no immediate need for Bear Creek coal, and an expenditure of an additional $630,000 to build a redundant railroad could not have seemed justified. As long as the MW&S continued to provide at least a modicum of service, the mine operators were unlikely to build their own railroad, and there remained the possibility that the owners of the MW&S would reconsider their asking price. So, much to the chagrin of the mine operators, work on the NP's Bear Creek branch line quietly came to an end. For the next eight years the NP would begrudgingly interact with the MW&S while the mine operators continued to complain about the rates they paid and the service received. By default, the MW&S had won its initial battle for survival, but its struggles were far from over.[5]

As war clouds descended on Europe, things gradually began to improve for both the mines and the MW&S. In April 1915, the railroad's performance still left much to be desired, delivering a total of only 430 cars to the NP, or about 16 per day. But as wartime demand for coal expanded, General Manager Maguire worked diligently to increase efficiency and improve service. By the end of the year, the railroad had handled 389,394 tons of freight, a 55 percent increase over 1910's volume, nearly all of it coal. In 1916, the railroad was handling almost 40 cars per day and by year's end had increased freight volume to 472,025 tons resulting in an operating income of about $220,000 and a remarkable net profit of $41,532. The increased cash flow allowed the MW&S to purchase another much needed locomotive. This engine was another Consolidation-type (2-8-0). Built in 1899 and purchased in May from the Pittsburgh & Lake Erie, it was a bit of an antique, but it allowed the retirement of Little Fifteen.[6]

The year 1917 showed continued operational improvement with 281,503 tons of freight handled in just the first six months. This was accomplished despite a washout near the Pierce and Damann ranches two and a half miles south of Bridger in late March. In May, General Manager Maguire announced that the mines were operating full time, and he expected that to continue through most of the summer. Montana Coal & Iron contributed 238,844 tons, or about a third of that year's total production, despite having suffered a mysterious fire in September 1916. The fire, which was presumed to be arson, completely destroyed the tipple

Seen here in Belfry around 1920, consolidation Number 6 was acquired from the Pittsburgh & Lake Erie Railroad in 1916 to help handle the increasing traffic load during the First World War. Note the lack of ballast and the widely spaced ties on this side track in the Belfry yard. (CCHS&M-Kidwell Collection).

and several nearby structures, all of which were quickly rebuilt. Year-end financials for 1917 showed that a total of 661,394 tons of freight had been hauled and operating revenue had jumped to over $306,000 resulting in a net profit of about $53,500. This allowed for the replacement of the original, used sixty-pound rail with new seventy-two pound in some areas, and by June, much of the mainline near Bearcreek had been upgraded.[7]

To address the increasingly problematic issue of inadequate passenger service (see chapter 9), in mid-June the railroad acquired a gasoline-powered McKeen railcar and by August had established dedicated passenger service from Bearcreek to Bridger. Also in August, a one-and-a-half-mile spur on a 2.5 percent grade was completed, running southwest from Bearcreek to Montana Coal & Iron's new mine in Foster Gulch. This new construction, which Elijah Smith had blocked in 1907, included a "wye" in Bearcreek for turning trains and locomotives. But trouble was never far away, and the railroad soon suffered its second work-related fatality.[8]

In October 1917, rear brakeman William McKenzie was riding in the caboose of a train headed south out of Bridger with a string of empties. Just north of Belfry, as the train slowly negotiated the narrow

This view looking north along the Clarks Fork River was taken about one mile north of Belfry between mile posts 10 and 11. This is the area where the railroad suffered its second fatality when William McKenzie was crushed by a derailed caboose. (General Photograph Collection, Railroad Museum of Pennsylvania, PHMC).

embankment along the Clarks Fork River the caboose derailed and abruptly tipped toward the river. Sensing impending doom McKenzie leaped off the opposite side where there was but little room between the tracks and the hillside. When the caboose suddenly righted itself and then fell in his direction McKenzie had no escape and was crushed when the car toppled off the tracks. According to locals, "it smashed his brains out and Chester Andrew (one of the railroad's engineers) scooped them up with a shovel and threw them in the river." The railroad offered McKenzie's widow a customary $25,000 death benefit, but when she could not produce a marriage certificate and admitted that they were not actually married, the offer was rescinded. McKenzie was the seventh person buried in the Belfry cemetery.[9]

Prior to the uptick in revenue generated by war time traffic, it was widely believed that the YPRR and MW&S's financial and operational problems were due to its greedy eastern investors siphoning off profits in order to pay themselves big dividends. While it was true that holders of preferred stock in the YPRR were allowed to receive up to a 6 percent dividend on net earnings, no dividends were ever paid. The real problem was the MW&S's burgeoning debt load. This, more than anything, explains why maintenance was curtailed and little or nothing was done to improve the company's inadequate infrastructure during the company's early years. Because Frank Hall had been forced to sell YPRR bonds at below face value, the MW&S had inherited a funded debt of $900,000. A year after its inception this number increased to $950,000 when an equipment loan was secured for the purchase of the railroad's first boxcars.[10]

By 1913, funded debt had grown to almost $970,000 and interest payments alone cost the railroad over $54,000 per year. Cash flow was further burdened in 1912 when a 2.5 percent sinking fund was established for the eventual retirement of corporate bonds. Although the release of funds held in escrow due to the rate dispute that began in 1909 allowed the MW&S to realize its first profitable year in 1912, it wasn't until wartime traffic increased in 1916 that profits began to surge. As the increase in coal haulage pushed the MW&S into profitability, Gannon and Maguire faced a dilemma. Should they reduce the company debt or improve its physical plant? There was a delicate balance to be realized here, and in the end, Gannon was probably forced to yield to pressure from the bondholders to make good on the interest payments while he worked to reduce the company's overall debt load. Minimal upkeep became the order of the day and regardless of whether Maguire, who had to deal with ongoing operational problems, agreed, there was probably little he could do about it. Progress was slow but by the end of 1918, the company's funded debt had been reduced to $835,000.[11]

As the MW&S struggled with its balance sheet, in late 1917 the mine operators were again complaining about car shortages forcing them to curtail production. This time they brought the problem to the attention of both the Federal Fuel Administrator and the Montana Railroad Commission. The investigation that followed again pointed to NP as the culprit, but NP officials innocently claimed that they had a car shortage of their own and that the Great Northern was creating the problem by refusing to supply cars destined for customers on that line. But car shortages weren't the only problem. The increase in traffic during the past two years coupled with a lack of maintenance had taken its toll. A report from the Railroad Commission disclosed that "the Montana, Wyoming & Southern has not adequate equipment to take care of the coal business and that its track is in deplorable condition." Because of these recurring problems, in December 1917 undisclosed parties (presumably the mine operators and local coal vendors) demanded that the federal government step in and force NP, or Great Northern, to assume control of the MW&S to ensure adequate service.[12]

Less than a month after the mine operators demand for government intervention, most of the country's railroads were nationalized and placed under the control of the United States Railroad Administration (USRA). The government takeover was meant to streamline nationwide operations during the world war. The MW&S, being a privately owned short line, was exempt from the government control. Using its independent status as leverage, the MW&S appealed to the Montana Railroad Commission to force NP to supply the needed cars. The commission claimed it did not have the authority to make such a ruling and referred the appeal to the USRA director general in Washington, DC. In April, the USRA ruled that the NP and Great Northern had to deliver cars to the Bear Creek mines in "any quantity their business requires." The result of this ruling was an increase in production during 1918 to over 692,000 tons, or more than forty carloads per day. This notable increase was accomplished despite a two-week lapse in mid-June when the tracks on Golden Flat were once again washed away by a flood on the Clarks Fork River. By the end of 1918, the increased traffic had resulted in the MW&S realizing a record profit of $70,510. This surplus cash allowed the railroad to finally begin making much-needed capital improvements. The decision to begin reinvesting in the company's infrastructure may have also been influenced by a change in management. Due to failing health, in late July 1918 Michael Maguire took an extended leave of absence. He was replaced by an energetic thirty-eight-year-old named William H. Bunney who immediately began implementing changes and working to improve the company's relationship with its powerful neighbor the NP.[13]

This photo shows MW&S locomotive Number 5 working with an NP pile driver to replace a damaged trestle. Although the location of this photo is uncertain, this may be the trestle that was damaged by fire in December 1919, or it may simply have been the victim of a cloudburst and flash flood. (CCHS&M-Kidwell Collection).

Short in stature, personable, and well liked, William Bunney's wavy hair and round wire-rimmed glasses gave him a fatherly, professorial look. A professional railroader, Bunney began his career with the NP in 1899 and worked in both St. Paul and Missoula before being promoted to chief clerk for the superintendent in Livingston, Montana, in 1912. Due to his energy and ability to get things done, Bunney was known as a "terrier" during his time with the NP. When he arrived in Belfry he was determined to turn things around for his new employer and made a point of getting personally acquainted with every MW&S employee. He soon knew all of them by their first name. Being both an avid fisherman and a devoted card player, Bunney and his wife further cultivated their relationship with his staff by often hosting bridge dinner parties at their home in Belfry for fellow employees Hugh Routh, Earle Romek, William Gullickson, and their wives.[14]

About a year after Bunney assumed the position of general manager, an article in the *Butte Miner* claimed that "according to local railroad men who have inspected the railroad recently," Bunney was "winning appreciation for efficient operation of the line." This observation corroborates other unidentified sources who claimed that it was under his direction that rock ballast and new ties were installed, and much of the remaining sixty-pound rail was replaced with seventy-two pound. To alleviate persistent car shortages, Bunney also authorized the purchase of twenty-five additional drop-bottom gondolas. His approach to solving the company's problems inspired both loyalty and respect among the employees. The physical improvements he implemented caused the MW&S to emerge from the war years in better shape than it had ever been.[15]

With the railroad now operating smoothly, 1919 saw the establishment of the last major mining operation in the Bear Creek valley. Because the best coal lands were controlled by large companies, the newly created Eagle Coal Company operated on land leased from Montana Coal & Iron. The agreement restricted Eagle to mining only bed number three on a defined tract in the upper reaches of Foster Gulch and included a $0.15 per ton royalty to Montana Coal & Iron. Negotiated in May 1919, by the time the agreement was finalized on June 2 operations were already underway. The MW&S now served seven mines, two of them, the Smith and Foster Gulch mines, operated by Montana Coal & Iron.[16]

Unfortunately the Eagle mine soon became a headache for the MW&S. Just a few weeks after operations began, Trainmaster H. C. Riddle was forced to send Eagle Coal a letter of complaint. In his letter he pointed out that after weighing their cars on Montana Coal & Iron's scale at Foster Gulch, Eagle was allowing unbilled loads to be mixed with cars from the Foster Gulch Mine. This, he pointed out, forced the MW&S to switch those cars out in Belfry or Bridger, which, according to Riddle, "consumes quite a little time." He also admonished Eagle Coal's management for repeatedly complaining about the delivery of empty cars. He advised them that the problem was theirs, not his, and that they needed to request cars as far in advance as possible. He pointed out that a daily car situation report was needed and that he could not supply cars on short notice since the NP was only running three trains per week. The

Montana Coal & Iron's Foster Gulch mine began full-scale operation in 1917. This photo, taken in 1920, shows the three tracks beneath the tipple used for loading different sizes of coal. The track nearest the hillside was used for slack. Cars on the other two tracks would have received nut or lump coal. To the left is the uncovered tipple used by the Eagle Coal Company, which hauled coal from its mine portal farther up the gulch to the tipple via an electric tramway. A small section of the tramway is visible behind the building on the far left. (Lot 026 B6F3.12, NP rail cars in front of Foster Creek Mine, Montana Historical Society Photograph Archives).

railroad's interaction with Eagle Coal quieted down for a few months after the receipt of Riddle's letter, but in February 1920 there were more issues. With spring thaws coming on, William Bunney felt it necessary to inform them that they needed to raise and ballast the tracks at their mine. He advised that if not done promptly "this track will sink into the mud very quickly and will be unsafe for operation." He added, helpfully, that they should look into getting cinders from the Foster Mine boiler house to use as ballast. This advice got things moving again, but within a year, there would be more trouble.[17]

While Eagle Coal presented periodic operational difficulties, in his continuing effort to reduce overall costs and improve efficiency, Bunney decided to experiment with using water from the mines in the locomotive boilers. All of the mines produced water from their underground workings and having multiple water sources in the Bear Creek valley would simplify operations, possibly even eliminating the need for the water tank at International Junction. Unfortunately, the results of these experiments were wholly unsuccessful. It was soon discovered that water from the mines contained excessive suspended fines and dissolved solids which caused foaming in the boiler as the temperature increased. The foaming resulted in water being carried from the steam dome through the dry pipe to the cylinders which forced engineers to constantly open the cylinder cocks to blow the water out. Being incompressible, water in the cylinders could cause a cracked or blown cylinder head, while constantly blowing the water out of the cylinders washed away critical lubricating oil. The suspended fines also increased the frequency of boiler washing and blow downs to remove accumulated sediment. These procedures, along with the chalky white evaporative crusts that formed around the safety valves and whistles, soon made a mess of the locomotives. Various water additives were tested to no avail, and after a short time, the experiment with mine water was abandoned.[18]

With William Bunney in charge, by 1919 the company had acquired a roster that included three 2-8-0 locomotives, sixty-nine boxcars, fifty gondolas, two cabooses, a combine, a baggage car, a gasoline-powered McKeen railcar, and a half dozen miscellaneous cars used for maintenance. Capital improvements during the year included continued replacement of old rails and ties, and the construction of a small engine house in Bearcreek called "the garage" to house the McKeen. Although derailments were now less frequent, in at least one case, the improvements being made were the direct cause of an accident.[19]

During the MW&S's early years, many of the Japanese laborers who had helped build the railroad, remained in the area and worked on section crews. In 1916, there were thirty-one Japanese immigrants on the railroad's payroll. Although well liked and respected, the Japanese were not fully accepted by the local community. This animosity forced many of them to live in a small enclave of dugout shacks and old boxcars west of Belfry on the flats between Bear Creek and the engine house. Here they maintained small gardens and subsisted on rice and occasional fish they

Yellowstone Park Railroad caboose Number 1 was a short, home-built, side-door design completed in early March 1907. Still in service forty years later, it is seen here in the Belfry yard. (Courtesy of California State Railroad Library & Archives).

Caboose Number 2 was similar to Number 1 but slightly longer. It is believed to have been built by the YPRR in late 1907. The boarded-up windows and stovepipe extending from the side door suggest that by 1947, it was no longer in revenue service. (Courtesy of California State Railroad Library & Archives).

This MW&S "armstrong" derrick car was built for the Yellowstone Park Railroad in 1906. The frequency of derailments during the early years of operation must have kept this piece of equipment busy. It is seen here in Belfry during May 1955 just prior to being scrapped. (PAc 97-93.12758, MWS Derrick car, Montana Historical Society Photograph Archives).

caught in the Clarks Fork River. Despite the prevailing prejudice, some of these men eventually attained positions of importance like roadmaster and section foreman.[20]

On one unfortunate occasion in early July 1919, possibly due to some miscommunication or language barrier, a section crew replacing ties and rail along the Clarks Fork River north of Belfry neglected to set out red warning flags. The crew had pulled the spikes holding the rails in place and moved on just as a northbound coal drag headed by engine Number 6 came rolling up the line. Moving at less than twelve miles per hour, the engine shivered when it hit the loose rails. As it rocked from side-to-side, engineer Charles Burns quickly closed the throttle and applied brakes. Number 6 bounced a few times and then slowly began to roll over. As the engine tipped toward the river the slow-motion disaster permitted Burns and Fireman George Miller to escape. They leaped from the cab and tumbled down the embankment as Number 6 rolled on its side. Then, having escaped with only minor cuts and bruises, they watched helplessly as the engine slid down into the river. The locomotive's tender and several cars were derailed but remained upright. For Burns and Miller, it was just another day at the office. After checking for broken bones, they brushed themselves off, collected the rest of the crew and

Ready for a day of hard work, a section crew composed of Japanese immigrants is headed north out of Belfry. A dugout-type dwelling used by some of these men is barely visible in the distance on the far right. (Author's collection).

In this view looking north along the Clarks Fork River about one and a half miles from Belfry, the railroad's lightly ballasted but otherwise well-maintained roadbed can be seen along with the water tank that used a steam jet to draw water from the river. This may have been the area where locomotive Number 6 took its unfortunate plunge during July 1919. (General Photograph Collection, Railroad Museum of Pennsylvania, PHMC).

hiked back to Belfry, where a call was placed to the NP requesting a wrecker. If this unfortunate event were not enough, the year ended with a fire ignited by a passing train that badly damaged three sections of a trestle on Golden Flat.[21]

Although things seemed to be going well, the prosperity the railroad and mines experienced during the war years was not permanent. When the world war ended, there was an immediate slump in the nation's economy. Manufacturing slowed, the demand for Butte copper and the coal to smelt it dropped off, and sales of commercial coal, which was the primary market for the mines at Bear Creek rapidly collapsed as well. The economic slump also caused a precipitous drop in wheat prices, which was exacerbated by the start of a prolonged drought that forced many dry land farmers to abandon their homesteads. This exodus further distressed an increasingly dismal market for commercial coal. The Spanish influenza pandemic that hit in late 1918 only added to the area's misery. Compounding these problems was a decision by NP's Northwest Improvement Company to start selling commercial coal from its mines in Red Lodge, with lower freight tariffs allowing them to under-cut Bear Creek prices. Demand for Bear Creek coal dropped so precipitously that according to the *Carbon County Journal*, by mid-May 1919 the Bear Creek mines were operating only four or five days a month placing the valley's residents in "desperate straits." The miners' plight was mirrored in the MW&S's financials, which saw an $80,000 swing from profitability in 1918 to an almost $11,000 loss the next year. The mines got some relief when the Montana Railroad Commission ruled that the NP had to raise the tariff on commercial coal shipped from Red Lodge to be the same as that being charged Bear Creek coal. This ruling eliminated the price discrimination against Bear Creek coal, but the mines and the railroad that served them were still having a hard time.[22]

Along with the drop in coal sales, the postwar economy also saw a dramatic increase in the cost of living. With fewer days of work at the mines, and pay frozen at wartime levels by the federal government, many miners gave up and left town. Those who stayed, along with other coal miners across the country, felt they should no longer have to work under wartime restrictions. At midnight on October 31, 1919, the United Mine Workers (UMW) called a nationwide strike and Montana coal miners walked off the job. Within two weeks, as temperatures in parts of Montana dropped to fifty below zero, the coal situation had become critical. Schools and businesses across the state were closed due to a lack of heating fuel. By late November, the fuel situation was so bad that the Yegen brothers began recruiting "volunteers" from Billings to work at their Bear Creek mine; the Smokeless & Sootless mine soon followed suit. The arrival of these nonunion workers, who called themselves the Billings Community Coal Miners Association, caused tensions to rise and there was concern about possible violence. In early December, at the request of Governor Sam Stewart, four companies of the US First Infantry were dispatched to Montana from Fort Lewis, Washington, to keep the peace and protect the mines and "volunteers." On December 7, about 150 troops of Company G arrived at the NP depot in Bridger where they transferred to a special MW&S train that bucked snow drifts all the way to Bearcreek. Not knowing what to expect, they arrived with machine guns mounted in the baggage car doors. But their martial preparations were unwarranted; all was calm in Bearcreek.[23]

As the troops disembarked into the snow along the tracks, they were greeted by a crowd of young boys with sticks on their shoulders who marched along beside them to the grinning amusement of the soldiery. Described by the *Billings Gazette* as being "picturesquely uniformed," the men wore big fur caps, heavy olive-green greatcoats, high overshoes, and shaggy bearskin gloves that reached above the elbows. With Springfield rifles slung over their shoulders, bayonets dangling ominously from their belts, they trudged through the snow to their billet in the machine shop of the Bear Creek mine and then on to their assigned guard posts. Guard duty must have been mostly a matter of fighting off boredom in the snow and subzero temperatures as there was no trouble from the miners.[24]

On December 10, President Woodrow Wilson intervened and presented a proposal to end the strike to UMW president John L. Lewis. The proposal was accepted and local officials instructed the miners to return to work. But the miners at Bear Creek were skeptical about the agreement and refused to return until December 17 and then only because the severe weather was causing widespread suffering. Having encountered no trouble during their two-week deployment, the army withdrew on December 20. The reason for the calm being that the miners knew that operating the mine machinery took considerable experience and believed that the untrained "volunteers" were no threat to their jobs. In fact, rather than dig coal, one group of "volunteers" spent most of their time shoveling snow off the McCarthy Branch so trains could reach the Smokeless & Sootless mine. The others managed to ship a few much-needed carloads of slack coal from the Yegen mine to Billings, most of it coming from piles that had already been mined. Due to their inexperience, the volunteer miners left behind damaged equipment and at least one burned out power generating unit. Beyond the damaged machinery, some of the more notable items that remained in Bearcreek after the strike were army-issue fur hats that many residents proudly wore for years to come; whether they were acquired through barter, sale, or outright thievery may never be known.[25]

By 1920, the country's economy had begun to rebound. With the miners back at work and coal bunkers across the state depleted, the MW&S got off to a good start by hauling a record 2005 carloads to Bridger during January; about eighty per day. Despite the lingering effects of the postwar depression, in terms of tonnage hauled, 1920 set a record for the MW&S. Operating revenue climbed to $478,548, and eclipsed the company's previous best year, 1918, by $133,690. But the postwar economy also resulted in increased expenses and despite the higher income, net profits for the year were less than half those achieved in 1918. Despite the railroad's record revenue, 1920 was not a good year for everyone. In early October, the Bear Creek Coal Company suffered a major disaster when a windstorm destroyed the trestle used to access its workings on the south side of Bear Creek. Having nearly mined out its holdings on the north side of the valley, the loss of the trestle was a crippling blow. With the bulk of its production shut down, Bear Creek Coal was unable to make the interest payments on its bonds and a year later, in November 1921, the company was forced into receivership. The mine was reopened by Triangle Fuel Company, with an option to purchase but was soon shut down. Similarly, the International Coal Company was also in deep financial trouble. When fire caused serious damage to its surface facilities the

One of the few photos of the Smokeless & Sootless mine. This snowy November 1929 photo is reminiscent of how things probably looked during the United Mine Workers strike ten years earlier. (CCHS&M-Kidwell Collection).

mine defaulted on its loans and it too was forced to close. In late 1922, the International mine was sold, and in January 1923, it reopened as the Carbon County Coal Company. Under lease agreements with various operators, both the Bear Creek and International properties were mined periodically for the next ten years, but production was never significant. The decline in these two operations had an immediate impact on the railroad and by 1922 operating revenue had dropped by about 35 percent. Despite this decrease, through his skillful financial management, in 1922 William Bunney increased annual profits to over $51,000.[26]

As the 1920s wore on, production from Anaconda's Washoe Coal Company mine became sporadic due to fluctuating demand for coal at the company's mines and smelters, and even though the Bear Creek and

A windstorm in October 1920 destroyed the Bear Creek Coal Company's trestle that spanned the valley and allowed access to mine workings on the south side. This disastrous event led to the company's financial collapse a year later. (CCHS&M-Kidwell Collection).

The International Mine, which was sold to the Carbon County Coal Company in 1923, shows no sign of activity in this September 1928 photo. The McCarthy Branch to the Smokeless & Sootless Mine is visible on the hillside to the left. (CCHS&M-Kidwell Collection).

International mines had slipped into insolvency, the economy overall was in an upswing. Production from the remaining mines soon stabilized at about half the wartime peak, and the railroad's physical plant remained in reasonably good condition. These factors supported a period of sustained modest prosperity and surplus cash-flow allowed the railroad to continue making improvements. These included the construction of a twenty-three-car siding and sugar beet loading ramp near the Ellis ranch south of Golden in October 1920 and the purchase a new locomotive from the Baldwin Locomotive Works in February 1921. The new engine, which was given the number ten, was a modern Consolidation-type (2-8-0) that weighed about 10 percent more than the older engines but exerted nearly 20 percent more tractive effort.[27]

This sugar beet dump near Rockvale on the NP Rocky Fork Branch is similar to beet dumps on the MW&S located on Golden Flat and just north of Belfry. (L. G. Webber photo, Joliet Public Library).

Plans for the Cooke City extension resurfaced in the early 1920s as well. The renewed interest was largely fueled by the activities of Gottwerth Tanzer and his Western Smelting & Power Company. With the support of East Coast investors, Tanzer had reopened the Henderson mine, built a smelter, hydroelectric power plant, and was in the process of installing a tram-line to haul ore down the mountain. Before the abrupt collapse of Tanzer's enterprise in 1925, all of this activity and the MW&S's newfound profitability made construction of a rail line to Cooke City seem feasible. The reluctance of MW&S management to abandon the idea is revealed in a 1930 Interstate Commerce Commission report that showed the railroad as still having ninety-five miles of line "under construction." This description, of course, was a gross exaggeration, as not a shovel full of dirt had as yet been turned. A year later, the effects of the Great Depression brought an end to all such speculation and two years after his death, Frank Hall's dream of a rail line that

MW&S locomotive Number 10, a 1921 product of the Baldwin Locomotive Works, came equipped with piston valves and Walschaerts valve gear, making it the railroad's first truly modern locomotive. The odd-looking air tank mounted on the pilot allowed for additional brake applications and was added after its arrival in Belfry. Later MW&S locomotives lacked this modification. This photo was taken in Livingston during 1943 after the engine had received an overhaul at the NP shops. (General Photograph Collection, Railroad Museum of Pennsylvania, PHMC).

followed Philip Gallaher's Clarks Fork route to Yellowstone National Park was finally laid to rest.[28]

While William Bunney's first priority was to improve the MW&S's equipment and physical plant, by late 1919 he was also making a determined effort to improve relations with the NP. When the NP complained about the inadequacy of the grain doors on cars they were receiving, Bunney immediately brought the issue to the attention of the mine operators. He reminded them that the "slabs," as he called them, had to be properly installed and at least two feet high. He also pointed out that the NP had an inspector in Bridger who opened the doors on every car and

The blast coming from Number 10's safety valve is a sign that the engine has a full head of steam and is ready for the next switching move at Anaconda's no. 2 mine in Washoe. Having done his job well, the fireman can be seen relaxing for a moment while gazing at the photographer. This photo probably dates from the 1930s. (DeGolyer Library, SMU, Everett DeGolyer Jr. Railroad Collection).

rejected those deemed to be improperly loaded. A little over a year later, his efforts to appease the NP precipitated more trouble with the Eagle Coal Company. This time the complaint focused on Eagle's habit of requesting cars they didn't need, loading them, and then seeking a buyer. This resulted in the MW&S having to make additional switching moves and paying demurrage charges while the cars sat in Belfry or hauling the unbilled loads to the NP yard in Bridger for storage. According to Bunney, when the cars were dropped in Bridger "the Northern Pacific complain bitterly account [*sic*] being obliged to switch cars around Bridger, have their yard cluttered with cars that are not moving and also to having their equipment tied up under loads that are not billed." He concluded by noting, "We can expect trouble with the Northern Pacific very soon if equipment is ordered then not returned promptly with billed loads."[29]

In addition to the issues with the NP, in June, Bunney advised Eagle Coal that its mine tracks were causing derailments because there were too few ties and many of those in place were too short. He also noted that the curve on their turnout was so sharp that it had caused the railroad's new locomotive, Number 10, to derail, and it had cost $200 to get it back on the tracks. He told the company it needed to add ties, replace the turnout, and flatten the curve. He finished by warning: "It is not practicable to try any longer to operate this track until this change is made."[30]

Bunney's attention to the complaints about grain doors and unbilled loads demonstrated his focus on establishing good relations with his ex-employer. His diligent efforts were rewarded in May 1921 when an agreement for joint agency was finally realized. Years in the making, this agreement brought an end to NP's antagonistic relationship with the MW&S. Although forced cooperation during and after the war may have made it inevitable, Bunney's forbearance and cooperation must be credited for bringing the two sides together. As Frank Hall had originally proposed to Howard Elliott in 1905, a single agent in Bridger would now handle all business for both railroads. Joint use of all yard tracks was agreed to as well. This change, the companies announced, was "in the interest of economy and efficiency." It signaled a clear departure from NP's previous attitude toward the MW&S and within a few years would result in joint passenger service as well.[31]

9

"You Will Be Wiser after You Have Tried It"

SOON AFTER THE FIRST TRAINLOAD OF COAL WAS SHIPPED IN September 1906, Frank Hall began to think about passenger service on his new railroad. Initially, with only one locomotive, passengers were obliged to ride in the caboose of a passing freight train, at whatever time the train happened through town. Hall knew this was unacceptable and began to search for an economical alternative. In early 1907, he believed he had found the answer when George Atkins, the YPRR's secretary-treasurer, alerted him to the presence of a derelict gasoline-powered railcar parked in Indianapolis, Indiana.

The railcar Atkins had found was a product of Vimotum Hydrocarbon Car Company. Located in Columbus, Indiana, Vimotum had begun experimenting with gasoline-powered railcars in 1899 and Atkins was an early investor. Although several experimental models, including an attempt to motorize the private railcar used by the president of the Pennsylvania Railroad, were built, none was successful. One of the company's later prototypes used a forty-one-foot car body built by the Jewett Car Company of Akron, Ohio, powered by a three-cylinder, twenty-four horsepower Wolverine engine. This car was tested by an East Coast railroad and then returned to Indianapolis, where it was abandoned. Named "Sunny Brook" and weighing only fifteen tons, it is described in contemporary accounts as looking like "an ordinary interurban car minus the trolley pole." Because of his involvement in the Vimotum company, Atkins believed that Sunny Brook would be a cost-effective solution to YPRR's passenger service problems.[1]

Based on Atkins's recommendation, Hall purchased the derelict and sent master mechanic Harry Reeves to Indianapolis with instructions to rebuild it inside and out. The hulk was hauled to the Interstate Company in the suburb of Brightwood where Reeves installed a new fifty-horsepower gasoline engine and leather upholstered seats. With three forward gears, the refurbished railcar had a top speed of thirty-five miles per hour. Resplendent in a fresh coat of bright yellow paint, Sunny Brook was ready for testing in mid-March 1907. After several successful demonstration runs at a local yard, due to an apparent fascination with modern technology, rather than have the car shipped Hall elected to test his new contraption by having Reeves "drive" the car back to Belfry with Hall and several other "officials" as passengers. Their route is uncertain, but it was reported that "the car perhaps will be run over Pennsylvania tracks to Chicago and then over the Chicago, Milwaukee & St. Paul to Omaha. From Omaha to the west the tracks of the Union Pacific will be used." A Union Pacific official informed Hall, "You are welcome to use our tracks. . . . We have tried to build these automobile cars and want to see how you do. We believe you will be wiser after you have tried it." His assessment was, quite possibly, a gross understatement.[2]

Sadly, no record of Hall's improbable 1,500-mile trundle across the country exists, but there can be little doubt that his little yellow trolley car made quite a scene as it rattled along through the countryside at its less than impressive top speed. How long the trip took is unknown, but it may account for Hall's prolonged absence during May and June, when, as described elsewhere, with the Yegen's foreclosure suit pending, his attorney was unable to locate him. What transpired during the long trip from Indiana can only be imagined. Whether Hall's new bride, Laura, was willing to accompany him on his cross-country ramble is a mystery as well. In the end, Sunny Brook somehow made it to Belfry and at least some effort was made to use it in passenger service. But as with most early attempts at coupling a gasoline engine to a passenger car, Hall's railcar did not live up to expectations. Although no record of its performance exists, it seems likely that the fifty-horsepower engine was unable to propel the fully loaded car up the nine-mile grade to Bearcreek without stalling or overheating. A year and a half later a frustrated reporter in Belfry stated, "If the expert at the round house will only fix up that motor car, and start it out on schedule time each day, there will be little the residents of the valley lack in the way of transportation facilities." This comment reveals that by late 1908 Sunny Brook was inoperable, and because Frank Hall had more pressing matters to deal with at that time, the YPRR was back to running unscheduled passenger service on its periodic coal drags. Sunny Brook never ran again and was destroyed in the engine house fire on July 3, 1910.[3]

Due to Sunny Brook's inadequate performance, by May 1907 the YPRR had acquired its first passenger car: a small "combine," or combination passenger coach-baggage car. Despite this addition, the YPRR never operated scheduled passenger service. It was not until November 18, 1909, three months after Frank Hall's departure, that the MW&S issued a passenger schedule that announced mixed-train service twice a day (except Sunday) between Belfry and Bearcreek with a single train continuing on to Bridger. In December a revised schedule added International Junction as the train's new terminus beyond Bearcreek. This service, which included a US mail contract awarded in January 1910, was a success. Records show that during the first ten months of operation the railroad carried 8,940 passengers or about 35 per day. Despite the traffic volume, passenger revenue accounted for only about 3 percent of total income, and whereas it was an important service for area residents, it was not a priority for the railroad. How closely the daily mixed freight-passenger trains adhered to the published schedule is a matter of conjecture.[4]

In addition to the regularly scheduled mixed-trains, as early as January 1909 the YPRR was running special trains for social events in the valley. On January 16, for example, the Modern Woodsmen held a big dance in Bridger. Music was supplied by Heinie's Orchestra and dinner was served at the Barlow Hotel. For this event a special train left Washoe at 7:30 p.m. with stops at Bearcreek and Belfry. Another special train was

Facing, The railroad's combine, which was the principal passenger conveyance until 1917, has left the rails, and the passengers onboard probably received "a good shake up." A Japanese section crew can be seen working to alleviate the problem. The railroad's narrow roadbed is clearly evident as are two loaded gondolas and an unidentified locomotive. (CCHS&M-Kidwell Collection).

Montana, Wyoming & Southern

The Only Railroad to the Famous Bearcreek Coal Fields

General Offices, Belfry, Montana

Connects at Bridger with Northern Pacific Railroad.
Connects at Belfry with stage for Chance and upper valley.
Connects at Bearcreek with stage for Red Lodge.

Passenger Time Table of the Montana, Wyoming & Southern Railroad.

3 Mixed Except Sunday	1 Mixed Except Sunday	STATIONS	2 Mixed Except Sunday	4 Mixed Except Sunday
Lv. P. M.	Lv. A. M.		Arr. P. M.	Arr. P. M.
2.00		Bridger	1.00	
f 2.20		Golden	f 12.35	
3.15	7.30	Belfry	L 12.15 A 11.45	5.05
f 3.35	f 7.50	Olivers	f 11.15	f 4.40
4.00	8.15	Bearcreek	11.00	4.25
4.10	8.20	International Junct.	10.45	4.15
Arr. P. M.	Arr. A. M.	f Stop on Signal.	Lv. A. M.	Lv. P. M.

M. W. MAGUIRE, General Manager.

MW&S passenger schedule issued on December 8, 1910.

planned for the big Independence Day celebration in Bearcreek in 1910. The engine house fire that damaged both MW&S engines on the night of July 3 nearly put an end to this excursion, but railroad officials were quickly able to lease an NP engine, and the special train and celebration went off as planned. Other special trains were run from Washoe or Bearcreek as needed to haul spectators and players to baseball games as far away as Fromberg.[5]

Because passenger service was not a priority and contributed little to the company's bottom line, as freight traffic increased, passenger schedules suffered and overall service declined, resulting in numerous

MW&S facilities in Bridger were kept to a minimum. The depot, seen here in 1923, was an unremarkable structure with an office and passenger waiting room. The only other railroad facility was a stand pipe for locomotive water that was connected to the town water supply. The MW&S and YPRR had a contract that allowed them to use the NP turntable located at the north end of town. (General Photograph Collection, Railroad Museum of Pennsylvania, PHMC).

In May 1954, twenty-two years after passenger service came to an end and almost a year after the railroad ceased operations, the MW&S depot in Bearcreek is a sad visage of its former self. (PAc 97-73.14420, MWS Depot Bearcreek, Montana Historical Society Photograph Archives).

complaints. One Bearcreek resident observed that due to the MW&S's inconvenient scheduling, a roundtrip to Billings took nearly three days and required an overnight stay in both Billings and Bridger. Because of this, many travelers were willing to pay the two-dollar fare to take the stagecoach over the hill to Red Lodge in order to catch an NP train rather than be subjected to the inconvenient and questionable service provided by the MW&S. To solve this problem, in June 1917, the MW&S acquired a slightly used McKeen Motor Car from the Charles City Western Railroad (CCW) in Charles City, Iowa. The McKeen was built in January 1911 and had been retired around 1914 when the CCW converted to electrical power. Like Sunny Brook, the McKeen was a gasoline-powered passenger car. A more successful design than earlier machines, it could be operated cheaply and required only a two-man crew, but its cantankerous nature made it a headache to operate.

The McKeen Motor Car was developed by William R. McKeen Jr., superintendent of Motive Power at Union Pacific's Omaha, Nebraska, shops, as a means of providing economical passenger service on that railroad's lightly populated branch lines. After several experimental units, McKeen settled on a design utilizing a vertical six-cylinder, two-hundred-horsepower gasoline engine mounted transversely on the car's four-wheel front truck. Power was transmitted through a chain drive to the front axle only. The car body design emphasized both strength and aerodynamics utilizing porthole-style windows advertised as being airtight, water-proof, and dust-proof, along with a unique "wind-splitter" front end to reduce air resistance. These features gave the McKeen a distinctive look not easily confused with other railcars. Two sets of gears allowed a top speed of about sixty miles per hour with gas consumption averaging three miles to the gallon.[6]

The McKeen cars were cutting-edge technology for their time and were therefore plagued by numerous problems, one of which was the lack of a reverse gear. Reversing the car's direction required stopping, shutting down the engine, and then shifting the cam shaft to cause the engine to run in reverse. This process did not endear the McKeens to the motormen assigned to operate them. They could also be tricky to start as they used compressed air fed into three of the cylinders to turn

Acquired in 1917, "Bear Creek" the MW&S's McKeen railcar appears to be ready to load passengers and head out. Based on the location of the grain elevator visible in the background, this photo was taken in Bridger. The car's quirky, indefatigable operator "Silent Ed" Bunnell is standing third from the left. (Courtesy of Montana Department of Transportation).

the engine over. If the other three cylinders did not "fire up" quickly the compressed air on board would be exhausted and some other means of starting the engine had to be found. Additionally, reports of clutch failures and a temperamental power plant that was easily damaged by the jolts and bumps encountered on branch line tracks, added to the operator's problems.[7]

Christened "Bear Creek" the MW&S put its McKeen to work in July 1917 making two round trips a day from Bearcreek to Bridger, often with a baggage car in tow. Despite the official name being prominently emblazoned on the side, locals quickly began referring to the McKeen as "the submarine" or "sub" because of its nautical look or the "Galloping Goose" due to its rhythmic rocking motion. It had seating for fifty-six passengers and the interior was described as being quite plush with red velvet seats and rosewood paneling. Passenger service with the McK-een was a great success because the new schedule allowed residents of

"Silent Ed" Bunnell proudly stands in front of "Bear Creek" as it is prepared for departure from Belfry in 1920. The baggage car and two boxcars coupled behind suggest that Bunnell is about to make the downhill run to Bridger and not the steep climb up the valley to Bearcreek. (PAc 97-93.14157, MWS "Bear Creek" McKeen car in Belfry, Montana Historical Society Photograph Archives).

Bearcreek and Belfry to make day trips to Billings via the NP connection in Bridger. But as with other railroads, engineers on the MW&S found the McKeen a challenge to operate—that is, until the job fell to Ed Bunnell.

Affectionately known as "Silent Ed" but sometimes referred to as "Chief," Bunnell was a quaint fellow of small stature with conspicuous ears and a great talker. He reputably had traveled widely and once worked as the foreman on a pineapple plantation in Hawaii. His move to Montana forced him to forsake his tropical garb, and he was often seen wearing a dark, brimmed engineer's cap with matching baggy, grease-stained coveralls. According to William Romek, one of the railroad's clerks, Bunnell was a marvel at the controls of the McKeen and could keep it "chugging up the steep grades to Bearcreek through all weather conditions." Proud of his work maintaining a critical service

Built in 1919 directly across the tracks from the Bearcreek Depot, the small engine house called "the garage" was home for the railroad's McKeen railcar between runs. (CCHS&M-Kidwell Collection).

for the people of Washoe, Bearcreek, and the Clarks Fork Valley, Silent Ed spent his days perched on the motorman's seat in the confined space at the front of the McKeen peering out its big square windows engulfed by the roar of the engine and the smell of exhaust and hot oil. When, in October 1919, a small engine house called "the garage" was built directly across from the depot in Bearcreek, light maintenance and daily operations became a bit easier.[8]

As with many others, Bunnell found shifting the engine cam shaft from forward to reverse and back again an annoying process. According to historian William Schopp, this oft-repeated complaint of McKeen motormen led them to use "considerable brainwork to avoid reversing." On the Virginia & Truckee Railroad in Nevada, for example, slight grades at the station in Carson City allowed them to reverse the car's direction for short distances by shifting into neutral and allowing gravity to roll the car backward. Bunnell may have heard of this tactic because a traveling salesman who had occasion to ride Bear Creek in 1923 reported that on their arrival at the Bearcreek depot, Bunnell did not bother to reverse its direction using the wye. As a result, the next morning the McKeen left

"Bear Creek" with a baggage car in tow is seen crossing the trestle over its namesake drainage just after departing the Belfry Depot. (PAc 97-93.14408, MWS McKeen car-Psgr Service Bridger 1920, Montana Historical Society Photograph Archives).

Bearcreek running backward. Bunnell rolled into Belfry in reverse but pointed in the right direction for the trip north to Bridger. This maneuver saved him a cam shaft change in both Bearcreek and Belfry. When questioned about the safety and propriety of this maneuver Bunnell reportedly grinned and, with a twinkle in his eye, admitted that he been warned about doing it "once or twice" but claimed that even in reverse, he had a good view of the track and had never once been late.[9]

Revenue from passenger service was never an important part of the company's income, contributing only $3,989 to the bottom-line in 1919, or just slightly more than when it started ten years earlier. By 1922, passenger haulage had increased slightly, but even with the increase, it accounted for only a little over 1 percent of total revenue. Regardless of its insignificant impact on the bottom line, it remained a critical service for area residents. The McKeen maintained a six-days-a-week schedule until December 1926, when Bunnell was reportedly "gassed while cranking the MW&S sub at Bearcreek." The incident must have been serious as Silent Ed immediately left for a vacation in California, probably hoping

IMPROVED SERVICE

BEAR CREEK TO BILLINGS

Service is improved by joint arrangement under which Northern Pacific Gas-Electric car runs through Billings to Bear Creek. Attend to business in Billings in one day. A warm comfortable ride.

Leave Bear Creek -	7:35 A. M.
Leave Belfry - -	8:10 A. M.
Arrive Billings - -	10:40 A. M.
Leave Billings - - -	3:45 P. M.
Arrive Belfry - - -	6:10 P. M.
Arrive Bearcreek - -	6:50 P. M.

Montana, Wyoming & Southern Railroad Co.

Joint passenger service was announced on December 16, 1926.

that after leaving his grease-stained coveralls behind, a return to more tropical climes would speed his recovery. This event sidelined Bear Creek but also resulted in improved service when an agreement was reached with the NP for direct through service from Bearcreek to Billings utilizing one of the NP's newly acquired Electro-Motive Company (EMC) gas-electric railcars. The EMC units used a 175-horsepower Winton six-cylinder gasoline engine to generate electricity to power traction motors on the car's front truck. The new service, with seating for forty-two passengers, provided a single round trip each day departing Bearcreek at 7:35 a.m. and returning at 6:50 p.m., with a crew change in Bridger. Initially the NP assigned railcar B-5 to this run, but when its engine burned out in 1927 while towing a baggage car (possibly on the steep grade up the

Through passenger service from Bearcreek to Billings was instituted in December 1926 utilizing one of the NP's new EMC gas-electric railcars. Railcar B-5, shown here in Centralia, Washington, in 1936, was the first to be used. An identical unit, B-7, replaced B-5 in 1927 (Emery Roberts Collection [2012.74], Washington State Historical Society, Tacoma).

Bear Creek valley), B-5 was replaced by B-7, an identical EMC railcar. Later NP's B-6 may have been used on this run as well.[10]

Due to declining patronage, by early 1929, through service to Billings had ended. The McKeen was repaired and put back into operation running only as far as Bridger, but its days were numbered. Ed Bunnell returned to work and later alleged that from March to May 1932, he was forced to operate the McKeen despite his repeated complaints about its poor condition. During this time, Bunnell claimed that he suffered chronic and debilitating health issues due to the railcar's worn piston rings, improperly enclosed crankcase, and defective exhaust pipe constantly leaking fumes into the cab. The McKeen was clearly on its last legs and with as few as four or five passengers riding it on a typical day, rail passenger service on the MW&S came to an end in early May 1932. When the McKeen was retired, a five-passenger highway bus was put into service hauling mail and light freight from the CB&Q depot in East

Rail passenger service ended in early May 1932 when the McKeen railcar was retired and replaced by the five-passenger bus seen parked at the Belfry Depot. (Courtesy of Montana Department of Transportation).

Bridger to Washoe with stops at Bridger, Belfry, and Bearcreek. The bus route was extended to include Red Lodge in 1934. Passenger service on the NP was also suffering and in February 1933, less than a year after the MW&S retired its McKeen, triweekly rail service on the NP from Billings to Bridger was terminated as well.[11]

Even though passenger rail service to Belfry had ended, maintaining the appearance of the depot and the surrounding six-acre park was just as important to William Bunney as it had been to Frank Hall. From the railroad's earliest days, Hall had used Japanese section-crew laborers to maintain the gardens, but due to austerity measures, by 1940, the depot was down to a single full-time Japanese gardener who resided in one of the depot's basement apartments. A well-liked and valued member of the community this individual had maintained the grounds for many years. But as tensions between the United States and Japan began to rise just prior to the Second World War, locals noticed that a well-dressed, briefcase-toting Japanese man would periodically come to visit. What the two men discussed is unknown. He may have been an insurance salesman for all they knew, but it looked suspicious. When Federal agents came and hauled the groundskeeper off to an internment camp at Fort Missoula in 1942, people believed their suspicions had been confirmed. Sadly, the whole episode was probably just "war time hysteria," but without a groundskeeper, the park and gardens inevitably fell into disrepair.[12]

The railroad continued its bus service until the MW&S ceased operations and the bus route was sold to an ex-employee. The railcar Bear Creek was junked in Belfry after its retirement. After scrapping the engine and running gear the car body was used as a storage shed alongside the engine house; a sad reminder of its glorious past. Sixty years later part of Bear Creek could still be found slowly rusting away in the weeds near where it once worked and served the communities of the upper Clarks Fork and Bear Creek valleys.

10

"A Lack of Sufficient Revenue"

ALTHOUGH FRIENDLY RELATIONS WITH THE NP GAVE THE MW&S a chance to prosper, its operational problems continued and the railroad soon suffered its third fatality. Edwin Kose, a handsome young man who lived on his parent's farm not far from Belfry, was hired as a brakeman shortly after returning home from the war in Europe, where he had served in the Ninety-First Infantry Division during the Meuse-Argonne Offensive "without receiving a scratch." On March 30, 1922, Kose was making his last run before being laid off due to another coal miners' strike and was riding in the caboose as his train pulled into Belfry after making the downhill run from the mines. Although there were no witnesses, it appears Kose left the caboose as the train rounded the curve into Belfry in order to release the brake retainers on the cars. As Kose went about his work, Engineer Charles Burns saw a kink in the rails and threw the train into emergency braking. The jolt of the sudden brake application apparently caused Kose to fall under the train. According to witnesses who found him, he was "cut square in two."[1]

Kose was buried in the Belfry cemetery and because negligence on the part of the railroad could not be proven, his horrified parents received only $7,100 from the railroad rather than the more customary $25,000. Stunned by the loss of his only son, Edwin's father died the following year. Devastated by the traumatic loss of her son and husband, Edwin's heartbroken mother died a year later. The immediate result of the accident was the establishment of a policy that prohibited the release of retainers before a train came to a complete stop.[2]

***Facing*, Sun-kinked rails like these were the cause of Edwin Kose's death in March 1922. This view down the Bear Creek valley was taken about three and a half miles west of Belfry near mile post 16. A short train with a derailed combine can be seen in the distance. (General Photograph Collection, Railroad Museum of Pennsylvania, PHMC).**

Later that year, on November 8, company president Frank S. Gannon, passed away at his home in New York at the age of seventy-one after having suffered a stroke two years earlier. During his funeral service the railroad ceased all activity for two minutes in respect for a man who was well known and respected by the people of Belfry. Gannon, who had helped guide the company through its difficult early years, was replaced by Vice President Morris A. Zook, a civil engineer and graduate of Phillip Gallaher's alma mater, the Polytechnic College of Pennsylvania. Zook lived in Plainfield, New Jersey, not far from the company's New York City office and, like Gannon, had previously worked for the Erie Railroad where he developed an extensive knowledge of railroad construction and economics. In 1910, while working as a consultant and expert witness, he had testified in support of the MW&S during the contentious rate hearing case in federal court.[3]

The 1920s were a time of periodic labor unrest for both the MW&S and the mines. Operational shutdowns caused by occasional washouts were a continuing headache as well. In May 1922, one such event, described by the *Bridger Times* as being caused by a "veritable cloudburst," took out several sections of track south of Bridger. A little over a month later, on July 1, the Railway Employees' Department, a division of the American Federation of Labor, went on strike, and more than 400,000 shopmen across the country walked off the job. The strike's lingering effects hampered operations for more than a year. Then, in September 1924, a mysterious fire, presumed to be arson, once again reduced Montana Coal & Iron's tipple at the Smith mine to a pile of smoldering rubble. The fire caused only a brief production hiatus as the structure was quickly replaced by the tipple from the abandoned Clark's Fork mine near Fromberg. Despite these interruptions, as the nation's economy began to recover, the MW&S averaged twenty-five to thirty-five carloads

Edward Bunney's improvements to the MW&S included the addition of rock ballast. This view taken at the south end of the Belfry yard in September 1929 shows a section of line ballasted with neatly manicured river rock. River rock appears to have been widely used by the MW&S as anomalous rounded cobbles can still be found along many parts of the old roadbed. (General Photograph Collection, Railroad Museum of Pennsylvania, PHMC).

per day. Freight totals for 1925 included 396,820 tons of coal, 10,766 tons of agricultural products, 155 tons of livestock and 19 tons of manufactured goods, and business continued to improve. During September 1927, for example, the railroad handled forty or more cars per day, including 1,015 loads of coal, fifty-nine cars of wheat, and forty-four cars of sugar beets.[4]

The company's steady cash flow and fewer mishaps during the twenties allowed it to purchase two additional locomotives. The first of these, a Mikado-type (2-8-2), built by the Baldwin Locomotive Works in 1924, was a departure from previous designs. It was both heavier and more powerful, and the trailing truck under the cab allowed it to operate in reverse with less risk of derailment, making it suitable for switching. But

One of three locomotives purchased from Baldwin during the 1920s, Number 20 was unique in being the MW&S's only 2-8-2 Mikado. All three locomotives acquired during the 1920s were delivered in Baldwin's 291 paint scheme with aluminum stripping and lettering highlighting an olive-green cab, tender, cylinders, and bands around the sand and steam domes. The boilers were probably finished in either Russian or American iron (light gray). (DeGolyer Library, SMU, Everett DeGolyer Jr. Railroad Collection).

Still wearing shiny factory paint the crew of Number 12 pose with their new engine while they await their next assignment in the Belfry yard. (CCHS&M-Kidwell Collection).

apparently the Mikado's capabilities were not sufficiently impressive to warrant a reorder. The railroad's final locomotive, acquired three years later, reverted to an earlier design identical to Number 10. The three Baldwin locomotives purchased during the 1920s allowed the retirement of the railroad's remaining prewar engines and would carry the company through to its final days of operation.[5]

With upgraded track and roadbed, by the late 1920s, operations on the MW&S had improved considerably, but there were still issues that made it a demanding road to work on. One persistent problem was the steep grades near the mines. This became an even more serious issue when there was ice or snow on the rails. Brakemen had learned that they needed to place blocks of wood, or whatever was available, in front of the wheels between moves or cars would often slide down the slick rails even with the brakes locked. On one wintry night, a crew working the Foster Gulch spur found it necessary to set out a car that had faulty brakes. After uncoupling it from the train, and before the wheels could be blocked, the car began to roll down the line toward Belfry. A shouted warning sent brakemen sprinting for the nearest phone. Hugh Routh, the Belfry stationmaster, was roused and ran out to make sure the yard switches were aligned for the mainline. He then waited for the fugitive car to make its appearance. In time, the clickety-clack of steel wheels on jointed rail echoed in the distance. Minutes later the car made its appearance rounding the curve into Belfry covered in snow and looking like a ghost in the night after its nine-mile flight down the valley. To the amazement of all, it negotiated the curve into the yard and rolled on through before disappearing into the darkness. The next morning the car was found sitting on the mainline a few miles north of Belfry. It must have seemed incredible that after its nighttime jaunt through Bearcreek, past farms and houses, and over several unprotected grade crossings, there were no injuries or damage to report.[6]

During the late 1910s and early 1920s, changes were afoot for NP that would soon impact the MW&S. Having been almost totally dependent on Red Lodge for its coal supply in eastern Montana and North Dakota for over twenty years, toward the end of the First World War, the NP began to investigate potential alternative sources. A January 1918 evaluation by the Northwest Improvement Company estimated that remaining reserves in Red Lodge would last about twelve years. This determination, along with rising production costs and frequent labor unrest, prompted the NP to begin a search for a new fuel source. After investigating several options, the company elected to begin development of a thick, near-surface coal seam located about thirty miles south of Forsyth, Montana. Referred to as the "Rosebud seam" this bed of subbituminous coal was over twenty feet thick and could be mined from the surface, using large shovels and draglines that were just then being developed. Engineers estimated that Rosebud coal could be mined for less than one dollar per ton, a huge savings over the three dollars per ton cost of Red Lodge coal. The disadvantage of this new fuel was that Rosebud coal had significantly lower heat content, which forced the NP to modify the firebox grates and ash pans in their locomotives. This seemingly minor change would in turn have a profound effect on the MW&S.[7]

The NP's decision to switch to Rosebud coal was quickly felt in Red Lodge when the West Side Mine was closed on July 31, 1924, due to mining difficulties and rising costs. A month later the NP completed a branch line from Forsyth to their new mine called Colstrip. With an initial production rate of 50,000 tons per month, Rosebud coal was soon powering NP freight locomotives from Mandan, North Dakota, to Spokane, Washington. By 1928 Colstrip was producing around 1 million tons per year; five years later, production had increased to 2.5 million tons. The increased production allowed closure of the East Side Mine in Red Lodge in June 1932, thus ending the town's more than forty-year history as a major coal mining center. A study completed the next year estimated that the switch to surface mining at Colstrip was saving the NP about $1 million annually.[8]

While the NP was transitioning to its new fuel supply, the stock market crash of October 1929 plunged the country into the Great Depression. For the Bear Creek mines, the damaging effects of the economic downturn were exacerbated by the increasing availability of natural gas. As pipeline construction spread across the state, homeowners and businesses alike began switching to this cleaner, more convenient fuel; commercial coal sales suffered accordingly. These factors were reflected in

Although production from Anaconda's Washoe no. 2 mine had become sporadic by the 1920s, this photo shows several boxcars ready for loading and evidence of new construction. (CCHS&M-Kidwell Collection).

Bear Creek's total production, which went from 465,768 tons in 1929 to 296,582 tons in 1931, nearly a 40 percent drop. In May 1931, the mine operators once again filed a complaint with the railroad commission and requested a rate reduction, claiming that the railroad was making excessive profits. When the commission investigated, it found that the railroad had suffered a decrease in revenue similar to that of the mines and refused to make a rate adjustment. With their appeal for a reduced tariff denied, by 1932 the mines were in dire straits. The first to suspend operations was the Smokeless & Sootless. This was followed by the final closure of the Bear Creek and International mines, which had been only minor contributors following their change in ownership in the 1920s. Anaconda hung on for a while longer but, after suffering an underground fire, finally shut down its Washoe mining operations in 1938. The remaining mines struggled on.[9]

Due to the higher quality of Bear Creek coal and the importance of maintaining more than one supply source, after shutting down its mining operation in Red Lodge, the NP was anxious to keep the Bear Creek mines and the MW&S in operation. With this in mind, in 1932, William Bunney, who had assumed the MW&S presidency in September after the passing of Morris Zook, began to work on agreements that would fundamentally change the relationship between the two railroads. The first agreement granted trackage rights to the NP over the twelve miles of MW&S track between Bridger and Belfry. The second guaranteed a reduced rate for the shipment of coal purchased by the NP.[10]

The trackage rights agreement, approved by the Interstate Commerce Commission (ICC) in early 1933, was different from most in that it established that MW&S trains would no longer operate north of Belfry. This restricted all MW&S operations to the track between Belfry and the mines. Due to the NP's larger, heavier locomotives, this change necessitated the strengthening of trestles and bridges, and flattening the curvature of the Belfry wye. Several yard tracks were added in Belfry as well. NP covered the cost of all of these improvements.[11]

The reduced rate Bunney agreed to for NP coal was a flat "switching charge" of $5.50 per car rather than the current tariff of $0.59 per ton for commercial coal. The assumption being that profits from commercial coal haulage would cover any potential loss incurred by the reduced rate given the NP. The bulk of the coal that the MW&S agreed to haul for the NP was slack, which the mines were willing to sell cheaply because it was considered a waste product, generally not salable on the commercial market. Due to the changes the NP had been forced to make to its locomotives to allow them to burn Rosebud coal, slack coal from Bear Creek was now a viable alternative. The lower costs agreed to by the MW&S and the mines made slack from Bear Creek price competitive. In 1932, the NP agreed to begin buying 100,000 tons per year. It was a small volume when compared to the output of Colstrip, but the agreement was crucial for the survival of the MW&S and the mines it served. Because of its higher heat content, Bear Creek coal was used by most NP passenger

Number 20 in factory-fresh paint running light on the outskirts of Bearcreek circa 1925. (General Photograph Collection, Railroad Museum of Pennsylvania, PHMC).

In this undated photo, two crewmen can be seen conversing in the cab while Number 20, with white "extra" flags showing, pauses along the Clarks Fork River near the water tank north of Belfry. (General Photograph Collection, Railroad Museum of Pennsylvania, PHMC).

At the time of abandonment there were three cabooses on the property numbered 1, 2, and 4. NP records indicate that in October 1933, a 1500-series bay-window caboose (1518) was sold to the MW&S. It is believed that this car was given the number 3. Since there is no record of this car serving on the MW&S, it may have been traded back to the NP shortly after its arrival for the 1600-series caboose seen here, which was given the number 4. Since no record of this transaction appears to exist, the history of caboose number 3 remains a mystery. (Courtesy of California State Railroad Library & Archives).

locomotives running between Jamestown, North Dakota and Spokane, Washington. It was also used by local and branch line engines between Mandan, North Dakota, and Missoula, Montana.[12]

Initially, the agreements were a "win-win-win" solution for the NP, the mines, and the MW&S. With operations now limited to the nine-mile branch from Belfry to the mines, the MW&S's three new locomotives easily handled the steady stream of traffic that originated from Montana Coal & Iron's Smith and Foster Gulch operations. Eagle Coal continued to generate some traffic, and until 1938, there were occasional shipments from Anaconda's Washoe mine as well. About the time the Anaconda operation shut down, the Smokeless & Sootless mine was reopened under a lease agreement with the Homer Coal Company. This brought renewed activity to the McCarthy branch and replaced some of the shipments lost due to the mine closure at Washoe.[13]

Although the agreement with the NP allowed Montana Coal & Iron to maintain production at around 300,000 tons per year, the benefit to

The engineer glances at the camera while working a switch job in the Belfry yard. After nineteen years of service, its factory paint long gone, Number 10 is looking a bit worse for the wear in this December 1940 view. (PAc 97-93.10394, MWS 10 Belfry, Montana Historical Society Photograph Archives).

The fireman watches for a signal as Number 20 works the yard at Belfry. This photo probably dates from the late thirties or early forties (Courtesy of California State Railroad Library & Archives).

Good photos of Number 12 are rare. In this shot from July1939, it sits in front of the Belfry engine house with its smokebox door open undergoing light maintenance. The low building on the left houses the winch for the coaling tower. A corrugated metal tank used for locomotive sand can be seen above Number 12's sand dome. (PAc 97-93.02935, MWS 12 Belfry 7/30/39, Montana Historical Society Photograph Archives).

the MW&S was fleeting. As the Great Depression grew worse commercial coal sales continued their inevitable decline. The NP contract kept the mines busy, but by 1942, the switching charge the MW&S was collecting had become a money-losing proposition. An analysis by the NP showed that the revenue derived from commercial coal shipments on the MW&S had decreased by 25 percent during the past ten years, resulting in a $41,000 decrease in annual operating income. An internal NP engineering analysis noted that "it is obvious that the switching charge . . . cannot possibly support the operation of this short line. As soon as the commercial coal decreases to a critical point this little railroad will have to fold up."[14]

As the company struggled along with an ever-decreasing revenue stream, in late 1939 the original thirty-year gold bonds issued in 1909 reached maturity. The amount due was $457,000, but the company didn't have the money. Seeking relief, the MW&S petitioned the ICC and the District Federal Court for a financial readjustment, which was

In this July 1939 photo, the white flags on Number 12's smokebox suggest that all trains on the MW&S operated as "extras." An indication of the railroad's ongoing maintenance program can be seen in the new and badly decayed ties stacked alongside the tracks. A string of company gondolas is visible in the distance. (PAc 97-93.02936, MWS 12 Belfry, Montana Historical Society Photograph Archives).

allowed under a recently passed provision of the Bankruptcy Act of 1938. In March 1940, with 85 percent of the bondholders in agreement, the court approved the restructuring of the company's debt and allowed it to redeem just 15 percent of its outstanding bonds (about $70,000), while extending the maturity date on the remaining bonds ten years. The ruling also allowed for a reduction in the interest rate from 5 to 3 percent. This decision gave the MW&S some breathing room, but its long-term financial situation remained uncertain. That uncertainty ended in 1942, when the exigencies associated with wartime production began to rapidly increase the need for coal.[15]

Facing top, Beginning in 1933, the NP operated all trains running between Bridger and Belfry. In this shot from November 1940, Number 1903, a W-2 class Mikado, is seen pulling into the Belfry yard burdened with seventy empties destined for the mines in the Bear Creek Valley. (PAc 97-93.10388, NP X1903W arriving Belfry, Montana Historical Society Photograph Archives).

After performing an air brake test, NP extra 1903E is ready to depart. The town of Belfry and the Occident grain elevator are visible in the far distance on the left. (PAc 97-93.10387, NP X1903E in Belfry 11/27/40, Montana Historical Society Photograph Archives).

In this 1938 view of Montana Coal & Iron's Smith Mine the trestle used to access the workings on the south side of the valley can be seen on the right. This was the site of the 1943 explosion that killed seventy-four miners and one rescue worker. (Courtesy Western Heritage Center, Billings, Montana).

As with many industries, the Second World War saved the mines and railroad from their Depression-time woes. As war production ramped up, commercial coal sales increased along with purchases by the NP. With three engines in good working order, the MW&S began employing two shifts to keep up with the increasing output. The bulk of the production still came from Montana Coal & Iron's Smith and Foster Gulch mines, with lesser output from the Eagle and the old Smokeless & Sootless property now called the Brophy Coal Company. But as production was being pushed to its limits, on February 27, 1943, the Smith mine suffered a massive underground explosion and cave-in that took the lives of seventy-four miners. It was the worst coal mining disaster in the state's history, and it resulted in that mine's permanent closure. The tragic loss of so many miners had an immediate and devastating effect on the small close-knit communities of Bearcreek and Washoe, where virtually everyone knew someone who had lost a family member.[16]

Despite the damage the explosion caused to both the mine and the local communities, Montana Coal & Iron still managed to ship 477,000 tons in 1943; 150,000 tons going to army and navy installations and another 150,000 to the NP. In 1944, coal production, mainly from the Foster Gulch mine, peaked at 576,000 tons, or about forty cars per day. But with the war's end in sight, by mid-1945 demand began to drop off. Only 500,000 tons were shipped in 1945, and by 1947, coal demand had returned to Depression-era levels. It was a harbinger of things to come when the Eagle Coal Company filed for Voluntary Dissolution at the end of 1947, leaving the railroad with only two customers. Since much of the profit generated during the war was used to retire the remaining $387,000 in first-mortgage bonds due in 1949, there remained little in the way of cash reserves to sustain the railroad through the hard times to come.[17]

As the 1940s wore on, commercial coal sales remained depressed. In an attempt to reduce costs and remain competitive with cheap natural gas that was beginning to flood the market, Montana Coal & Iron began a strip-mining operation along Scotch Coulee and in Foster Gulch. These efforts met with only limited success. Due to the steep topography, the amount of coal that could be mined was limited, and as the coal was dug from the hillsides, the volume of overburden that had to be removed rapidly increased. This added to the cost of mining and resulted in contamination as the overlying soil and siltstone increasingly sloughed into the coal as it was mined. Complaints from customers soon brought these operations to a close. The strip mine in Scotch Coulee was abandoned in 1947; the Foster Gulch operation shut down in February 1948. Despite these setbacks Montana Coal & Iron managed to produce around 200,000 tons per year through the late 1940s, much of it going to the NP, but as production from the mines gradually dropped off, so did the fortunes of the MW&S.[18]

Trouble loomed in 1950, when the Great Western Sugar Company in Billings, a steady customer for over forty years, converted to natural gas and did not renew its contract with Montana Coal & Iron. Within a few months, both Anaconda Copper and Montana Power followed suit. In December of the next year, the Ideal Cement plant near Three Forks also converted to natural gas and as the NP continued its conversion from steam to diesel power, sales to the railroad began to decline as well.[19]

The reduction in coal sales was telling, and for the MW&S, the end came quickly. By 1951, with fewer than ten cars being loaded each day, coal drags were cut back to an every other day schedule. In an effort to reduce costs, additional austerity measures were implemented, including layoffs and doubling up on jobs. When William Bunney retired and William Gullickson took over as company president in September 1951, even more severe measures were taken that included wage cuts, much reduced track maintenance, and a reduction to only two trains per week. Gullickson knew what he was doing, having worked for the MW&S since 1928, but despite his best efforts, the railroad continued to hemorrhage money. Gullickson appealed to the county government for tax relief and lobbied the state for higher tariffs without success. By 1953, the track was in such poor condition that a serious accident had become a real concern. The final blow came when the NP announced that it would not renew its coal contract after June 30, 1953.[20]

NP's announcement forced the MW&S board of directors in New York to make a decision. After enduring losses for the previous seven years, they had no choice but to call it quits and shut down the railroad. With little advance warning, the last train ran on July 30, 1953. An embargo was placed on the line three days later that allowed the MW&S to refuse cars from other railroads due to its unsafe condition, effectively ending cooperation with the NP. When asked about the decision, Gullickson told the *Billings Gazette* that the railroad had hauled only 6,191 tons of coal during the first five months of 1953 and had suffered a loss of nearly $25,000 in the process. A month later, on September 4, the MW&S filed a petition for abandonment with the ICC.[21]

An abandonment hearing was held in Billings on March 8, 1954, before both the ICC and Montana Board of Railroad Commissioners. Numerous parties testified in protest including the United Mine Workers and representatives from both the Brophy and Montana Coal & Iron Company mines. The mine operators complained that the cost of trucking their coal to Red Lodge or Bridger would force them out of business and the UMW stated that at least three hundred jobs would be lost as a result of the shutdown. William Romek, representing Montana Coal

During the summer of 1955, just months before meeting the scrapper's torch, Number 10 rests cold and silent in the Belfry yard, a sad reminder of the railroad's glory days (DeGolyer Library, SMU, Everett DeGolyer, Jr. Railroad Collection).

& Iron, let it be known that his company was contemplating a $150,000 modernization project that would allow it to compete favorably with other mines, but the investment could only be sanctioned if the railroad continued to operate.[22]

William Gullickson, whose position as president had been terminated in January 1954 following an unspecified disagreement with company officials in New York, testified on the railroad's behalf. In response to the various complaints, Gullickson stated that the abandonment decision was based on "a lack of sufficient revenue, deterioration of the system, both in its trackage and locomotion, and the prohibitive cost of rendering these in a serviceable [*sic*] condition." He went on to say that few ties had been replaced since 1947 and that all three locomotives needed work. Gullickson estimated the cost to repair the engines at $18,000, and went on to state that with no hope of making a profit, he did not know where the company could borrow the money to get the work done. When asked about possible alternatives, he said they had evaluated the possibility of buying a diesel locomotive but found it to be too expensive. He also pointed out that the company's management had been trying to sell the railroad to the NP for several years without success. A financial statement provided by the company's New York attorney showed that as of March 3, 1954, the MW&S had less than $845 cash on hand and that there were still bills to be paid.[23]

Complainants were given until April 26 to submit their briefs and after reviewing these the ICC approved the abandonment petition in May. Due to the Montana Railroad Commission's refusal to sanction abandonment, final authorization was not given until March 1955. The ICC stipulated that should any party come forward within forty days with plans to continue operations and offer to purchase the line at net salvage value, the company must make the sale. While grass grew between the rails and ranchers built fences across the right-of-way, the railroad lay dormant awaiting a buyer. In Belfry, the three Baldwin locomotives sat cold and silent near the engine house among a menagerie of worn-out cars and equipment. Final abandonment did not begin until October, when the Hyman-Michaels Company of Chicago began tearing up the track. By the end of the year, the locomotives, equipment, and track were all gone, leaving the three depots, engine house, timber trestles, cement culverts, and an accumulation of almost fifty years of black cinders along the right-of-way as the MW&S's only physical reminders.[24]

In 2012, more than a hundred years after Frank Hall's struggle to build a railroad to Cooke City had ended, state and local historians had the Belfry Depot, one of the few remaining monuments to his efforts, added to the National Register of Historic Places. Long may it stand as a tribute to Hall, Maguire, Gannon, Bunney, Gullickson, and all the other railroaders who kept the trains rolling and helped fuel the state's industry, heat its homes and businesses, and add much to the wealth of the Treasure State.[25]

EPILOGUE

DURING THE ENTIRE FORTY-SEVEN-YEAR HISTORY OF BOTH the Montana, Wyoming & Southern and Yellowstone Park Railroads, the companies were overshadowed, manipulated, and controlled by the Northern Pacific. From the beginning, outright hostility was manifest in the efforts of Howard Elliott and James N. Hill's attempt to crush Frank Hall and his fledgling enterprise through harassment, intimidation, and limiting his car supply. When, in 1913, the NP abandoned its plans for a branch line to Bear Creek, hostility gradually morphed into benign indifference as the NP made no special effort to help or hinder MW&S operations.

As coal production increased during the First World War, the NP begrudgingly began to cooperate with the MW&S and was finally forced by government edict to work with the short line in order to maximize wartime production and efficiency. This interaction and changes in management at both companies, along with the exigencies of the postwar depression, led to a period of cooperation exemplified by the establishment of joint agency in 1921 and shared passenger service a few years later.

As the country slipped into the Great Depression, cooperation became full-scale support when the NP saw the need to prop up the mines and the railroad that served them. Had Howard Elliott and the NP assumed this posture in 1905 and elected to support the YPRR rather than attempting to eliminate it, the history of this little short line might have been quite different. Although YPRR's shoddy construction and financial instability during its early years were a huge liability, had the NP supported Hall's railroad by supplying the needed cars and perhaps even loaning much-needed equipment, such as plows and flangers for winter operations, the YPRR would probably have been able to generate enough cash flow to overcome its disabilities. A positive relationship with the NP might have provoked Elijah Smith into applying his considerable influence in support of the railroad as well. This, in turn, could have resulted in even greater output from the mines. Taken together these changes may have allowed Frank Hall to retain his position as company president and allowed him to pursue his dream of a rail line to Cooke City and Yellowstone National Park. Although such an extension probably would not have been an economic success, it would have undoubtedly stimulated the expansion of agriculture and mining in both Wyoming and Montana.

In the end, a series of inevitable factors combined to spell doom for the MW&S. Due to its inability to expand its purpose beyond that of a coal hauling industrial railroad, when coal, especially expensive coal from underground mines, fell out of favor, the railroad's fate was sealed. The final blow came when the NP canceled its supply contract with the Bear Creek mines. Ironically, due to the advent of efficient diesel-electric locomotives, it was the NP, without malice, that wrote the final chapter in the history of the tough little short line railroad that Frank Hall built to serve the mines and people of the Clarks Fork and Bear Creek valleys.

APPENDIX A

The Yellowstone Park Railway (1900–1940)

FOLLOWING FRANK HALL'S DEPARTURE IN LATE 1899, AND subsequent negotiations between the Turner brothers, John Kendrick, and Charles Mellen, the Northern Pacific (NP) agreed to operate the Yellowstone Park Railway (YPRy) under contract for ten years. At the end of that period the agreement was extended to December 31, 1911. When the NP announced it would cease operations at the end of 1911, the mine operators filed a complaint with the Montana Railroad Commission. Although the commission refused to intervene, with the shutdown of the railroad imminent and the welfare of the local communities at stake, J. C. Williams, the YPRy's secretary-treasurer, offered to drop all rental charges if the NP would continue to operate the line. The NP agreed to this arrangement and operations continued on that basis until April 15, 1913.[1]

Between 1900 and 1913 the YPRy functioned as part of the NP, and according to local historian Edward L. Nowels, two locomotives based in Livingston were routinely assigned to the branch. Most often these were number 403, a D-6 class Mogul (2-6-0), and number 662, a class "B" American-Standard (4-4-0). Operations on the branch were demanding and due to the steep grades between Chimney Rock and Hoffman, these locomotives were capable of moving only four or five loaded cars at a time to the divide between Meadow and Trail Creek. When fifteen or more cars had been assembled, they would be cautiously worked down grade to Chestnut. Although NP crews were for the most part diligent and careful, on one occasion when work had been delayed at Chimney Rock and the crew was in a hurry to finish before dark, they neglected to hook up the air brake line on the last thirteen cars of an eighteen-car train. When the train headed down grade to Chestnut and the engineer made his first brake application the crew immediately knew that they were in trouble. Despite a desperate scrambling attempt to tie down the hand brakes, the train was soon careening down the line out of control. According to Nowels, the train was "squealing around curves and swinging wide, and hitting only the high spots on the short tangents." At some point, after the train broke in two, the runaway cars derailed on a curve scattering coal over several acres of the Harrison ranch. Due to their negligence, the crew spent thirty days off payroll.[2]

Despite improvements made by the NP, operations on the YPRy remained a challenge. The worst wreck the line experienced occurred in 1903 when, after dropping a caboose and a load of lumber on the mainline, a crew switching at the Hoffman mine had a loaded coal car break loose. The car gained speed quickly and a shouted warning from the conductor prompted passengers Mr. and Mrs. McCormick to jump from the caboose just before the collision. The impact sent the coal, lumber, and caboose rolling down grade toward Chimney Rock with ever increasing speed. The runaway sped past the Chimney Rock mine tipple, jumped Trail Creek, and piled up in a heap three hundred feet beyond the end of the tracks. Fortunately, there were no injuries to be reported.

When the NP ceased operations in April 1913, the only remaining mine on Trail Creek was the old Cook and Bell, or Maxey brothers', mine at Chimney Rock. Daniel Maxey had opened this mine in 1889, sold it to A. B. Cook around 1895 and then reacquired the property at a foreclosure sale in 1903. He put the mine back into operation with the help of his four sons John, William, David, and George. In late 1912, or early 1913, ownership of the mine was transferred to the Washington and Montana Coal and Development Company. According to railroad historian Thomas T. Taber, this new company was headed up by J. C. Williams and George Maxey of Montana, and A. A. Kraft and M. M. Kelliher of Spokane. A November 1912 article in the *Anaconda Standard* indicates that two Spokane businessmen named Lloyd and Sherman were involved as well. When the NP ceased operations, George Turner, who had become president of the YPRy, agreed to lease the railroad to the Washington and Montana Coal and Development Company.[3]

When the new company assumed operations, it contracted with the NP to continue providing the necessary trains and crews. This arrangement was short-lived as the NP soon deemed the tracks to be unsafe and refused to allow their locomotives or personnel on the line. This forced the mining company to acquire its own motive power. The first locomotive purchased was a small, aged saddle-tank (0-4-0T) engine reportedly built by the H. K. Porter Company of Pittsburgh that had previously been employed by the Anaconda Company at its coal mining operation at Electric, Montana. This little locomotive was capable of moving only one loaded car at a time from Chimney Rock to the divide. When three or four cars were assembled, the train was hauled to Chestnut. According to the Maxey brothers, this often resulted in an exciting ride because as the train eased its way down the grade along Meadow Creek, the cars would begin to push the little engine. As the speed increased, whichever brother was at the throttle would throw the locomotive into reverse while his sibling attempted to "club down" the hand brakes. Sometimes this worked, but due to the line's poor condition, derailments were common. William and George Maxey explained that for some reason the coupler on the locomotive was lower than the car couplers and when the cars began to bounce the coupler on the first car would slide on top of the locomotive coupler. This caused the engine's front drivers to lift off the tracks. When the engine derailed and rolled on its side the brothers would shut things down and make the long walk home. The next day, they would return with jacks and timber, put the engine back on the rails and complete the trip. One of them commented, "It was fancy railroading all right, but nobody ever got hurt." Around 1915 a second locomotive was acquired. This engine was another diminutive saddle-tank (0-6-0T) locomotive that reportedly came from Anaconda's East Helena smelter.[4]

According to Nowels, shortly after Washington and Montana Coal leased the YPRy, the railroad was sold to Livingston businessman Charles Garnier and Wilfred Johnson of Lewistown for $50,000. Garnier and Johnson hoped to make a quick profit by selling the line to the Milwaukee Road which they believed was about to build a branch line from Bozeman to Gardiner via Trail Creek. When the rumored Milwaukee branch line failed to materialize and production from the Maxey mine at Chimney Rock dropped off, Garnier and Johnson began to look for a way

This 0-4-0T is believed to have come from Anaconda Copper Mining's coal mine and coking operation at Electric, Montana. It was sold to Washington and Montana Coal and Development Company around 1913. This photo was taken in October 1931, long after the railroad had ceased operations. (Museum of the Rockies, RVN04037, Ron V. Nixon).

out. According to Taber, Garnier and Johnson petitioned the Montana Railroad Commission for permission to abandon the line in 1917, but the commission refused to authorize abandonment claiming they had no jurisdiction because the YPRy was not a common carrier. Nowels makes no mention of the abandonment petition but states that rising steel prices during the First World War prompted Garnier and Johnson to sell the line to a scrapper.

Believing they still had a legitimate lease, the Maxey brothers met the scrapping crew with brandished shotguns and ordered them off the property. The scrappers departed but soon returned with a work train. This time, the Maxeys blocked the line with their small steam engine and again forced the scrappers to retreat. Nowels asserts that the issue went to court and was not resolved until the spring of 1918. The resulting agreement allowed all but the first two miles of track to be removed. The

The second locomotive acquired by the Washington and Montana Coal and Development Company was an 0-6-0T. This engine reportedly came from Anaconda's East Helena smelter. Presumed to be an H. K. Porter product, it may have been put to use by the Maxey brothers around 1915. With its drive and connecting rods removed, this 1931 photo finds the engine rusting away near Chestnut. (Museum of the Rockies, RVN04036, Ron V. Nixon).

Maxey brothers purchased that section from the scrapping company and continued to operate the line after abandoning their operation at Chimney Rock and opening the Meadow Creek no. 2 mine located about two miles from Chestnut. In 1921, the Maxey brothers sold the no. 2 mine to the Meadow Creek Coal Company, which continued to operate it until 1924.

The sequence of events outlined here is put to question by an official NP map of Chestnut dated May 1917. That map depicts the YPRy right-of-way with the word *removed* next to it, clearly indicating that by that date the entire line had been scrapped. If the NP map is dismissed as the work of a misinformed draftsman, then it seems likely that at least two miles of the YPRy remained in place until the Meadow Creek mine closed in 1924. When operations ceased both locomotives were unceremoniously parked on a siding near Chestnut and left to rust away. Taber claims that due to confusion regarding the line's ownership, the rails and locomotives were not removed until 1940.[5]

At some point the YPRy acquired the moniker "Turkey Trail Railroad." How or when this came about is unknown, but this unflattering name, no doubt an allusion to the line's poor track, appears to have been widely used by both locals and NP trainmen for much of the railroad's existence. The line's original name, and Frank Hall and William Turner's visionary goal of building a railroad to Yellowstone National Park, was by then just a distant memory.

APPENDIX B
Coal

COAL CLASSIFICATION

Coal is classified or ranked, based on its hardness, moisture, and heat content, measured in British thermal units (BTUs). Anthracite is the hardest and highest class, while lignite, or brown coal, is the softest and lowest class; bituminous and subbituminous occupy intermediate steps between the two. Within each of these ranks, there are numerous subdivisions, but in general, as the hardness increases from lignite to subbituminous, bituminous, and anthracite, the moisture decreases and the heat content increases. Broadly speaking, bituminous coal was the preferred fuel for steam locomotives.

COAL SIZES

The size of the coal being removed from mines has an important bearing on its commercial value. Larger pieces are generally preferred. The smallest size, called "slack," is often considered a waste product, unsalable in the commercial market because its small size causes it to burn too rapidly. It also tends to fall through standard stove grates. Although definitions vary somewhat, the following sizes were established for bituminous coal by the US Department of Energy:

- Run of mine: passes through 8-inch holes
- Lump: passes through 5-inch holes
- Egg: passes through 5-inch holes and retained by 2-inch holes
- Nut: passes through 2-inch holes and retained by 1.25-inch holes
- Stoker coal: passes through 1.25-inch holes and retained by 0.75-inch holes
- Slack: passes through 0.75-inch holes and under

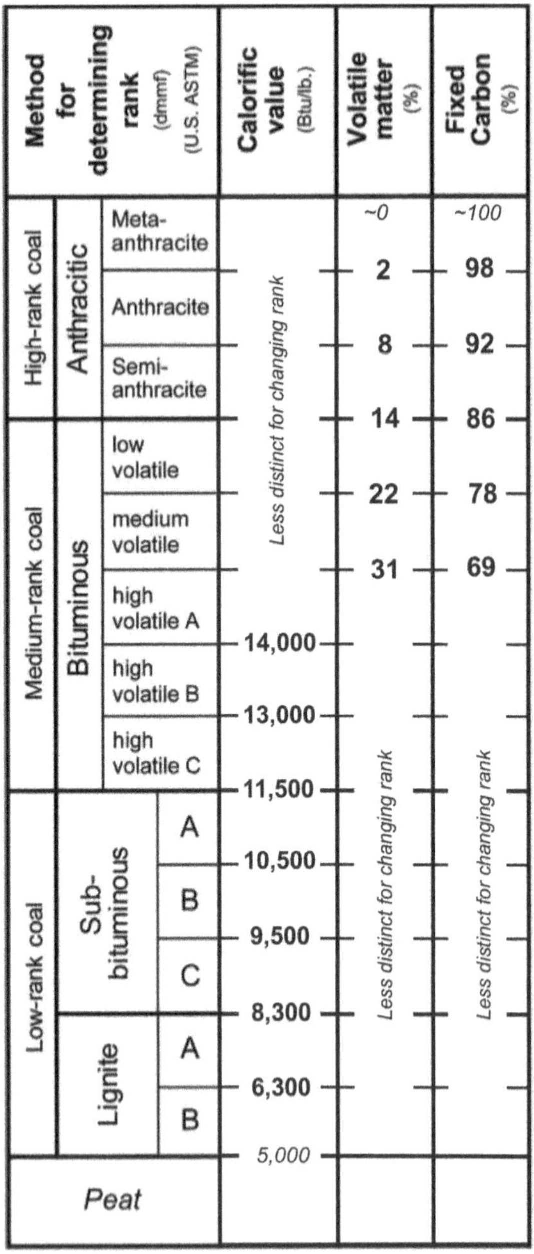

Coal classification chart. (Kentucky Geological Survey).

(References pertaining to slack in this volume reflect the Montana Railroad Commission's 1915 definition of slack as "all coal that will pass through a 1½" mesh or through a ¾" bar screen.")[1]

COAL ANALYSES

Each type of coal referred to in this volume had its own particular characteristics. Coal mined at Trail Creek, Bozeman Pass, and near Bridger was deposited about 82 million years ago as part of the Upper Cretaceous Eagle Formation. It is of bituminous rank and has a relatively high heat content which makes it suitable for conversion to coke used for smelting. It was also a preferred locomotive fuel, especially in western Montana, where its low sulfur content served to reduce toxic combustion gases that posed a danger to engine crews in long tunnels. Its principal drawback was its high ash content. Coal's ash content is determined by the volume of noncombustible materials, such as clay, silt, and fine sand, within the coal. Coal with high ash content tends to produce a smoky fire. When used as a locomotive fuel, it forced engine crews to dump locomotive ash pans more frequently.[2]

Coal from the Red Lodge–Bear Creek Coal Field was deposited about 60 million years ago as part of the Paleocene Fort Union Formation and ranges in rank from high-grade subbituminous to low-grade bituminous. Most of the higher-grade coal is found on the Bear Creek side of the field. This coal is slightly inferior to Bozeman Pass coal in terms of heat content but is easier to mine because the beds are thicker and nearly horizontal. Although coal from the Red Lodge–Bear Creek Field generally produces less smoke and ash than coal from Bozeman Pass, the Northern Pacific found that it tends to produce sparks, which forced the NP to take measures to protect the roofs of line side structures and expend a great deal of effort devising spark arrestors for its locomotives. Because Red Lodge coal often has thin layers, or partings, of shale within it, it has a tendency to form "clinkers," which reportedly "took careful and skillful firing to avoid the creation of 'heavy slugs'" that had to be cleared from the firebox grates. It also possesses a relatively high sulfur content. For this reason, after the mines on Bozeman Pass shut down, low-sulfur coal from Roslyn, Washington, was shipped as far east as Helena. This practice ended when Rosebud coal became available in the 1920s.[3]

Aside from being inexpensive to mine, Colstrip (Rosebud) coal produced fewer sparks than Red Lodge coal and had low sulfur and ash contents. The problem with this coal is its low heat content. As discussed elsewhere, conversion to this fuel during the 1920s forced the Northern Pacific to modify the fireboxes of its locomotives. This conversion allowed it to burn slack coal from Bear Creek as well.

Representative analyses of the various coals discussed in this volume are given as follows:

Livingston Coal Field: Trail Creek Area (Hoffman Mine, Storrs Number 3 Bed)[4]

- high-volatile bituminous A, B, C (Eagle Formation, Upper Cretaceous)
- moisture (12.4%); ash (8.51%); sulfur (0.67%); BTU 10,950

Livingston Coal Field: Bozeman Pass Area (Mountain Side Mine, Cokedale Bed)[5]

- high-volatile bituminous A, B, C (Eagle Formation, Upper Cretaceous)
- moisture (5.4%); ash (30.63%); sulfur (0.33%); BTU 9,030

Bridger Coal Field (Bridger Coal & Improvement Co.)[6]

- high-volatile bituminous A, B, C (Eagle Formation, Upper Cretaceous)
- moisture (14.83%); ash (13.35%); sulfur (0.33%); BTU 10,037

Red Lodge Coal Field (East Side Mine, Bed Number 1)[7]

- subbituminous A to high-volatile bituminous C (Fort Union Formation, Paleocene)
- moisture (11.69%); ash (11.98%); sulfur (1.05%); BTU 9,787

Bear Creek Coal Field (Unspecified Mine, Bed Number 3)[8]

- high-volatile bituminous C (Fort Union Formation, Paleocene)
- moisture (8.60%); ash (13.65%); sulfur (2.85%); BTU 11,444

Colstrip: Rosebud Coal Bed (Average of Twenty-Eight Samples)[9]

- subbituminous B to C (Fort Union Formation, Paleocene)
- moisture (24.22%); ash (8.24%); sulfur (0.65%); BTU 8,768

APPENDIX C

Red Lodge–Bear Creek Coal Field: Geology and Mining Methodology

COAL IN THE RED LODGE-BEAR CREEK COAL FIELD OCCURS IN the Fort Union Formation, a geological unit that was deposited during the Paleocene Epoch of the Tertiary Period about 60 million years ago. Comprised of a nearly 8,000-foot-thick sequence of interbedded siltstone, sandstone, and shale, the Fort Union was deposited when south-central Montana was covered by dense forests, swamps, bogs, and slowly meandering rivers and streams. In the Red Lodge–Bear Creek area, coal is found within an 825-foot-thick section composed of mostly sandstone and shale within the Tongue River Member, about 5,700 feet above the base of the formation. Within this 825-foot-thick section, there are nine mineable coal horizons. Some are made up of multiple thin coal beds separated by thin layers of sandstone or shale; others contain a single bed up to twelve feet thick. Aggregate thickness of coal within the section is about 60 feet. The nature and extent of these coal beds was recognized early on, and Red Lodge mining engineers numbered them one through seven starting with the stratigraphically highest. When it was later discovered that two coal horizons had been overlooked, these beds were designated 1 ½ and 4 ½, in order to maintain the preexisting scheme. The same nine coal horizons are present to the east along the upper reaches of Bear Creek.

According to the US Geological Survey, the coal in the Red Lodge–Bear Creek Coal Field is variable in composition and defies simple classification. Samples from various horizons place its rank between high-volatile bituminous "C" and subbituminous "A." A report published in

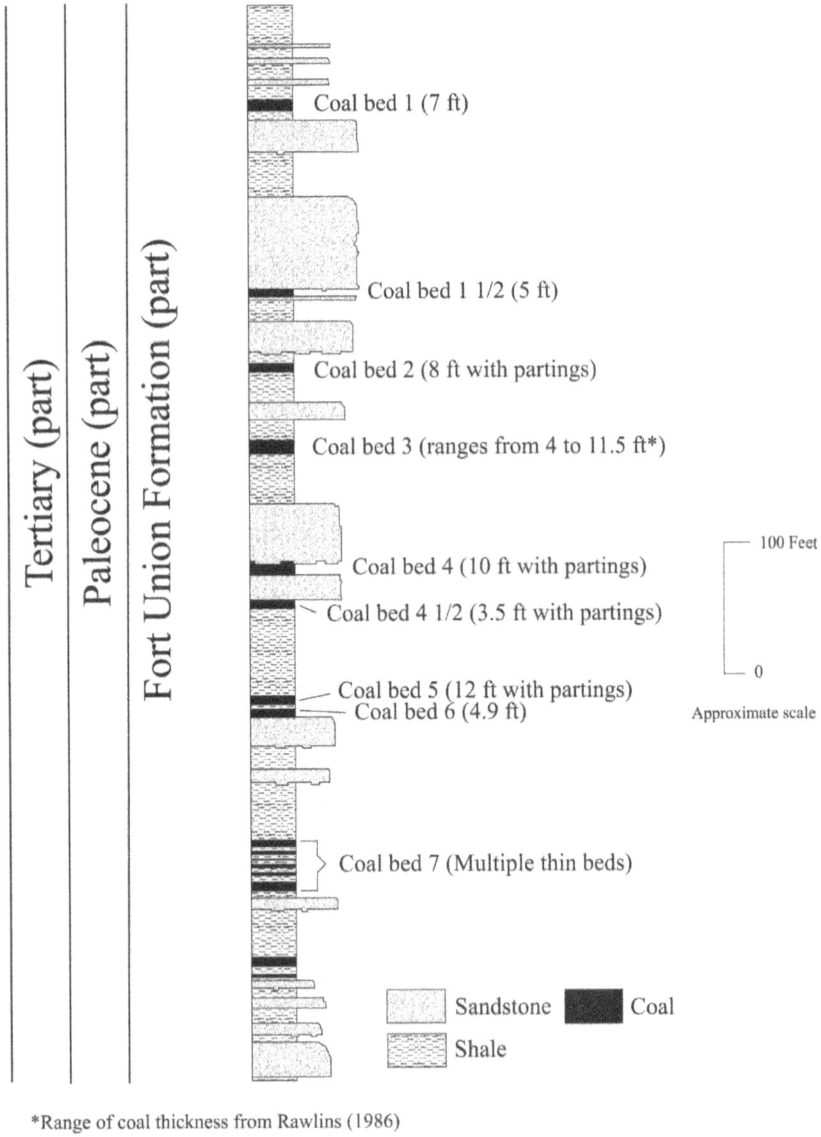

Generalized stratigraphic section of the coal-bearing portion of the Fort Union Formation in the Red Lodge-Bear Creek Coal Field. (After Roberts and Rossi 1999).

1949 attempted to settle this discrepancy by classifying all of the coal as bituminous based on its "resistance to weathering," but some of it is probably more accurately described as subbituminous. One of the geologically interesting aspects of this coalfield is that the coal at Bear Creek is of slightly higher quality than the coal in the same beds a few miles away at Red Lodge. The Bear Creek coals typically possess both lower moisture and higher heat content. The reason for this is unclear, but it might be related to slightly higher heat flow (temperature of the rocks) near Bear Creek due to the intrusion of thin vertical layers of molten rock called dikes after the coal was formed. This may also explain Bear Creek coal's resistance to weathering, or "slacking," meaning that it can be stored for long periods. The ability to store the coal, along with its higher heat content, are the reasons Bear Creek coal was preferred by commercial vendors.[1]

Until the late 1940s, all of the mining in the Red Lodge–Bear Creek area was done through underground workings, which began at the surface and followed the nearly horizontal coal beds into the hillsides. Coal was mined using the "room and pillar" method. This involved building a main "haulageway" or gangway into the coal bed from the mine portal or heading and then extending laterals at a right angle to the haulageway. These laterals were then connected by perpendicular crosscuts that left a checkerboard pattern of unmined coal "pillars" in place to support the mine roof while the coal was removed. Depending on the topography, multiple surface entries into different coal beds might be utilized at a single mine. Coal beds that lacked surface exposure were exploited by driving an inclined shaft through the intervening sandstone and shale from one bed to another. As described elsewhere, the Montana Coal & Iron Company briefly employed surface, or strip mining in the late 1940s, but with only limited success.[2]

Due to their surface exposures, coal beds two, three, and four in the Bear Creek area were the most easily developed and accounted for the bulk of the production. As development continued, some mines used inclines to allow mining of beds five and six as well. Development of bed number one was limited to Anaconda's mines in the upper reaches of Keucking Creek. The International mine's initial entry was in bed five.

Table 15.1. Locomotive roster

Number	Type	Builder	BN	Date Built
1	4-4-0[1]	Rhode Island	1195(?)	1882
3	2-8-0[2]	Alco–Rhode Island	40681	December 1906
5	3-T-Shay[3]	Lima	2083	October 1908
5	2-8-0[4]	Lima	1124	September 1910
6	2-8-0[5]	Alco		1899(?)
10	2-8-0[6]	Baldwin	54486	January 1921
12	2-8-0	Baldwin	59778	January 1927
20	2-8-2	Baldwin	57975	September 1924
Sunny Brook[7]	motor car	Vimotum		1905(?)
Bear Creek[8]	motor car	McKeen	67(?)	January 1911

1. Formerly Butte, Anaconda & Pacific Number 15; acquired from Great Northern (née St. Paul, Minneapolis & Manitoba); b/n between 1195 and 1200 exact number is unknown; purchased by Yellowstone Park Railroad in January 1906; probably scrapped around 1917.

2. Purchased new by Yellowstone Park Railroad; final disposition unknown.

3. Purchased new by Yellowstone Park Railroad; sold in August 1910 to Laquin Lumber Co., Laquin, Pennsylvania; sold in 1913 to Northwest Lumber Co., Kerriston, Washington, as Number 3; sold in 1930 to Brix Logging Co., Holbrook, Oregon; sold to Alaska Junk Co., Portland, Oregon, scrapped in 1940.

APPENDIX D

Locomotive Roster

YELLOWSTONE PARK AND MONTANA, WYOMING & SOUTHERN RAILROADS

Drivers (in inches)	Cylinders	Operating Weight	Boiler Pressure	Tractive Effort
64	17 × 24			
50	20 × 26	157,000		
36	13.5 × 15	160,000		35,100
56	20 × 26	160,000	200	31,600
54	21 × 28	175,000	200	37,000
54	21 × 28	176,000	200	37,000
56	21 × 28	208,000	200	39,100
42				

4. Built new for MW&S; disposition unknown.

5. Taber (1960) claims this is a former Pittsburgh & Lake Erie locomotive. The rectangular builder's plate indicates ALCO as builder. It may have been sold for scrap around 1926.

6. Locomotives 10, 12, and 20 were all built new for MW&S; probably scrapped in 1955.

7. Destroyed in engine house fire on July 3, 1910, Belfry, Montana.

8. Built for Charles City Western Railroad as Number 51; sold to MW&S in 1917; junked in Belfry, Montana, in 1933.

NOTES

1. "TREAT HIM IN EVERY WAY AS AN IRRESPONSIBLE FELLOW"

1. *Helena Independent*, January 26, 1891; *Helena Independent*, January 9, 1893.

2. *Racine Daily Journal*, April 14, 1886; *Green Bay Weekly Gazette*, May 1, 1886. The 1910 US census for Milwaukee indicates Hall was born in New York; the 1920 census says Wisconsin. Census records also indicate a birth date of 1868. His obituary in the *Long Beach Sun* from September 21, 1929, says he was born in 1864. In both cases, I have adhered to the 1910 census data.

3. *Wisconsin State Journal*, March 24, 1887; *Waukesha Journal*, June 21, 1890; *Independent Record-Helena*, February 3, 1892; (Lindman's age was estimated from his wife's obituary in the *Weekly Wisconsin* from February 19, 1898. She was forty-five in 1898).

4. *Oshkosh Northwestern*, November 15, 1892; *Oshkosh Northwestern*, December 27, 1893; *Anaconda Standard*, July 22, 1895; *Independent Record-Helena*, November 15, 1896.

5. *Daily Inter-Mountain-Butte*, November 27, 1897; *Billings Gazette*, November 16, 1897.

6. *Anaconda Standard*, March 1, 1898; *Spokane Chronicle*, February 25, 1898.

7. *Anaconda Standard*, March 1, 1898; Spokane *Spokesman-Review*, February 25, 1898; "Willis Ritche (1864–1931)," Historic Preservation Office, Spokane City | County, www.historicspokane.org/spokane-architects/willis-ritchie (accessed July 23, 2021); Wikipedia, s.v. "Willis Ritchie," last updated July 14, 2022, en.wikipedia.org/wiki/Willis_Ritchie; Wikipedia, s.v. "William D. Turner," last updated December 4, 2022, en.wikipedia.org/wiki/William_D._Turner; "William Wallace Davenport Turner," Find a Grave memorial page, May 22, 2010, 52725489, www.findagrave.com/memorial/52725489/william-wallace_davenport-turner. Also see "A Story of Pioneer Struggles during Early Days in Los Angeles and Southern California," *Los Angeles Times*, 1904.

8. Spokane *Spokesman-Review*, February 25, 1898; *Anaconda Standard*, September 26, 1898; *Butte Miner*, April 4, 1898; *Spokane Chronicle*, February 25, 1898.

9. *Butte Miner*, April 24, 1898.

10. *Anaconda Standard*, September 26, 1898.

11. *Anaconda Standard*, June 17, 1898; *Helena Independent Record*, July 3, 1898; Taber 1960, 6.

12. Roberts 1966, A32–A47; *Phillipsburg Mail*, June 7, 1888; *Livingston Enterprise*, June 16, 188; Taber 1960, 6. For a review of coalfields and geology, see Weed 1891; Calvert 1912; and Roberts 1966.

13. *Helena Independent Record*, June 28, 1898; *Helena Independent Record*, July 7, 1898; *Helena Independent Record*, August 16, 1898; Nowels n.d., 1.

14. Wikipedia, s.v. "Charles Sanger Mellen," January 9, 2022, https://en.wikipedia.org/wiki/Charles_Sanger_Mellen; Mellen to Hall, July 25, 1898, Northern Pacific Railway Archives, Minnesota Historical Society, St. Paul.

15. Mellen to Hall, July 25, 1898, Northern Pacific Railway Archives, Minnesota Historical Society, St. Paul.

16. *Helena Independent*, August 11, 1898; *Helena Independent*, August 16, 1898; Nowels n.d., 1.

17. *Bozeman Daily Chronicle*, January 19, 2002 (Chesnut, when the post office was established, a clerk added a *t* to the name); Roberts 1966, 32A, 40A.

18. *Poor's Manual of Railroads*, 1909, v.42, 674, Yellowstone Park Railway; Roberts 1966, plate 8; *Helena Daily Independent*, August 4, 1898. Railroad rail is classified by its weight per yard. Fifty-six pound is light rail; mainline track at this time would typically have used ninety pound or heavier. Railway curvature is found by connecting two points on an arc with a one-hundred-foot chord, drawing radii from the center of the arc to the chord end points and then measuring the angle between these radii lines (grades are author's calculations).

19. *Anaconda Standard*, September 26, 1898; *Helena Independent*, February 2, 1899.

20. *Helena Daily Independent*, August 11, 1898; *Helena Daily Independent*, November 19, 1898; *Livingston Enterprise*, November 19, 1898; *Anaconda Standard*, December 25, 1898.

21. *Helena Daily Independent*, August 2, 1898; *Helena Daily Independent*, August 26, 1898; *Helena Independent Record*, November 19, 1898.

22. Taber 1960, 6; Hall to Kendrick, December 1, 1898, Northern Pacific Railway Archives, Minnesota Historical Society, St. Paul; transcript, *Cook et al. v. Gallatin RR*, Supreme Court of Montana, June 6, 1903, *Pacific Reporter*, vol. 72 (St. Paul, MN: West Publishing, 1903), 678–84.

23. Mellen to Kendrick, March 24, 1899; Mellen to Kendrick, April 28, 1899, Northern Pacific Railway Archives, Minnesota Historical Society, St. Paul.

24. Taber 1960, 6–7; *Anaconda Standard*, September 9, 1900.

25. *Butte Miner*, June 7, 1903; *Billings Gazette*, September 1, 1899.

26. *Anaconda Standard*, October 15, 1899; Kendrick to Mellen, September 29, 1899, Northern Pacific Railway Archives, Minnesota Historical Society, St. Paul.

27. Turner to Kendrick, October 30, 1899; superintendent to Pearce and Kendrick, May 3, 1900; auditor to Pearce, July 27, 1901, Northern Pacific Railway Archives, Minnesota Historical Society, St. Paul; *Anaconda Standard*, September 9, 1900.

28. Railroad Commission of Montana, 1912, Fifth Annual Report, 18; transcript, *Cook et al. v. Gallatin RR*, 678–84; "William Wallace Davenport Turner," Find a Grave memorial page. Also see appendix A.

2. "THE LINE IS REMARKABLE FOR CHEAPNESS"

1. Doris Withorn, "Yankee Jim George," in Zupan and Owens 1979, 6–7.

2. "Jefferson Standifer," in Thrapp 1988, 1351; Robert A. Murray, "Historic Background," in Anderson 1983, 9; also see "History of Red Lodge," *Livingston Enterprise*, March 2, 1889; "Yellowstone Pioneers," *Livingston Enterprise*, December 25, 1889.

3. Woodruff 1907, 92–107; Roberts and Rossi 1999, SB9-SB13; Combo et al. 1949, 13. The physical characteristics of this coal place on the boundary between subbituminous "A" and high-volatile bituminous "C." (see appendix B).

4. "Yellowstone Pioneers," *Livingston Enterprise*, December 25, 1889; "Chronicles of the Yellowstone," *Bozeman Weekly Chronicle*, June 27, 1883; Hartman 2019, 16–18; Lovering 1929, 44, 77; also see Wolle 1963, 389–90. According to the *Bozeman Weekly Chronicle* (June 27, 1883), Miller's partners were James Gourley, Ed Hibbard, and Bart Henderson. T. S. Lovering (1929) does not mention Hibbard but includes J. H. Moore instead. Credence is given the *Chronicle*'s account because it was written just thirteen years after the events discussed.

5. The Clarks Fork of the Yellowstone, or simply the Clarks Fork, should not be confused with the Clark Fork River in western Montana. The Clarks Fork follows an easterly course through the Beartooth Mountains and then turns north, emptying into the Yellowstone River near Laurel, Montana (see Lovering 1929 and Van Gosen 2007 for an overview of the geology and ore bodies).

6. Hartman 2019, 19–20, 25–28; Smith 1986, 30–31.

7. "History of Red Lodge," *Livingston Enterprise*, March 2, 1889; *Anaconda Standard*, July 1, 1923.

8. Lovering 1929, 45.

9. Schrenk and Frey 1997, 18–20; Taylor and Taylor 1999, 14–15; Renz 1980, 79–80. Independence Creek was renamed Gold Creek by Henry Villard as a promotional gimmick.

10. Taylor and Taylor 1999. 29–36; Wolle 1963, 400; *Helena Weekly Herald*, May 8, 1884.

11. Taylor and Taylor 1999, 32; Townsend 2013, 11.

12. Townsend 2013, 14–15; Wikipedia, s.v. "George Bird Grinnell," last updated April 28, 2022, https://en.wikipedia.org/wiki/George_Bird_Grinnell (see Townsend 2013 for overview of legislative activities).

13. Townsend 2013, 17–18.

14. See Townsend 2013, 14, with footnote on Park boundary.

15. Taylor and Taylor 1999, 35; Townsend 2013, 41. The company name was intended to dispel suspicious legislators of the notion that the goal was something other than the New World Mining District.

16. Lovering 1929, 48; Van Gosen 2007, 448.

17. *New Northwest*, April 9, 1886.

18. *Billings Gazette*, Illustrated edition, July 1, 1894, 13, 43–44; *Progressive Men of the State of Montana* 1902, 1553–54.

19. *Philipsburg Mail*, March 7, 1889; Taylor and Taylor 2008, 9–14; *Rocky Fork & Cooke City Railway*, prospectus map, Montana Historical Society Archives, Helena. Also see Townsend 2013, 42. For a more complete history of the Rocky Fork & Cooke City Railway, see Taylor and Taylor 2008, 9–32.

20. Townsend 2013, 23; Taylor and Taylor 2008, 9–14. A 3 percent grade (158 feet/mile) is the maximum locating engineers generally consider acceptable for a standard-gauge railroad. James George's partners were Enoch Ferguson, Alex Hudley, and Rosa G. Black. Given the timing of this transaction, it is likely that each party had homesteaded an adjoining 160-acre tract; a copy of the claim is on display at Carbon County Historical Museum, Red Lodge, Montana.

21. *Livingston Enterprise, June 26, 1886; H. R. Rep. No. 790, 50th Cong., 1st Sess., 1888;* Townsend 2013, 23.

22. *Billings Gazette*, July 5, 1886; Merritt to Kendrick, November 23, 1889, in Taylor and Taylor 2008, 27.

23. Taylor and Taylor 2008, 9–14; Smith 1986, 27; *Bozeman Weekly Chronicle*, February 23, 1887; Platt to Harris, in Townsend 2013, 40. A railroad called the Stillwater & Cooke City was incorporated in February 1887 by a group representing the Minnesota Mining & Smelting Company. The line was to run from Columbus, Montana, to the copper-nickel deposits at Nye City with a further extension up the Stillwater River to Lake Abundance north of Cooke City. The proposed Cooke City extension seems to have been a political device aimed at blocking right-of-way approval for the Billings, Clark's Fork & Cooke City Railroad in order to preserve that opportunity for itself. Failing to attract investors, the Stillwater & Cooke City Railroad disappeared shortly after its incorporation papers were filed (*Billings Gazette*, February 19, 1887).

24. Taylor and Taylor 2008, 9–20.

25. Zupan and Owens 1979, 48.

26. *Billings Gazette*, quoted in *Helena Weekly Herald*, March 1, 1888.

27. *Billings Gazette*, in the *Helena Weekly Herald*, March 1, 1888; *Fort Benton River Press*, June 13, 1888; *New Northwest*, July 6, 1888; *Livingston Enterprise*, August 18, 1888; *Livingston Enterprise*, December 29, 1888; *H. R. Rep. No. 790, 50th Cong., 1st Sess., 1888; Progressive Men of the State of Montana* 1902, 1554.

28. Taylor and Taylor 2008, 14; *Livingston Enterprise*, August 11, 1888; *Fort Benton River Press*, August 1, 1888.

29. Taylor and Taylor 2008, 9–20; Malone, Roeder, and Lang 1976, in regard to Daly and Butte. In 1895, Anaconda Mining Co. became Anaconda Copper Mining Co. In 1899, the name was changed to Amalgamated Copper Co., and in 1915, it was changed back to Anaconda Copper Mining Co.

30. Taylor and Taylor 2008, 9–20; Zupan and Owens 1979, 48; *Livingston Enterprise*, February 16, 1889; *Fort Benton River Press*, December 19, 1888.

31. Lewty 1995, 16–17; Oregon Improvement Company records, 1877–1935, Archives West (orbiscascade.org); Wikipedia, s.v. "Henry Villard," last updated December 13, 2022, en.wikipedia.org/wiki/Henry_Villard; *Coos Bay Times*, April 11, 1912; also see *Eugene Daily Guard*, April 8, 1912, and *Boston Globe*, April 14, 1912; *Helena Independent*, August 17, 1889; Montana & Wyoming Railroad incorporators: Elijah Smith, Prosper W. Smith, John S. Tuney, E. R. Bell, and Edward J. Berwind of New York and A. G. Horley, Philip M. Gallaher, and O. F. Goddard of Montana. Capital stock $2 million.

32. *Helena Weekly Herald*, December 12, 1889; Montana Coal & Iron Co. incorporators: Elijah Smith, Edward J. Berwind, John E. Berwind, Elias L. Frank, and John S. Finley of New York; Prosper W. Smith of Boston; S. Davis of S. Oyster Bay, Long Island; and Philip M. Gallaher, C. E. Bond, and O. F. Goddard of Billings. Capital stock $2 million); Helena Independent, August 17, 1889.

33. Smith 1986, 34; *Progressive Men of the State of Montana* 1902, 1553–1554; *Helena Independent*, August 17, 1889; *Red Lodge Picket*, August 5, 1893.

3. "WE CAN CONTROL THE COAL TRADE OF MONTANA"

1. *Billings Gazette*, Illustrated Edition, July 1, 1894.

2. *Anaconda Standard*, January 24, 1894; *Red Lodge Picket*, October 27, 1894. After Gallaher and Chowning struggled to haul in dredging equipment and worked the stream gravels for some period of time, news of this "discovery" abruptly ends.

3. *Billings Gazette*, Illustrated Edition, July 1, 1894.

4. *Billings Gazette*, March 5, 1896; *Billings Gazette*, August 12, 1896; *Billings Gazette*, September 8, 1896; *Red Lodge Picket*, May 16, 1896; *Billings Weekly Gazette*, September 22, 1896.

5. Gallaher to Kendrick, August 22, 1896, Northern Pacific Railway Archives, Minnesota Historical Society, St. Paul.

6. Coke is created by roasting coal in an air-tight kiln or oven to drive off volatile components. The resulting product, which is nearly pure carbon, burns hotter and more evenly than coal and is used in smelting ore. In its simplest sense, coke is to coal as charcoal is to wood. For discussion of coal deposits and mines, see Darton 1906; Washburne 1907; and Knappen and Moulton 1930. Bridger, the town, was first established in 1864 as a river crossing on a wagon road pioneered by mountain man and explorer Jim Bridger. When William A. Clark opened his Bridger Coal and Improvement Company mine in 1898, the town was named Georgetown in honor of a local resident. The name Bridger was not officially adopted until 1902.

7. After reaching an output of eight hundred tons per day, the Carbonado Mine was closed in January 1901 due to its high operating costs.

8. The Clark's Fork Coal Company mine and the associated settlement of Gebo (later called Coalville) were served by a spur off the Clarks Fork Branch. The small station located where the spur diverged from the mainline was given the name Fromberg in honor of a major NP stockholder. An undated internal NP memo (circa late 1905) reviews terms and date of deal with Clark, and a letter lays out terms of proposed agreement (Northern Pacific Railway Archives, Minnesota Historical Society, St. Paul; Mellen to Clark, December 23, 1897, Northern Pacific Railway Archives, Minnesota Historical Society, St. Paul).

9. Smith to Mellen, February 7, 1898; Smith to Mellen, January 31, 1899, Northern Pacific Railway Archives, Minnesota Historical Society, St. Paul; Wikipedia, s.v. "Charles Sanger Mellen," last updated January 9, 2022, en.wikipedia.org/wiki/Charles_Sanger_Mellen.

10. Lewty 1995. 5–17; *Coos Bay Times*, April 11, 1912; also see the obituary in *Eugene Daily Guard*, April 8, 1912.

11. Daly to Kendrick, August 22, 1899; Mellen to Bush, July 5, 1899; Northern Pacific Railway Archives, Minnesota Historical Society, St. Paul.

12. Kendrick to Mellen, August 12, 1899; Kendrick to Daly, August 14, 1899; Daly to Kendrick, August 22, 1899, Northern Pacific Railway Archives, Minnesota Historical Society, St. Paul; Darton 1906, 189.

13. Pearson to Elliott, January 19, 1904, Northern Pacific Railway Archives, Minnesota Historical Society, St. Paul; Schrenk and Frey 1997, 29–31; Malone 1996, 181–82;

Wikipedia, s.v. "Charles Sanger Mellen," last updated January 9, 2022, en.wikipedia.org/wiki/Charles_Sanger_Mellen; also see Renz 1980.

14. *Helena Independent Record* November 19, 1899; Trail Creek Coal and Land Company incorporators: Henry Elling, George Cox, J. Kountz, George W. Boyce, and Frank A. Hall; capital stock $100,000 (*Helena Independent Record*, December 29, 1899; on December 19, 1899, the same paper reported the incorporators as George W. Boyce, Frank A. Hall, and W. F. Meyers, all of Bozeman. The later account is believed to be accurate, as Hall is known to have been involved in the "Kountz mine." Incorporation papers show Boyce and Hall held 50 percent of the company stock. *Butte Daily Inter-Mountain*, December 26, 1899; *Butte Daily Inter-Mountain*, December 29, 1899; *Butte Daily Inter-Mountain*, December 21, 1899; Incorporation Papers YPT&T (Montana Historical Society, Helena). Yellowstone Park Telephone and Telegraph Company incorporators: Frank A. Hall, George W. Boyce, and George Cox, all of Bozeman; capital stock $10,000. Capital stock was increased to $40,000 on August 5, 1901; principal place of business changed to Livingston on September 21, 1901.

15. *Butte Miner*, April 29, 1900. The Hellinger/Kountz Mine was closed permanently by 1909 (Biennial Report of the Inspector of Coal Mines of the State of Montana 1907–8, J. B. McDermott, inspector, Montana State Library, Helena).

16. Wolle 1963, 406–8. The copper-nickel ore body at Hicks Park and Nye City is part of a geological formation called the Stillwater Complex. Although copper-nickel mining was quite limited, the 2.7-billion-year-old complex, known as a layered ultra-mafic intrusion, saw significant chromite mining during the Second World War and later became the site of the only platinum-palladium mine in the United States.

17. *Butte Miner*, March 26, 1900.

18. *Red Lodge Picket*, June 22, 1900; *Red Lodge Picket*, August 31, 1900; *Red Lodge Picket*, August 10, 1900; *Billings Gazette*, February 22, 1901; Lovering 1929, 48. The *Billings Gazette* (February 22, 1901) states the agreement was made "late in the fall," but the *Red Lodge Picket* mentions it on June 22, 1900. So it must have been negotiated during the summer, which links it to Hall's trip up the Boulder.

19. *Bozeman Avant Courier* in the *Red Lodge Picket*, August 31, 1900.

20. *Red Lodge Picket*, August 10, 1900.

21. *Billings Gazette*, October 3, 1900.

22. *Butte Miner*, September 20, 1900; *Butte Miner*, September 21, 1900. Three newspaper accounts each give Mr. Hart different initials, C. T., E. L., and E. F.

23. *Billings Gazette*, October 20, 1900; *Billings Gazette*, October 21, 1900; *Red Lodge Picket*, November 16, 1900. Yellowstone Park Railroad incorporators: Alexander Morrison, Hackensack, NJ; E. N. Everitt, Jersey City, NJ; J. B. Clark, Hoboken, NJ; Frank A. Hall, Livingston, MT; and C. E. Barrett, Indianapolis, IN; capital stock $2,500,000.

24. *Red Lodge Picket*, February 15, 1901; *Billings Gazette*, February 22, 1901; *Billings Gazette*, May 25, 1901.

25. *Big Timber Pioneer*, in Hartman 2019, 93–95.

26. *Bozeman Weekly Chronicle*, April 13, 1887.

27. *Red Lodge Picket*, February 15, 1901; *Billings Gazette*, March 19, 1901; *Big Timber Pioneer*, in Hartman 2019, 93–95.

28. Polk's City Directory 1902; *Butte Inter-Mountain*, July 8, 1901; *Red Lodge Picket*, August 2, 1901; *Anaconda Standard*, September 30, 1901; *Anaconda Standard*, November 4, 1901.

29. *Butte Inter-Mountain*, July 9, 1901; *Butte Miner*, October 16, 1903; *Butte Miner*, November 3, 1904; *Anaconda Standard*, September 26, 1903.
30. *Great Falls Tribune*, June 16, 1902.
31. *Butte Miner*, July 20, 1902.
32. *Butte Miner*, December 29, 1901.
33. *Billings Gazette*, June 20, 1902; Whithorn and Withorn n.d., 26.
34. *Billings Gazette*, April 15, 1903; *Billings Gazette*, October 27, 1903.

4. "A RAILROAD WILL BE BUILT"

1. Interview with Charles Yegen, Billings, Montana, April 2021; *Billings Gazette*, Illustrated Edition, July 1, 1894; *Progressive Men of the State of Montana* 1902, 1879.
2. *Billings Gazette*, November 27, 1903. Bear Creek Coal Company incorporators: Christian Yegen, Billings, Montana; Philip M. Gallaher, Bozeman, Montana; B. E. Vaill and Miss L. H. Yerkes, Red Lodge, Montana; and Walter Lamport and Robert Leavens, Bearcreek, Montana; capital stock $200,000.
3. *Billings Gazette*, November 28, 1903.
4. *Anaconda Standard*, January 31, 1904; Pearson to Elliott, January 19, 1904, Northern Pacific Railway Archives, Minnesota Historical Society, St. Paul.
5. Menzies to Claghorn, May 5, 1905, Northern Pacific Railway Archives, Minnesota Historical Society, St. Paul; Taber 1960, 2; Axline 1999, 53.
6. Lovering 1929, 46; Ferguson 2002, 1–5.
7. *Butte Miner*, July 22, 1905; *Great Falls Tribune*, September 1, 1905; Axline 1999, 54; YPRR incorporation papers (Montana Historical Society, Helena, MT). Yellowstone Park Railroad Board of Directors: Frank A. Hall, George J. Atkins, Louis Rosenfeld, O. M. Belfry, George R. Heisey, John A. Monk, and S. N. Mumma; officers: Frank Hall, president; S. N. Mumma, vice president; George Atkins, secretary-treasurer.
8. Schrenk and Frey 1997, 41; en.wikipedia.org/wiki/Howard_Elliott_(railroad executive).
9. Elliott to C. W. Bunn, July 10, 1905; Elliott to Hannaford, July 10, 1905, Northern Pacific Railway Archives, Minnesota Historical Society, St. Paul.
10. Elliott to Lamont, July 10, 1905 ; Pearson to Elliott, January 19, 1904, Northern Pacific Railway Archives, Minnesota Historical Society, St. Paul; Taylor and Taylor 1999, 28. Combined production from the Mountain Side and Rocky Canyon mines in 1905 was 124,380 tons. This was the year of peak production. For details see Roberts 1966, 42.
11. Elliott to C. W. Bunn, July 10, 1905, Northern Pacific Railway Archives, Minnesota Historical Society, St. Paul.
12. Menzies to Claghorn, May 5, 1905; Elliott to Lamont, July 10, 1905, Northern Pacific Railway Archives, Minnesota Historical Society, St. Paul.
13. *Billings Gazette*, January 2, 1905; *Billings Gazette*, April 25, 1905.
14. Author's calculations and opinions.
15. *Gazette (York, PA)*, May 30, 1905. Attendees at meeting: Frank Hall, Livingston, Montana; S. N. Mumma, Landsville, Pennsylvania; E. E. Brunner, York Haven, Pennsylvania; O. M. Belfry, Philadelphia; H. S. Rich, Marietta, Pennsylvania; E. R. Heisey, Dallastown, Pennsylvania; John A. Monk, George R. Heisey, Charles A. Fondersmith, Lancaster; and R. H. Shindle and N. Sargent Ross, York, Pennsylvania.

16. Annual Statement YPRR, July 27, 1905, Carbon County, Clerk & Recorder's Office, file 115.

17. Elliott to Hannaford, July 10, 1905; unknown to Elliott, August 28, 1905, Northern Pacific Railway Archives, Minnesota Historical Society, St. Paul. Trouble first surfaced for Hall and his telephone company eight months earlier when, in October 1904, the Montana Electric Company filed a claim for $1,463.80 in unpaid bills. Numerous other small creditors soon followed suit, and on June 14, 1905, W. B. Dolenty, part owner and cashier of the First State Bank of Livingston commenced a legal action in district court against Hall for over $8,400. Before further action could be taken, Hall sold the company to Rocky Mountain Bell for $25,000, with $20,000 earmarked for the retirement of a mortgage likely facilitated by George Atkins and held by American Trust & Savings Bank of Chicago. Rocky Mountain Bell used the remaining $5,000 to satisfy outstanding liens. The deal, which was signed on June 23, allowed Hall to sidestep his looming financial problems and left his unsecured creditors, including Dolenty, out in the cold (*Dolenty v. Rocky Mountain Bell Telephone Co., Supreme Court of Montana, Pacific Reporter*, vol. 108 [St. Paul, MN: West Publishing, 1910], 921–27).

18. *Anaconda Standard,* August 3, 1905; *Billings Gazette,* August 25, 1905; undated internal NP memo circa 1905, Northern Pacific Railway Archives, Minnesota Historical Society, St. Paul.

19. Axline 1999, 54–55.

20. *Clarke Fork Herald,* May 2, 1907; *Anaconda Standard,* July 22, 1905; *Billings Gazette,* November 30, 1905; *Butte Miner,* April 15, 1906; *Butte Miner,* November 30, 1906; Axline 1999, 54–55; Dutton 1967, 10–11.

21. *Billings Gazette,* August 24, 1905; *Billings Gazette,* August 29, 1905; *Billings Gazette,* September 3, 1905; Sharkey to Hannaford, August 22, 1905, Northern Pacific Railway Archives, Minnesota Historical Society, St. Paul.

22. *Billings Gazette,* September 25, 1905; *Butte Miner,* November 26, 1905; *Butte Miner,* December 4, 1905.

23. *Lancaster New Era,* November 20, 1905; *Butte Inter-Mountain,* November 30, 1905.

24. *Billings Gazette,* November 28, 1905.

25. *Billings Gazette,* November 19, 1904; *Billings Gazette,* July 1, 1905; *Billings Gazette,* September 22, 1905; *Billings Gazette,* July 12, 1907; *Billings Gazette,* November 26, 1907; *Billings Gazette,* May 29, 1934; *Progressive Men of the State of Montana* 1902, 1554. Gallaher died in Azusa, California, May 18, 1934.

26. *Billings Gazette,* November 1, 1905; *Billings Gazette,* November 29, 1905; US Census Milwaukee 1910. Laura's obituary in the *Long Beach Daily Telegram* on November 1, 1921, gives her birthdate as 1878; the census indicates it was 1875. I have adhered to the census date.

27. *Butte Inter-Mountain,* January 8, 1906; *Butte Inter-Mountain,* January 8, 1906; *Butte Inter-Mountain,* January 22, 1906; *Billings Gazette,* January 23, 1906; Chief Engineer to Elliott, March 8, 1907, Northern Pacific Railway Archives, Minnesota Historical Society, St. Paul.

28. *Butte Miner,* January 22, 1906; *Laurel Sentinel,* October 5, 1906.

29. *Butte Miner,* January 8, 1906; *Billings Gazette,* January 23, 1906; Mutschler 2002, locomotive roster.

30. *Butte Miner,* January 29, 1906; *Butte Miner,* February 19, 1906; *Butte Miner,* March 19, 1906.

31. *Butte Miner*, April 10, 1906; *Billings Gazette*, April 29, 1906; Elliott to Miller, December 19, 1908, Northern Pacific Railway Archives, Minnesota Historical Society, St. Paul.

32. *Butte Miner*, April 15, 1906; *Anaconda Standard*, May 29, 1906.

33. *Butte Miner*, April 15, 1906; *Carbon County Republican*, May 25, 1906.

5. "IN ITS UTILITARIAN ADVANTAGES THE NEW STATION IS UNSURPASSED"

1. *Billings Gazette*, June 26, 1906; *Billings Gazette*, July 3, 1906; Regan and Andrew 1962, 2.

2. *Billings Gazette*, July 5, 1906; *Carbon County News*, August 11, 2005; Regan and Andrew 1962, 2. Lose (1920) suggests that there was only one train and that NP locomotive only went to Bridger. This view is supported by Shirley Zupan and Harry J. Owens (1979). Jetta Regan and Bertha Andrew (1962) indicate there were two trains, as does the *Carbon County News*, August 11, 2005.

3. *Bridger Advocate*, February 7, 1906; *La Crosse Tribune*, November 22, 1906, May 31, 1907.

4. *Carbon County News*, October 2, 1930.

5. Regan and Andrew 1962, 5.

6. National Register of Historic Places Registration Form, Montana, Wyoming and Southern Depot, Belfry, Montana, 2012, 3–4; *Carbon County News*, October 2, 1930.

7. National Register of Historic Places Registration Form 2012, Montana, Wyoming and Southern Depot, Belfry, Montana, 3–4; *Red Lodge Picket*, Illustrated Industrial Edition, February 1907.

8. *Butte Miner*, April 15, 1906; Regan and Andrew 1962, 7–8; *Carbon County News*, August 11, 2005.

9. *Red Lodge Pickett*, August 1906, in National Register of Historic Places Registration Form, Bearcreek Bank, Bearcreek, Montana, 2004, 1; Zupan and Owens 1979, 265; Axline 1999, 55; McNeish 2009, 45.

10. Zupan and Owens 1979, 266; *Butte Miner*, November 27, 1906; *Great Falls Tribune*, April 15, 1907. In April 1907, Novota was convicted of second-degree murder and sentenced to ten years to life.

11. MW&S timetable no. 5, July 9, 1917, Railroad Museum of Pennsylvania.

12. Robertson 1991, 329. When the NP first contemplated a line to Bear Creek in 1897 the cost estimate was $10,000 per mile. Seven years after the YPRR was completed, the NP estimated the cost of a line duplicating the YPRR to be $30,000 per mile or nearly twice what Hall spent (*Billings Gazette*, September 16, 1907). Anaconda's mining operation at Washoe was conducted by the Washoe Coal Company a wholly owned subsidiary. For simplicity, this operation is referred to as the Anaconda mine.

13. Romek 1976, 45; L. M. Perkins to W. L. Darling, March 1, 1907, Northern Pacific Railway Archives, Minnesota Historical Society, St. Paul.

14. Perkins to Darling, March 1, 1907, Northern Pacific Railway Archives, Minnesota Historical Society, St. Paul; Railroad Commission of Montana Fifth Annual Report 1912, 79; Regan and Andrew 1962, 2. In 1915, slack coal was defined by the Railroad Commission of Montana as coal that will pass through a 1.5-inch screen (see appendix B).

15. Zupan and Owens 1979, 265; Taber 1960, 4; *Anaconda Standard,* November 2, 1906; Poor's Manual of Railroads 1909, v. 42, 674, report on YPRR. Zupan and Owens, as well as Taber, give the date of first shipment as September 15; Jon Axline (1999) indicates it was August 22.

16. *Red Lodge Picket,* August 17, 1917; *Coos Bay Times,* April 8, 1912; Sharkey to Hannaford, August 22, 1905, Northern Pacific Railway Archives, Minnesota Historical Society, St. Paul. Born in New Bedford, Massachusetts, in April 1840, Smith died in Portland, Oregon, on April 5, 1912, aged seventy-two, after a two-month illness. He had been placed in a sanatorium during the summer of 1911 due to both physical and mental health issues. He died intestate and apparently with little money. His body was shipped to his sister Annie Smith in New Bedford for burial.

17. Yellowstone Park Railroad Stations: Bridger MP 0; Jennings MP 3; Golden MP 8; Belfry MP 13; Bearcreek MP 23; Smith MP 24; McCarthy MP 25; Amalgamated (Anaconda) MP 26.

18. Retainers are manual valves on the air brake system that allows cars to be set with a certain level of brake application independent of applications made by the engineer. They are important for controlling trains on steep grades where multiple brake applications might be necessary. The retainers must be manually released when no longer needed.

19. *Billings Gazette,* January 8, 1907; *Clarke Fork Herald,* June 27, 1907; Mellen to Kendrick, April 28, 1899, Northern Pacific Railway Archives, Minnesota Historical Society, St. Paul.

20. *Clarke Fork Herald,* April 18, 1907.

21. *Indianapolis Morning Star,* March 18, 1907; *Clarke Fork Herald,* June 27, 1907; *Billings Gazette,* July 2, 1907; *Billings Gazette,* July 26, 1907; Ancestry.com, Select Marriages Index.

22. Woodworth, internal NP memo "YELLOWSTONE PARK RAILROAD," July 28, 1907, 2, Northern Pacific Railway Archives, Minnesota Historical Society, St. Paul; *Lancaster Intelligencer Journal,* July 1, 1909; Axline 1999, 57.

23. *Billings Gazette,* August 27, 1907; *Billings Gazette,* September 16, 1907.

24. Hill to Elliott, October 26, 1907, Northern Pacific Railway Archives, Minnesota Historical Society, St. Paul.

25. Hill to Elliott, October 26, 1907; Elliott to Hill, October 27, 1907, Northern Pacific Railway Archives, Minnesota Historical Society, St. Paul; *Billings Gazette,* August 30, 1907.

6. "PHYSICALLY . . . A BROKEN-DOWN MAN"

1. *Bridger Advocate,* February 7, 1907; *Carbon County News,* Belfry edition, December 3, 1908; *Carbon County News,* Belfry edition, August 4, 1910; Railroad Commission of Montana Fifth Annual Report 1912, 67. Thomas T. Taber (1960, 14) claims number 3 came from Duluth, Rainy Lake & Western, but no record of that railroad exists; therefore, it appears that Taber actually meant the Duluth, Rainy Lake & Winnipeg, which was formed at about that time.

2. Railroad Commission of Montana Fifth Annual Report 1912, 67–68; *Billings Gazette,* September 16, 1907; *Clarke Fork Herald,* July 18, 1907. In 1907, the YPRR owned

a few flat cars, some bunk cars, a hand-powered derrick car, and a small home-built side-door caboose.

3. *Billings Gazette,* July 6, 1906; *Billings Gazette,* September 27, 1907; *Billings Gazette,* September 9, 1908; *Billings Gazette,* March 10, 1909.

4. *Billings Gazette,* November 15, 1907; *Butte Inter-Mountain,* November 12, 1907; Railroad Commission of Montana First Annual Report 1907, 140.

5. *Butte Inter-Mountain,* November 22, 1907; Slade to Levey, telegram, November 16, 1907, Northern Pacific Railway Archives, Minnesota Historical Society, St. Paul. Also see *Billings Gazette,* November 15, 1907. These were twenty-nine-foot Rodgers Convertible Ballast cars purchased in the late 1890s. Designed for multipurpose use, by 1907 the BA&P was replacing these wooden cars with new fifty-ton capacity steel hopper cars, which is another reason they were available for lease.

6. Elliott to Hill, December 3, 1907; Elliott to Harrison, December 3, 1907, Northern Pacific Railway Archives, Minnesota Historical Society, St. Paul.

7. *Billings Gazette,* January 7, 1908; *Billings Gazette,* February 2, 1908; Regan and Andrew 1962, 7.

8. *Billings Gazette,* January 3, 1908; *Carbon County News,* Belfry edition, September 17, 1908.

9. *Carbon County News,* Belfry edition, November 19, 1908; Shay Locomotives website, accessed April 15, 2021. https://www.shaylocomotives.com.

10. *Carbon County News,* Belfry edition, December 3, 1908; *Carbon County News,* Belfry edition, April 27, 1910.

11. *Carbon County News,* Belfry edition, November 26, 1908.

12. Author's calculations based on *Poor's Manual of Railroads* 1909, v. 42, 674.

13. *York Dispatch,* August 26, 1908; *York Dispatch,* October 22, 1908; *(York, PA) Gazette,* October 28, 1908. Bondholders committee: C. C. Frick, H. W. Heffener, M. B. Gibson, W. S. Bond, L. G. Brown.

14. *York Dispatch,* November 19, 1908; *(York, PA) Gazette,* November 11, 1908; *(York, PA) Gazette,* November 14, 1908. New YPRR Board: E. W. Meisenhelter, E. A. Rice, H. Weist, H. W. Heffener, F. A. Hall, G. J. Atkins, and S. N. Mumma. Officers: H. W. Heffener, president; S. N. Mumma, vice president; L. G. Brown, secretary-treasurer.

15. Ryan to Elliott, November 20, 1908, Northern Pacific Railway Archives, Minnesota Historical Society, St. Paul.

16. Ryan to Elliott, November 20, 1908, Northern Pacific Railway Archives, Minnesota Historical Society, St. Paul.

17. *Anaconda Standard,* November 30, 1908; *Billings Gazette,* December 1, 1908.

18. Elliott to Miller, December 19, 1908, Northern Pacific Railway Archives, Minnesota Historical Society, St. Paul.

19. *Carbon County News,* Belfry edition, December 3, 1908.

20. *Carbon County News,* Belfry edition, December 31, 1908; *Carbon County News,* Belfry edition, January 28, 1909; Mutschler 2002, 61–62.

21. Elliott to Scallon, March 9, 1909; Elliott to Goodell, May 5, 1909; Chief Engineer to Elliott, March 8, 1907, Northern Pacific Railway Archives, Minnesota Historical Society, St. Paul.

22. Elliott to Goodell, May 5, 1909; Goodell to Elliott, May 28, 1909, Northern Pacific Railway Archives, Minnesota Historical Society, St. Paul; *Missoulian,* June 1, 1909

(*Bozeman Avant Courier*, BC&W incorporation), Bear Creek and Western Railroad directors: William Wallace Jr., John G. Brown, H. K. Jones. Capital stock $10,000.

23. Sketch map by R. E. Thian, January 14, 1913, attached to memo from Thomas Cooper, August 22, 1913, Northern Pacific Railway Archives, Minnesota Historical Society, St. Paul; *Billings Gazette*, October 29, 1909.

24. Taber 1960, 5; Revocation of Appointment of Agent, Yellowstone Park Railroad Co., June 14, 1909, misc. file 529, Carbon County Clerk & Recorder's Office. Taber's story is questionable and has not been independently verified. He claims the meeting took place on May 28, but the document removing Hall as company agent states that the meeting was held on May 20. Taber also claims that the proceedings took place in Maine, which seems unusual given that all previous board meetings had been held in Pennsylvania.

25. *Lancaster Intelligencer Journal*, July 1, 1909; *Lancaster News-Journal*, November 9, 1909.

26. *Billings Gazette*, June 8, 1909; *Billings Gazette*, June 29, 1909; *Billings Gazette*, June 30, 1909; *Billings Gazette*, July 1, 1909; *Billings Evening Journal*, August 12, 1909; Taber 1960, 5–7.

27. *Billings Evening Journal*, August 12, 1909; 1910 US census, Milwaukee, ancestry.com.; *Long Beach Daily Telegram*, March 2, 1920; *Long Beach Daily Telegram*, May 13, 1920; *Long Beach Daily Telegram*, November 20, 1920; *Long Beach Daily Telegram*, December 31, 1920; *Long Beach Daily Telegram*, November 1, 1921; *Santa Ana Register*, September 8, 1920; *Long Beach Times*, May 13, 1920; Romek 1976.

28. *Long Beach Daily Telegram*, November 1, 1921; *Long Beach Press*, May 9, 1923; *Long Beach Press*, January 25, 1922.

29. *Long Beach Daily Telegram*, August 13, 1922.

30. Regan and Andrew 1962, 7; *Long Beach Sun*, September 21, 1929; *Long Beach Sun*, May 10, 1931.

7. "THE TRACK-BED IS IN FIERCE CONDITION"

1. *Billings Gazette*, May 26, 1909. The *Bridger Times*, May 28, 1909, claims there were "twenty-five New York capitalists" in the group.

2. *Billings Gazette*, May 28, 1909.

3. Railroad Commission of Montana Fifth Annual Report 1912, 73.

4. Montana, Wyoming & Southern Railroad, Board of Directors: Frank S. Gannon, William H. Langley, W. H. Siebert, C. M. Hall, W. C. Langley, New York; C. C. Frick, York, Pennsylvania; H. S. Rich, Marietta, Pennsylvania; Charles W. Fernald, Fanwood, New Jersey. Officers: Frank S. Gannon, president; William H. Langley, vice-president; Charles W. Fernald, treasurer; Frank S. Gannon Jr., secretary. Capital stock $5,500,000. Certificate of Incorporation of Montana, Wyoming & Southern RR Co., Carbon County Clerk & Recorder's Office, file 210. Frank Hall created the Yellowstone Park Railway (1898), Yellowstone Park Telephone & Telegraph Co. (1899), Yellowstone Park Railroad (1900), and a second Yellowstone Park Railroad (1905). A Union Pacific affiliate called the Yellowstone Park Railroad was also created in 1905.

5. *Butte Miner*, December 15, 1908; *Butte Miner*, December 25, 1908; *Butte Miner*, February 20, 1909; *Butte Daily Post*, December 29, 1909; *Billings Gazette*, December 29, 1909. The railroad proposed one hundred years later was called the Tongue River Railroad,

its purpose was to expedite the development of coal reserves near the town of Decker, Montana. Although not intended as a bridge line, had it connected with the Burlington Northern–Santa Fe Railroad at Decker, it would have created the Sheridan to Miles City rail link proposed in 1908. The plan was dropped in 2016 after an adverse ruling by the Federal Surface Transportation Board.

6. *Poor's Manual of Railroads* 1910, v. 43, 1434–35; assignment, Albert P. Broomell et al., YPRR to MW&S, September 1, 1909, Carbon County Clerk and Recorder's Office, Misc. Records Book 2. Langley & Company did not make its first quarterly payment of $225,000 until November 1909 (*Lancaster News-Journal*, November 9, 1909).

7. *New York Herald*, November 9, 1922; *Brooklyn Standard Union*, November 9, 1922; *Brooklyn Times Union*, January 9, 1922; *Bridger Times*, November 23, 1922.

8. Railroad Commission of Montana Third Annual Report 1910, 116; *Bridger Times*, September 4, 1909; *Billings Gazette*, September 28, 1909.

9. *Carbon County News*, Belfry edition, October 14, 1909; *Billings Gazette*, October 9, 1909. Note: These two accounts differ. The October 14 story is believed to be more accurate because several days had elapsed between the time of the wreck and when the story was written.

10. *Billings Gazette*, October 19, 1909.

11. Gannon to Elliott, October 2, 1909; memo from Elliott, October 12, 1909; Elliott to Hannaford, November 27, 1910, Northern Pacific Railway Archives, Minnesota Historical Society, St. Paul. Following George Atkins unsuccessful attempt to sell the YPRR to private investors during May and June, this offer to the NP reinforces the assumption that transferring ownership to Langley & Company was merely an expedient to remove Frank Hall from office. Langley & Company probably had no interest in owning a railroad and were probably dismayed when Atkins attempt at a quick sale fell through.

12. *Billings Gazette*, January 30, 1910; *Billings Weekly Gazette*, February 4, 1910. A little over a year after making these comments, due to failing health and the fact that his brothers had predeceased him, Elijah transferred control of Montana Coal & Iron to Charles R. Smith of Menasha, Wisconsin. Charles was the son of Elisha Smith, founder of the Menasha Wooden Ware Company and appears to have not been related to Elijah. Beginning in the summer of 1911, it was Charles who dealt with the continuing frustrations associated with the MW&S.

13. Railroad Commission of Montana Third Annual Report 1910, 115–118.

14. *Bridger Times*, February 4, 1910.

15. Railroad Commission of Montana Third Annual Report 1910, 117; Railroad Commission of Montana Fifth Annual Report 1912, 66; *Carbon County News*, Belfry edition, January 27, 1910.

16. Railroad Commission of Montana Third Annual Report 1910, 119–121.

17. *Carbon County News*, Belfry edition, May 5, 1910; MW&S representatives included J. F. Trumbo, Frank S. Gannon, M. W. Maguire, and A. R. Clement. Also present were W. C. Langley, the New York broker who helped finance the railroad; R. E. Riggs, an attorney from New York; and G. W. Pierson, an attorney from Red Lodge. The Bear Creek Coal Co. was represented by Messrs. Yegen, Leavens, Hopka, Vaill, Herford, and Dirby; the International Mine by H. Rosetta; Washoe Coal Co. by P. E. Egan; and the Smokeless & Sootless Mine by J. R. Brophy.

18. *Carbon County News*, Belfry edition, April 27, 1910; Shay Locomotives website, https://www.shaylocomotives.com. Accessed April 15, 2021.

19. *Butte Miner*, January 22, 1906; *Carbon County News*, Belfry edition, May 12, 1910.

20. *Carbon County News*, Belfry edition, July 4, 1910; *Billings Gazette*, July 5, 1910.

21. *Carbon County News*, Belfry edition, August 11, 1910, September 1, 1910.

22. *Carbon County News*, Belfry edition, October 27, 1910; *Laurel Sentinel*, November 24, 1910; *Billings Gazette*, January 15, 1910; Railroad Commission of Montana Fifth Annual Report 1912, 73.

23. Railroad Commission of Montana Second Annual Report 1909, 66–68; Railroad Commission of Montana Third Annual Report 1910, 33–34.

24. Railroad Commission of Montana Fifth Annual Report 1912, 65–87.

25. Railroad Commission of Montana Fifth Annual Report 1912, 122.

26. Spurling to Hannaford, April 15, 1911, Northern Pacific Railway Archives, Minnesota Historical Society, St. Paul.

27. *Billings Gazette*, August 6, 1912; Railroad Commission of Montana Sixth Annual Report 1913, 230.

28. Railroad Commission of Montana Sixth Annual Report 1913, 231, 233; *Bridger Times*, June 13, 1913 (twenty-five gondolas, but only fifteen boxcars, not twenty-five; see *Moody's Analyses of Investments*, part 1, *Steam Railroads*, Eighth Annual 1917. New York: Moody's Investors Service, 983–4).

29. *Butte Miner*, January 17, 1913.

8. "IN THE INTEREST OF ECONOMY AND EFFICIENCY"

1. Elliott to Hill, March 20, 1912, Northern Pacific Railway Archives, Minnesota Historical Society, St. Paul.

2. Report by Thomas Cooper on BC&WRR, August 22, 1913; Elliott to Spurling, December 6, 1912; Northern Pacific Railway Archives, Minnesota Historical Society, St. Paul.

3. Elliott to Gannon, April 4, 1913, Northern Pacific Railway Archives, Minnesota Historical Society, St. Paul; *Great Falls Tribune*, April 29, 1913.

4. Internal NP memo from Thomas Cooper, August 22, 1913, Northern Pacific Railway Archives, Minnesota Historical Society, St. Paul.

5. *Billings Gazette*, December 14, 1913.

6. *Great Falls Tribune*, July 9, 1915; Railroad Commission of Montana Tenth Annual Report 1917, 228; *Bridger Times*, May 12, 1916; Taber 1960, 15.

7. *Bridger Times*, March 30, 1917; *Poor's Manual of Railroads* 1918, v. 51, 223–24; 1920, v. 53, 705–706; MW&S ROW map 6/17.

8. *Red Lodge Picket*, August 17, 1917; *Missoulian*, August 26, 1917.

9. Regan and Andrew 1962, 6; *Carbon County Journal*, October 10, 1917.

10. *Butte Miner*, December 14, 1917; *Poor's Manual of Railroads* 1910, v. 43, 1434–35; Railroad Commission of Montana Fifth Annual Report 1912, 65–87; YPRR incorporation papers, Montana Historical Society, Helena.

11. *Moody's Analyses of Investments*, part 1, *Steam Railroads*, Eighth Annual 1917. New York: Moody's Investors Service, 983–4; *Poor's Manual of Railroads* 1920, v. 53, 705–6.

12. *Carbon County Journal*, December 19, 1917.

13. *Billings Gazette*, July 21, 1918. Bunney's position was not made permanent until January 1, 1919; Maguire died on January 17, 1920, in New York. Production totals for 1918 were: Montana Coal & Iron 307,606; Anaconda 147,774; Bear Creek 135,000; International 53,620; Smokeless & Sootless 48,385 (Montana Bureau of Mines, December 1919). *Red Lodge Picket*, April 25, 1918; *Poor's Manual of Railroads* 1920, v. 53, 705–6; *Bridger Times*, June 14, 1918, June 28, 1918.

14. *Missoulian*, April 16, 1911; *Missoulian*, December 15, 1912; *Carbon County News*, October 2, 1930; *Missoulian*, April 16, 1911; *Billings Gazette*, April 14, 1931; *Billings Gazette*, March 27, 1932.

15. *Butte Miner*, February 3, 1920; Official Railway Equipment Register, September 1919; Dutton 1967, 14–15.

16. Eagle Coal Incorporation papers, Montana Historical Society, Helena; Eagle lease agreement, Hubert Alfred Simmons papers 1906–67, Montana Historical Society, Helena. Eagle Coal Company was incorporated December 30, 1918, by J. T. Flaherty, J. V. Flaherty, and T. E. Frasure; capital stock $75,000; voluntary dissolution on December 29, 1947 (Montana Coal & Iron may have been a majority shareholder in the company with as much as 90 percent of the stock).

17. Riddle to Eagle Coal, June 5, 1919; Bunney to Eagle Coal, February 4, 1920 , Hubert Alfred Simmons papers, Eagle Coal Co. 1906–67, Montana Historical Society, Helena.

18. Dutton 1967, 15.

19. Official Railway Equipment Register, September 1919; *Bridger Times*, October 2, 1919.

20. Rossillon 1986, 5.

21. *Bridger Times*, July 10, 1919; Dutton 1967, 19; Regan and Andrew 1962, 6; *Bridger Times*, December 18, 1919.

22. *Carbon County Journal*, May 19, 1919; *Poor's Manual of Railroads* 1920, v. 53, 705. Established in 1897, Northwestern Improvement Company was a wholly owned NP subsidiary that handled all of the company's nonrailroad land and mining business.

23. *Billings Gazette*, December 11, 1919; *Butte Miner*, December 19, 1919; Romek 1976, 42; Zupan and Owens 1979, 134.

24. *Billings Gazette*, December 10, 1919.

25. Romek 1976, 42– 43; *Billings Gazette*, December 11, 1919.

26. *Bridger Times*, February 5, 1920; Taber 1960, graph; Romek 1976, 45; Carbon County Museum photo; *Red Lodge Picket*, November 30, 1921; *Billings Gazette*, November 14, 1921; *Billings Gazette*, October 12, 1922; *Billings Gazette*, January 14, 1923; McNeish 2009, 39.

27. Golden beet ramp, see ROW map Railroad Museum of Pennsylvania; *Poor's Manual of Railroads* 1923, v. 56, 1988; Baldwin Locomotive Works Spec. sheets v. 65, 124–25.

28. Official Railroad Equipment Register, December 1930; Lovering 1929, 46–47; Ferguson 2002, 1–5; Van Gosen 2007, 448.

29. Bunney to all mines, October 16, 1919; Bunney to Eagle Coal, January 17, 1921, Hubert Alfred Simmons papers, Eagle Coal Co. 1906–67, Montana Historical Society, Helena.

30. Bunney to Eagle Coal, June 7, 1921, Hubert Alfred Simmons papers, Eagle Coal Co. 1906–67, Montana Historical Society, Helena.

31. *Billings Gazette*, May 28, 1921; Schrenk and Frey 1997, 255–63.

9. "YOU WILL BE WISER AFTER YOU HAVE TRIED IT"

1. *Indianapolis Morning Star,* March 18, 1907; *Columbus Republican,* April 5, 1900; "Railway Car Builders of North America," Rollingstock.com, www.midcontinent.org/rollingstock/list/bldr_list_V.htm (Vimotum & Jewett). Accessed November 20, 2020. Originally called Atkins, Milliken & Thompson, in April 1900 the company was reorganized as the Vi-Motum Car and Engine Company, George J. Atkins, treasurer. It was later renamed Vimotum Hydrocarbon Car Company.

2. *Indianapolis Morning Star,* March 18, 1907.

3. *Clarke Fork Herald,* June 27, 1907; *Carbon County News,* Belfry Edition, November 19, 1908; *Carbon County News,* Belfry Edition, July 7, 1910.

4. Official Railway Equipment Registry, May 1907; Taber 1960, 6; *Carbon County News,* Belfry edition, March 3, 1910; *Carbon County News,* Belfry edition, December 8, 1910; *Billings Gazette,* January 15, 1910; *Poor's Manual of Railroads* 1911, v. 44, 1251. A mixed-train means that a "combine" or passenger car was included in a freight train or "coal drag."

5. *Carbon County News,* Belfry edition, January 14, 1909; *Carbon County News,* Belfry edition, July 7, 1910.

6. Railroad Commission of Montana, Tenth Annual Report 1917, 226–29; McKeen Motor Car Company Historical Society website, mckeencar.com; Wikipedia, s.v. "McKeen Motor Car Company," lasted updated January 4, 2023, https://en.wikipedia.org/wiki/McKeen_Motor_Car_Company; N. J. Pull, "McKeen Motor Car: History of the McKeen Motor Car Company," Historic Views of Owosso and Corunna Michigan website, shiawasseehistory.com/mckeen.html. Accessed July 30, 2021.

7. Schopp 1951; Zeitler 1921, 37–39, 113–15; also see Hilton and Due 1960; McKeen Motor Car Company Historical Society website, mckeencar.com. Accessed July 30, 2021.; Wikipedia, s.v. "McKeen Motor Car Company," lasted updated January 4, 2023, https://en.wikipedia.org/wiki/McKeen_Motor_Car_Company; N. J. Pull, "McKeen Motor Car: History of the McKeen Motor Car Company," Historic Views of Owosso and Corunna Michigan website, shiawasseehistory.com/mckeen.html. Accessed July 30, 2021.

8. *Bridger Times,* August 27, 1917; *Bridger Times,* October 2, 1919; Regan and Andrew 1962, 5; Romek 1976, 43–45.

9. Schopp 1951; White 1941, 10–11.

10. *Poor's Manual of Railroads,* 1920, v. 53. 706 and 1923, v. 56. 1988; *Carbon County News,* December, 16, 1926; Schrenk and Frey 1997, 255–63.

11. *Billings Gazette,* March 30, 1934; *Carbon County News,* May 12, 1932; *Carbon County News,* March 28, 1934; *Carbon County News,* Februrary 1, 1933; *Carbon County News,* May 23, 1934.

12. Dutton 1967, 24.

10. "A LACK OF SUFFICIENT REVENUE"

1. *Powder River County Examiner,* April 28, 1922; *Billings Gazette,* April 1, 1922; Regan and Andrew 1962, 6.

2. Regan and Andrew 1962, 6.

3. *New York Herald*, November 9, 1922; *Bridger Times*, November 23, 1922; *Plainfield (NJ) Courier News*, September 9, 1932.

4. *Bridger Times*, May 25, 1922; McNeish 2009, 27; *Bozeman Courier*, October 8, 1926.

5. Baldwin Locomotive Works Spec. sheets, v. 73, 131–32; v. 77, 412–13.

6. Dutton 1967, 26.

7. Locomotive Fuel Supply, Thomas Cooper, March 15, 1919, Northern Pacific Railway Archives, Minnesota Historical Society, St. Paul.

8. *Helena Independent-Record*, July 31, 1924; *Billings Gazette*, September 28, 1928; *Billings Gazette*, August 1, 1924; *Billings Gazette*, June 29, 1932; *Laurel Outlook*, May 10, 1933; Office of the General Fuel Supervisor (NP Coal Territorial Distribution), November 1, 1927, Northern Pacific Railway Archives, Minnesota Historical Society, St. Paul.

9. Bunney to Sweet, November 18, 1932, Northern Pacific Railway Archives, Minnesota Historical Society, St. Paul; *Billings Gazette*, May 16, 1931; Anderson 1993, 19.

10. *Carbon County News*, September 14, 1932; *Carbon County News*, September 28, 1932.

11. Yager to Stevens, July 24, 1933; Bunney to Sweet, Nocember 18, 1932, Northern Pacific Railway Archives, Minnesota Historical Society, St. Paul.

12. Bunney to Yager, June 24, 1932; Bunney to Sweet, November 18, 1932; Office of the General Fuel Supervisor (NP Coal Territorial Distribution), November 1, 1927, Northern Pacific Railway Archives, Minnesota Historical Society, St. Paul.

13. James F. Brophy sold the Smokeless & Sootless mine to his son James R. Brophy in 1940. Following the transfer of ownership, the company name was changed to Brophy Coal Company and later to the Clean Coal Company. This was the last mine to operate in the district; it shut down in 1967.

14. Assistant Chief Engineer to Smith, November 25, 1942, Northern Pacific Railway Archives, Minnesota Historical Society, St. Paul; Anderson 1993, 34.

15. *Billings Gazette*, December 8, 1939; *Great Falls Tribune*, January 7, 1940; *Great Falls Tribune*, March 16, 1940.

16. Anderson 1993, 34–35; Axline 1999, 62.

17. Anderson 1993, 36.

18. Anderson 1993, 36.

19. Anderson 1993, 36; *Billings Gazette*, September 26, 1951.

20. Taber 1960, 12; *Great Falls Tribune*, September 26, 1951; *Helena Independent Record*, October 2, 1951; Anderson 1993, 37.

21. Taber 1960, 12; *Bridger Times*, September 10, 1953; *Billings Gazette*, August 20, 1953; *Billings Gazette*, September 9, 1953; *Billings Gazette*, January 1, 1954.

22. *Billings Gazette*, March 9, 1954; *Billings Gazette*, March 10, 1954.

23. *Billings Gazette*, March 9, 1954.

24. *Billings Gazette*, March 10, 1954; *Billings Gazette*, March 29, 1955; Taber 1960, 14.

25. National Register of Historic Places Registration Form 2012, Montana, Wyoming and Southern Depot, Belfry, Montana.

APPENDIX A

1. Railroad Commission of Montana Fifth Annual Report 1912, 18–19.

2. Nowels, n.d.

3. *Anaconda Standard*, November 1, 1912; *Poor's Manual of Railroads*, 1909, v. 42, 674; Taber 1960, 8.

4. *Butte Miner*, December 2, 1915; Taber 1960, 8; Nowels, n.d.

5. Taber 1960, 9; Nowels, n.d.

APPENDIX B

1. Data from US Department of Energy, Energy Information Administration, Coal Data: A Reference, Washington, DC, 1982, 60; *Billings Gazette*, September 25, 1915 (coal definitions: Montana Railroad Commission).

2. James C. Dick, historian-archivist, NPRHA, email to the author, January 3, 2021; Schrenk and Frey 1997, 63.

3. James C. Dick, historian-archivist, NPRHA, email to the author, January 3, 2021; Schrenk and Frey 1997, 63 and 128; Office of the General Fuel Supervisor (NP Coal Territorial Distribution), November 1, 1927, Northern Pacific Railway Archives, Minnesota Historical Society, St. Paul, Minnesota.

4. A. E. Roberts 1966.

5. A. E. Roberts 1966.

6. Washburne 1907.

7. Woodruff 1907.

8. Woodruff 1907.

9. S. B. Roberts et al. 1999.

APPENDIX C

1. Combo et al. 1949; Gunderson and Wheaton 2020; Rawlins 1986.

2. Roberts and Rossi 1999; S. B. Roberts et al. 1999; Washburne 1907; Woodruff 1907.

BIBLIOGRAPHY

Anderson, Paul. 1983. "Cultural Resource Inventory and Evaluation: Red Lodge East Bench – Washoe – Highway – Burns – Smith Mines: Montana Department of State Lands." Unpublished report, GCM Services, Inc., Butte, Montana.

Anderson, Paul. 1993. "Definition and Evaluation of the Bear Creek Mining District, Carbon County, Montana." Unpublished report, GCM Services, Inc., Butte, Montana.

Axline, Jon. 1999. "Something of a Nuisance Value: The Montana, Wyoming and Southern Railroad 1905–1953." *Montana: the Magazine of Western History*, 48–63.

Calvert, W. R. 1912. "The Livingston and Trail Creek Coal Fields, Park, Gallatin, and Sweetgrass Counties, Montana." *U.S. Geological Survey Bulletin* 471, *Contributions to Economic Geology*, 384–405.

Combo, John X., Donald M. Brown, Helen F. Pulver, and Dorothy A. Taylor. 1949. "Coal Resources of Montana." *U.S. Geological Survey Circular* 53:1–25.

Darton, N. H. 1906. "Coals of Carbon County, Montana." *U.S. Geological Survey Contributions to Economic Geology*, 174–93.

Dutton, Daniel. 1967. "A Brief Look at the Montana, Wyoming and Southern Railroad Company and Some Towns of the Area." Unpublished manuscript, Carbon County Historical Society Archives, Red Lodge, Montana.

Ferguson, David. 2002. "Three Historical Mining Properties in the New World District, Park County, Montana." Unpublished report, GCM Services, Inc., Butte, Montana.

Gunderson, J. A., and John Wheaton. 2020. "Coal Resources of Montana." Montana Bureau of Mines and Geology Special Publication 122, *Geology of Montana*, vol. 2, Special Topics: 1–27.

Hartman, Kelly S. 2019. *A Brief History of Cooke City*. Charleston, SC: History Press.

Hilton, George W., and John F. Due. 1960. *The Electric Interurban Railways in America*. Stanford: Stanford University Press.

Knappen, R. S., and G. F. Moulton. 1930. "Geology and Mineral Resources of Parts of Carbon, Big Horn, Yellowstone and Stillwater Counties, Montana." *U.S. Geological Survey Bulletin* 822, *Contributions to Economic Geology* (Short Papers and Preliminary Reports), part 2, *Mineral Fuels*, 1–70.

Lewty, Peter J. 1995. *Across the Columbia Plain*. Pullman: Washington State University Press.

Lose, I. H., 1920. "Fourth of July in Belfry – 1906 Style." Unpublished manuscript, Carbon County Historical Society Archives, Red Lodge, Montana.

Lovering, T. S. 1929. "New World or Cooke City Mining District, Park County, Montana." *U.S. Geological Survey Bulletin* 811-A, *Contributions to Economic Geology* (Short Papers and Preliminary Reports), part 1, *Metals and Nonmetals Except Fuels*, 1–88.

Malone, Michael P. 1996. *James J. Hill: Empire Builder of the Northwest*. Norman: University of Oklahoma Press.

Malone, Michael P., Richard B. Roeder, and William L. Lang. 1976. *Montana: A History of Two Centuries*. Seattle: University of Washington Press.

McNeish, Jeff. 2009. *Bear Creek Valley*. Charleston, SC: Arcadia.

Mutschler, Charles V. 2002. *Wired for Success: The Butte, Anaconda & Pacific Railway 1892–1985*. Pullman: Washington State University Press.

Nowels, Edward L. N.d. "Old Trail Creek Track." Unpublished manuscript, Gallatin History Museum, Bozeman, Montana.

Polk's City Directory, Livingston, including Big Timber, Park and Sweet Grass Counties, R.L. Polk & Co., New York, 1902.

Progressive Men of the State of Montana. 1902. Chicago: A. W. Bowen & Co.

Rawlins, J. H. 1986. "Bearcreek Coal Field." In *Geology of the Beartooth Uplift and Adjacent Basins: Montana Geological Society and Yellowstone-Bighorn Research Association Joint Field Conference and Symposium*, 253–255. Montana Geological Society, Billings.

Regan, Jetta, and Bertha Andrew. 1962. "Review of Belfry's Founding and Development." Unpublished manuscript, Carbon County Historical Society Archives, Red Lodge, Montana, 8 pages (also see *Bridger Times*, November 12, 1925).

Renz, L. T. 1980. *History of the Northern Pacific Railroad*. Fairfield, WA: Ye Galleon Press.

Roberts, Albert E. 1966. "Geology and Coal Resources of the Livingston Coal Field Gallatin and Park Counties Montana." U.S. Geological Survey Professional Paper 526-A.

Roberts, S. B., and G. S. Rossi. 1999. "A Summary of Coal in the Fort Union Formation (Tertiary) Bighorn Basin, Wyoming and Montana." In *Resource Assessment of Selected Tertiary Coal Beds and Zones in the Northern Rocky Mountains and Great Plains Region*, U.S. Geological Survey Professional Paper 1625-A, SB-1–SB-14.

Roberts, S. B., E. M. Wilde, G. S. Rossi, Dorsey Blake, L. R. Rader, M. S. Ellis, G. D. Stricker et al. 1999. "Colstrip Coalfield, Powder River Basin, Montana: Geology, Coal Quality, and Coal Resources." In *Resource Assessment of Selected Tertiary Coal Beds and Zones in the Northern Rocky Mountains and Great Plains Region*, U.S. Geological Survey Professional Paper 1625-A, PC-1–PC-37.

Robertson, Donald B. 1991. *Encyclopedia of Western Railroad History*. 3 vols. Dallas, TX: Taylor.

Romek, William A. 1976. "Reminiscence." Oral history transcript. Montana Historical Society Archives, Small Collection 1453, Helena, Montana.

Rossillon, Mitzi. 1986. Cultural Resource Inventory. Belfry North Highway Project, Montana Department of Transportation.

Schopp, William, M. 1951. "Born Thirty Years Too Soon." *Railroad Magazine*. January (n.p.).

Schrenk, Lorenz P., and Robert L. Frey. 1997. *Classic Steam Era*. Mukilteo, WA: Hundman.

Smith, Burton, M. 1986. "Politics and the Crow Indian Land Cessions." *Montana: the Magazine of Western History*, 24–37.

Taber, Thomas T. 1960. "Shortlines of the Treasure State." Unpublished manuscript, Montana Historical Society, Helena, Montana.

Taylor, Bill, and Jan Taylor. 1999. *Rails to Gold and Silver*. Vol. 1, *1883–1887*. Missoula, MT: Pictorial Histories.

Taylor, Bill, and Jan Taylor. 2008. *Rails to Gold and Silver*. Vol. 2, *1888–1898*. Missoula, MT: Pictorial Histories.

Thrapp, Dan L. 1988. *Encyclopedia of Frontier Biography*. Vol. 3, *P–Z Index*. Glendale, CA: Arthur H. Clark.

Townsend, Craig E. 2013. "The Struggle to Build a Railroad to Cooke City Montana." Unpublished master's thesis, Montana State University, Bozeman, Montana.

Van Gosen, Bradley S. 2007. "The Life Cycle of Gold Deposits Near the Northeast Corner of Yellowstone National Park: Geology, Mining History, and Fate." In Integrated Geoscience Studies in the Greater Yellowstone Area—Volcanic, Tectonic, and Hydrothermal Processes in the Yellowstone Geoecosystem, edited by L. A., Morgan, U.S. Geological Survey Professional Paper 1717.

Washburne, Chester W. 1907. "Coal Fields of the Northeast Side of the Bighorn Basin, Wyoming, and of Bridger, Montana." *U.S. Geological Survey Bulletin* 341: 165–99.

Weed, Walter H. 1891. "The Cinnabar and Bozeman Coal Fields of Montana." *Geological Society America Bulletin* 2:349–64.

White, Victor H. 1941. "The Traveling Salesman." *Trains Magazine*. Reprinted in *Great American Railroad Stories*. Waukesha, WI: Kalmbach Publishing, 2014, 10–12.

Whithorn, Bill, and Doris Whithorn. N.d. *Photo History of Livingston-Bozeman Coal Country*. Livingston, MT: Yellowstone Gateway Museum.

Wolle, Muriel S. 1963. *Montana Pay Dirt: A Guide to the Mining Camps of the Treasure State*. Athens: Sage/Swallow Press of the University of Ohio.

Woodruff, E. G. 1907. "The Red Lodge Coal Field, Montana." *U.S. Geological Survey Bulletin* 341:92–107.

Zeitler, Raymond S. 1921. Self-Contained Railway Motor Cars and Locomotives. Chicago: American School.

Zupan, Shirley, and Harry J. Owens. 1979. *Red Lodge: Saga of a Western Area*. Red Lodge, MT: Carbon County Historical Society.

INDEX

Abbreviations: MW&S, Montana, Wyoming & Southern Railroad; NP, Northern Pacific; YP, Yellowstone Park; YPRy, Yellowstone Park Railway; YPRR, Yellowstone Park Railroad. Italic page numbers indicate maps and photographs.

Robert A. Schalla is a retired geologist who splits his time between Billings and Red Lodge, Montana. He is a registered professional geologist in Wyoming and holds a bachelor's degree from the University of California–Riverside and a master's degree from Oregon State University. During his professional career, he worked for several major oil companies before becoming an independent consultant in 1997. He has published numerous articles and coedited several volumes on oil exploration in the western United States. Having a lifelong interest in railroads, he has been engaged, since retiring, in researching the history and interrelationship of railroads and coal mining in southern Montana.

For Indiana University Press

Tony Brewer *Artist and Book Designer*

Dan Crissman *Trade and Regional Acquisitions Editor*

Samantha Heffner *Trade Acquisitions Assistant*

Brenna Hosman, Production Coordinator

Katie Huggins, Production Manager

David Miller, Lead Project Manager/Editor

Dan Pyle, Online Publishing Manager

Pamela Rude, Senior Artist and Book Designer

Stephen Williams, Marketing and Publicity Manager